AF395124

In the Shadow of the Ripper

In the Shadow of the Ripper

How Forensic Science Failed to Catch Jack

M.J. Trow

PEN & SWORD TRUE CRIME

An imprint of
Pen & Sword Books Ltd
Yorkshire - Philadelphia

First published in Great Britain in 2026 by
Pen & Sword True Crime
An imprint of
Pen & Sword Books Ltd
Yorkshire - Philadelphia

ISBN 978 1 03614 440 1

Typeset in INDIA by IMPEC eSolutions
Printed and bound in England by CPI Group (UK) Ltd, Croydon, CR0 4YY

The Publisher's authorised representative in the EU for product safety is
Authorised Rep Compliance Ltd., Ground Floor, 71 Lower Baggot Street, Dublin
D02 P593, Ireland.
www.arccompliance.com

For a complete list of Pen & Sword titles please contact

PEN & SWORD BOOKS LIMITED
47 Church Street, Barnsley, South Yorkshire, S70 2AS, England
E-mail: enquiries@pen-and-sword.co.uk
Website: www.pen-and-sword.co.uk

or

PEN AND SWORD BOOKS
1950 Lawrence Rd, Havertown, PA 19083, USA
E-mail: uspen-and-sword@casematepublishers.com
Website: www.penandswordbooks.com

Contents

Chapter 1

The Washing Away of Wrongs

The dead man lay by the side of the road. His throat had been cut and he had bled to death. Violence like this was common in thirteenth-century China, as it was the world over, but the headman of the local village wanted to get to the bottom of what had happened. The victim was a prominent landowner and a friend of his. He sent for the philosopher Sung Tz'u who was a magistrate and, as it turned out, a man centuries ahead of his time.

The magistrate believed that the murder weapon was a sickle, an agricultural implement with a curved, single-edged blade. But no such weapon had been found at the scene and in rural China there were thousands of them. It made sense to begin his inquiries with the victim's own workforce, so he had them assembled, complete with their sickles. He examined the blades and handles one by one – there was no trace of blood.

Then he tried an experiment and let nature provide a suspect. He stood the labourers under a hot sun with their sickles on the ground in front of them. Within minutes, the blowflies swarming in the summer air collected on one blade. That was the one with invisible bloodstains. A man could not see them, but a hungry fly could. The sickle's owner duly confessed and was executed for murder.

I have taken part in a re-enactment of this case. On behalf of the *Ancient Discoveries* television series made by the Wild Dreams company, I hacked a pig's carcase with a sickle and we all stood back, camera at the ready, to record the result. Unfortunately, it was November in a damp and chilly South Wales, not thirteenth-century China in high summer, so results were disappointing. The test *did* work, proving Sung Tz'u still right after all those centuries, but the flies did not arrive in the numbers we had hoped for and they had to be 'flown in' (pun intended) in an incubator in order to fly at all.

China underwent a renaissance in the thirteenth century as surely as Europe did in the twelfth and sixteenth centuries and with it came scientific advancement. Three inventions in particular changed the world: the printing press (the result of which you are reading now); the compass, which made international exploration possible; and, more ominously, gunpowder which formed the most devastating killing mechanism in history.

The European Renaissance produced astonishing art, architecture and scientific breakthroughs, but nothing as tangible in forensic science as Sung Tz'u. As we shall see, it was not until the nineteenth century that scientific fact began to replace ill-informed mumbo-jumbo, which in turn led to hard evidence that could be produced in court to solve crimes, which is the definition of forensics. Sung Tz'u's works were called *The Washing Away of Wrongs*, which implies that before (and long after) his time, miscarriages of justice were commonplace. Rational science washed away supposition and plain nonsense, but it took six centuries to reach the West.

Let us take the Chinese murder and see what would happen today. A passer-by finds the body (this is the 'first-finder', on whom suspicion always fell in the past). He/she contacts the police, probably by mobile phone and a murder operation kicks in. The police themselves will determine whether the man by the roadside is the victim of an accident or foul play. There is no sign of any attacker, nor vehicle, nor weapon. Yet the victim's throat has been cut and the assumption must be made that this is now a murder scene.

The road is closed and taped off (in the UK with blue and white tape, in the United States with yellow). A welter of officers arrives, as well as an ambulance and crew. Plain clothes detectives manage the area, the most senior assuming the role of SIO (senior investigating officer). All concerned will be automatically following what is often called the 5WH principle – Who? What? Where? When? Why? How?

The Who covers two aspects. Who is the deceased? There is an old adage in policing: to find out why a man died, you need to know how he lived. It may be that the first-finder knows him, but if not, enquiries must be made, the victims' clothes searched for an ID, photographs taken. The second aspect is who are the suspects? And that immediately takes us on to another WH question.

The What is sometimes obvious from the scene of crime. The man at the roadside has had his throat cut and he is clearly dead. In cases of poisoning, however, the 'what happened' will not be revealed until later.

The Where is also obvious. Or is it? Was the dead man killed where his body was found or was he killed elsewhere and his body dumped? In 1936, a pimp and small-time crook, Max Kessel, was murdered in London but his body was dumped in a ditch in St Albans, 40 miles away.

The When is exclusively the work of the pathologist. While today's SOCOs (Scenes Of Crime Officers) all wear protective clothing and senior officers can make intelligent guesses, only a forensic pathologist is able to pinpoint the time of death and even today, with a welter of scientific method and expertise, this is an inexact science.

The Why is the most intriguing of all. Motive is not always obvious and in some cases is never explained. We *assume* that the Whitechapel murderer known to the press as Jack the Ripper had a visceral hatred of prostitutes or women or both. But this is only an assumption because he was never caught. And one of the imponderables throughout this book is what makes a killer tick?

The How, in the case of our roadside victim, is fairly obvious, but nothing can be taken for granted.

Although a murder investigation team is large and its remit wide-ranging, involving all sorts of specialists, the specialist we are concerned with is the forensic pathologist, the expert witness in the courtroom, the guru of what used to be called 'the beastly science'.

If, like me, you are a fan of *Midsomer Murders*, the long-running television series, you will be familiar with Dr George Bullard (Barry Jackson) and his successors who have to cope with the weekly bloodbaths entirely on their own. Time of death? Ask Bullard. Blood group? Bullard. Mobile phone usage by the deceased? Bullard again. Motivation of the murderer? George Bullard probably has a few ideas! All this is to keep the storyline simple and, cynically, not to have to pay too many actors. In reality, the work of the pathologist is exclusively the body and what it can tell us. There would actually be a dozen people investigating the medical aspects of every Midsomer corpse.

Today, pathologists have very specific skills. Some of them work on fingerprint technology; others on DNA. An odontologist will provide expertise on teeth and bite marks on victims. An anthropologist will be brought in to advise in the case of skeletal remains. Other specialists will be cranio-facial experts, building a human face from such remains. Blood-pattern analysis is a world of its own, with spatter, droplets, cast-off and stains, all of which tell a story. Every police and pathology service in the world has large databases relating to every aspect of crime, and digitization has speeded up what is still often a slow and painstaking process. There are specialists in ballistics, burns, bomb blasts and documents, in photography and voice recognition. But after all that, it still often descends to a 'he said, she said' difference of medical opinion in a courtroom, exploited by cynical lawyers, for the prosecution and defence, whose job it is to make a case stick or to get their clients off.

Such minute expertise was not available to the pathologists in this book. The science was not there for them. Most of them were general practitioners. A few, as time wore on, were police surgeons, called to crime scenes in dark alleys in the middle of the night. Most, perhaps all of them, gave their work their best shot, but it was often not enough. Guilty men and women sometimes walked free; innocent ones sometimes went to the gallows.

The 'beastly science' did not always get it right.

Chapter 2

Dead Men's Tales

The mill door being shut, there stood a woman … with her hair about her head hanging down and all bloody, with five large wounds upon her head … 'I am the spirit of Anne Walker, who lived with John Walker … He promised to send me to a private place … And accordingly, I was one night, late, sent away with one Mark Sharp who upon a moor … slew me with a pick, such as men dig coal with, and gave me these five wounds, and after threw my body into a coal-pit hard by and laid the pick under a bush, and his shoes and stockings being bloody, he endeavoured to wash them, but seeing the blood would not part, he hid them there.

The above account of the murder of Anne Walker in Great Lumley, County Durham in 1631 is taken from Ernest Rhys's *The Haunters and the Haunted* (1921) which itself comes from an obscure text in the Bodleian Library. The appearance of the ghost has transferred the story into one of supernatural folklore, but the murder itself is real. Anne was a housekeeper to John Walker who made her pregnant and, out of embarrassment, decided to get rid of her. He either paid a hitman, local miner Sharp, or the pair together, told the girl that she would be taken to Lancashire (Sharp's home) for her confinement and would, along with the baby, be looked after.

Instead, Sharp killed her on the moors at Yellow Bank Head near Chester-Le-Street, where her decomposed body was found weeks later. Anne's ghost duly appeared to a local miller named Graham who reported the incident to the magistrate, Henry Davenport. This was a time when all kinds of impossible, supernatural events were accepted even by otherwise logical authorities and Walker and Sharp were arrested.

At the trial, held in August on Durham Palace Green, the judge and at least one jury member saw the apparition of Anne and a child (probably her baby) in the courtroom itself. Walker and Sharp were found guilty and, in an unprecedented move, sentenced that same day. They were duly hanged.

Davenport can have had no evidence against them. Even if Sharp's shoes and stockings had been found and even if they were bloodstained, there was no means of tying them to him – shoes and stockings were broadly similar. The same went for the coal-pick – seen one, seen them all. With no forensic science, all Davenport could go on was the ramblings of Graham's dream. And they may well have hanged two innocent men. As one blogger on the case online today says, 'Personally, I don't trust the testimony of ghosts. I can see right through them!'

And that is the problem for crime and criminology at any time before the nineteenth century. Despite the extraordinary science of Sung T'zu, for the next 700 years, superstition and mumbo-jumbo took the place of hard, rational fact.

One of the most famous murders in the ancient world was the assassination of Julius Caesar in March 44BC. The most detailed account comes from Gaius Suetonius Tranquillus, describing the knife attack on Caesar by senators in Rome. 'And at that moment, as he turned away, one of the Casca brothers with a sweep of his dagger stabbed him just below the throat. Caesar grabbed Casca's arm and ran it through with his stylus [pen]; he was leaping away when another dagger blow stopped him.' And so it went on until twenty-three stabs had been delivered. Slaves took the body to a doctor, Antistius, who carried out a post-mortem.

Suetonius does not tell us exactly how or where this was carried out but the doctor believed that the fatal wound had been the second, to the chest, delivered by Caesar's protégé, Marcus Junius Brutus. So far, so plausible, but at the funeral, 'two divine forms' brandishing flaming spears appeared and immediately we are in the realms of hocus-pocus. Civil war and chaos followed and the historians of Rome move on to later events. As to the murderers, we only have the traditional hit-list, because no forensics could establish who did what. As with the coal-pick in seventeenth-century County Durham, seen one Roman dagger, seen them all. And of course, Suetonius was writing well over a century after the events he was describing.

Violence and sudden death were far more common in the past than today. In the records of the King's Town of Brading in the Isle of Wight in the fourteenth century, half the murders committed (the place was a rough and ready port) were the results of fights between men and the most common weapon was a 'whirtle' (knife). There is much concern today about knife crime, especially in London, but if you use today's population figures compared with those of the Isle of Wight at the time, you were 400 times more likely to be stabbed to death in the fourteenth century than you are today.

Perhaps because murder was so commonplace, the criminal records compiled by the Saxon kings tend to cover blood feuds, theft, property frauds and the cover-all 'wergeld' (man price) which was the compensation paid to a victim's family. As with the case of Anne Walker above, the supernatural element kicks in all too quickly, obscuring hard evidence if, indeed, any was collected. Writers from Chaucer to Shakespeare contend that 'murder will out', that God will not let an injustice be done and that ghosts will return to point a finger at the accused. One of the major reasons for juries viewing a corpse was that, if the murderer was present in court, the body would rise up and denounce the killer. And money never *quite* left the equation. When the playwright Christopher Marlowe was killed in an 'ordinary' (eating house) on Deptford Green in May 1593, one of the most important points at the inquest was to establish the value ('deodand') of the murder weapon.

One murder that shocked the Medieval world as much as Caesar's rocked the ancient one was the assassination of Thomas Becket, the

Archbishop of Canterbury, in December 1170. Thanks to the five accounts of the death, two of them by eyewitnesses, we know the names of those responsible – Reginald FitzUrse, Hugh de Morville, William de Tracy and Richard Le Breton. Whether these 'hit men' were acting under the orders of Henry II (Becket's former friend but by 1170 a bitter enemy) is still under discussion, but the events of 29 December do not seem to be in doubt.

The knights arrived at the cathedral in Canterbury and left their swords, in time-honoured custom, outside. They found Becket on his way to evening prayers and confronted him, accusing him of treason against his king. One of the Archbishop's aides was Edward Grim who has left the best-known account of what happened. Becket refused to go anywhere with the knights and they collected their swords before crashing back into the cathedral and, tussling with the Archbishop, hacked him to death, slicing off the top of his head. Grim was injured trying to fend them off but Becket offered no resistance at all.

The other monks had vanished, except one, Hugh, later given the surname Malclerc (evil cleric) who trod on the dead man's neck and scattered his brains all over the floor. Ghastly though the details are, they have a ring of truth about them – a twelfth-century broadsword was a fearsome weapon and could inflict terrible wounds.

Becket's body was left where it fell, the whole cathedral – and later, as news spread, the city – in shock. It was buried the next day, but all accounts then move on to the supposed miracles connected with Thomas the Martyr; and the mechanics of his death were not recorded. There was no post-mortem, no accurate description of his wounds. Grim's was a genuine eyewitness account but in a twenty-first century court of law, he would have faced fierce cross-examination from the defence counsel determined to get the killers off. As it was, and perhaps tellingly, there was no direct accusation against the four knights who went on to live full lives. As for the king who may have hinted 'Will no one rid me of this turbulent priest?' Henry did penance by walking barefoot to Canterbury. It hardly equated with being 'hanged by the neck until he be dead'.

Even more vagueness – and the supernatural – crept into a series of child murders in the twelfth and thirteenth centuries. Seven boys, ranging in ages from 8 to 12, were murdered in England between 1144 and 1255. Collectively, they are often referred to as 'saints' because they were believed to have been Christian martyrs murdered by the Jews. This was the infamous 'blood libel', a belief that Jews carried out ritual murders of Christian children as part of their religious rites. Anti-Semitism was rife throughout Europe for centuries before the Nazis took up the idea and William of Norwich (murdered 1144), Harold of Gloucester (1168) and Robert of Bury (1181) were examples of what was believed to be a lethal cult.

The most famous example was Hugh of Lincoln, a 9-year-old tanner's apprentice who disappeared from his daily routine on 31 July 1255. His body was found (according to some accounts, by his mother) stuffed into a well in Lincoln's Jewish quarter nearly a month later. The well, it was believed, had been chosen by the boy's killers because the earth would not accept the body of an innocent so cruelly murdered. There was another interpretation too – when the Black Death (Bubonic Plague) struck Europe less than a century later, one supposed cause was that the Jews were deliberately poisoning water supplies.

The chronicler Matthew Parris, popular in his own day and revered ever since, was as anti-Semitic as everybody else. He wrote that Hugh had been kidnapped by a Jew named Capin and kept prisoner while word was sent to Jewish communities in all the major cities. They were invited to a ritual sacrifice in which Hugh would be treated as Christ had been treated. He would be made to wear a crown of thorns, be whipped and spat at, stabbed with a spear and ultimately nailed to a cross. Parris went a step further, claiming that Hugh was then disembowelled 'it is said, for the purpose of their [Jews'] magic arts'.

All this could be dismissed as the usual mumbo-jumbo of Medieval chroniclers, except that a month after the murder, Henry III arrived in

Lincoln with his usual entourage, had Capin hanged and sent ninety local Jews to the Tower of London, where eighteen of them were executed.

Had such a murder occurred today, little Hugh's body would have been examined minutely by a forensic pathologist. He or she could say how long it had been in the well, when (to within a few hours) he had died and what had caused death. There would have been visible signs of torture – the thorns lacerating the head, the whip marks on the back, the spear wound to the side. The evidence of disembowelling would have been obvious. But no such examination ever took place because science as we know it did not exist and to tamper with a dead body was sacrilege.

In a feeble attempt to establish the truth, Hugh's shrine in Lincoln Cathedral was opened in 1790. There was indeed a child's skeleton inside a 3ft 3in long stone coffin, but the science of the day could not tell the gender, still less make note of any wounds. As to the well 'discovered' inside the Jewish quarter many years later, this was found to have been a scam to boost the tourist trade; the well was built in 1910!

A possible clue to the boy saints' murders comes from the case of William of Norwich. His body was found in Thorpe Wood, north of the city, by a forester, Henry de Sprowston, who said that the boy had been gagged and was still wearing his jack (jacket) and shoes. There is no mention of hose or stockings and it may be that, apart from footwear, the boy was naked below the waist. This would indicate a sex crime, something which very rarely gets a mention of any kind in Medieval criminal records. Throughout Central Europe, grisly sex attacks which involved mutilation were often attributed to werewolves in the mistaken belief that humans could not be responsible for such atrocities.

Perhaps the best-known Medieval murder cannot be called a murder at all; today it would be a missing persons case. The 'murder' of the princes in the Tower is still attributed by most people to their uncle, Richard III. In the frantic power politics of the 1480s, the boys (the elder, Edward, was actually already king before his disappearance) were too much of a risk to Richard, who had usurped Edward's throne. Bizarrely, we have considerable forensic evidence for this case and, equally bizarrely, we still have it in our power to solve it, at least partially.

The boys, aged 13 and 9, were kept by Richard 'for their safety' in the royal apartments of the Tower and were not seen after the middle of July 1483. The assumption was made that they had been murdered but no bodies were found. Fast forward to 1674 and workmen digging in rubble near the White Tower found human bones. Royal surgeon John Knight decided, on no evidence whatsoever, that these were the skeletons of Edward and his brother Richard, Duke of York, the sons of Edward IV and nephews of Richard III. Accordingly, the bones were placed in an urn and an alabaster tomb was built in Westminster Abbey, traditional burial place of kings, designed by the architect Christopher Wren.

All very noble and poetic, except for one thing – the bones could belong to anybody. No one in 1674 had any scientific means by which to identify skeletons.

Fast forward again to 1933 when the urn was officially opened and forensic tests carried out. Bearing in mind that astonishing advances had been made by that time in terms of forensic science and pathology, the results were woeful. The expert called in was not, for example, the redoubtable Home Office Pathologist Bernard Spilsbury but Professor William Wright, Fellow of the Royal College of Surgeons. He found two or perhaps three bodily remains (the confusion here speaks for itself) and Laurence Tanner, Keeper of Muniments wrote in his report: 'only the right half of the lower jaw of the younger child, whom I shall now presume to call Richard, was present ...' This is presumption with a capital 'P'. As in 1674, there was still no way of identifying an individual by a partial mandible, so the assumptions of the seventeenth century were repeated in the twentieth!

Since the bones were reburied, today's experts can only go by Wright and Tanner's report and the photographs they took. Dr Foxley Norris, Dean of Westminster, had actually told the Society of Antiquarians in the 1930s that the tear ducts of one skull were enlarged, probably due to constant weeping, due to the harrowing experience of imprisonment! 'And that,' wrote P. Lindsay in far too mild a rebuttal, 'is how traditions are made.' Dr Juliet Rogers of the University of Bristol, has recently summed up the controversy perfectly: 'the only certain evidence here available is that [the bones] are pre-1674.'

But we could at least *prove* the lineage of the bones today. When the body of Richard III was discovered buried under the famous car park in Leicester in 2013, his identity was proved beyond a reasonable doubt by comparing his DNA with those of the existing Plantagenet family. Similar tests could be carried out on the princes' bones, all that is required is permission from King Charles III and the trustees of Westminster Abbey. And so far, these have not been forthcoming. If the case of the princes' murder is still wide open, His Majesty is actually obstructing the police in the course of their enquiries!

But mumbo-jumbo did not end with the Middle Ages. In 1612, Jennet Preston of Gisborne-in-Craven, Yorkshire, was put on trial accused of witchcraft and, more relevantly for us, murder. Her victim was Thomas Lister and we still have a record of the proceedings. Anne Robinson swore under oath that when Lister was dying in bed 'he cried out in great extremity, Jennet Preston lays heavy on me … help me, help me.' Other witnesses contended that while the dead man was being laid out 'the said Jennet Preston coming to touch the dead corpse, they bled fresh blood presently in the presence of all.' Preston was one of the victims of the infamous Pendle witch trials which exposed the legal authorities in all their rabid idiocy. Puritanism had taken hold in England by 1612 and in the hysteria that followed, anyone could be accused of witchcraft, held to account and executed without evidence. As Preston's trial account reads, 'And against these people [witches] you may not expect such direct evidence, since all their works are the works of darkness, no witnesses are present to accuse them, therefore I pray God direct your consciences.' In other words, evidence, even circumstantial, does not matter in the topsy-turvy world in which the

King James version of the Bible appeared. All that mattered was that 'Thou shalt not suffer a witch to live'. There was no post-mortem on Thomas Lister; we have no idea what caused his death, but it was certainly not being pressed on by Jennet Preston. They hanged her anyway at York on 26 July 1612.

And the nonsense of bleeding corpses lasted for many years to come. In 1684, Elizabeth Ridgway murdered her husband, Thomas, with white mercury which she mixed into his broth. She used it as a hair treatment but taken internally, it was fatal. He vomited 'in great torment' before dying in his bed twelve hours later. The local magistrate in Ashby-de-la-Zouch, Beaumont Dixie, ordered an inquest and had the man's body exhumed. There is no record of what, if anything, was found in the corpse but Elizabeth faced a trial for murder. At the inquest, the victim's father had forced her to touch his son's body and it 'burst out at nose and mouth bleeding, as fresh as if newly stabbed'. Nobody seemed to notice that stabbing was not the MO of the killer, but poison.

Elizabeth was found guilty and in a confession to a parish priest, John Newton, she admitted to killing her mother, a servant, her husband and a lover. She also had plans to kill two apprentices and finally take her own life. This would make Elizabeth a serial killer, two and a half centuries before such a concept existed. But since she was a proven liar, it is uncertain whether any of this was true or what her motives may have been. At least the jurist John Croke had an official view of murder by poison, which would run like a vicious thread through the nineteenth century. 'Of all murders poisoning is the worst and more horrible 1 because it is secret 2 because it is not to be prevented 3 because it is most against nature and therefore, heinous 4 it is also a cowardly thing.'

The Newgate Calendar or Malefactor's Bloody Register published from the 1770s onwards was a macabre mish-mash of crimes with so much fabrication that it was virtually fiction. It also harked back to earlier times for which actual evidence was extremely scant. The edition of 1816 covered, among others, the 'life' of the cannibalistic Beane family who waylaid, robbed, murdered and ate travellers near Edinburgh in the reign of James VI. Lying through his teeth, George Wilkinson, who wrote it, said, 'The following narrative presents such a picture of human barbarity, that were it not *attested by the most unquestionable historical evidence* [my italics] it would be rejected as altogether fabulous and incredible,' (which goes for most of the tales in the collection). The Beanes lived in a cave, the family growing in size in incestuous liaisons, and the king himself, with a huge armed escort, located the killers' lair which looked like a butcher's slaughterhouse. There was no trial and the whole family was executed. The men had their genitals cut off as well as their hands and feet and they bled to death. The women were burned. There was no sign of repentance.

No body parts, no contemporary reportage, no trial or inquest. Nothing, in short, but a grim fairytale which *may* have a basis in fact to a very limited extent. We know that the Bender family in Kansas in the 1870s behaved in a similar way, robbing and murdering travellers. Their body count was ten (as opposed to the Beanes' hundred plus), the skeletons were found behind their shack in Cherryvale and there was no sign of cannibalism.

If the Beane murders are lost in the mists of time and legend, the case of Eugene Aram is well documented. He was executed in York on 6 August 1758 for a murder that happened fourteen years earlier. Thomas Hood wrote a poem about it in 1831:

> Two sudden blows with a ragged stick
> And one with a heavy stone.
> One hurried gash with a hasty knife
> And then the deed was done.
> There was nothing lying at my feet
> But lifeless flesh and bone.

On 1 August 1758, a labourer working in a field at Thistle Hill, Knaresborough in Yorkshire stumbled on human remains. At the inquest, the coroner's jury decided, with no evidence at all, that these were the remains of Daniel Clark, who had disappeared on 7 February 1745. Some of Clark's goods (he was a shoemaker) were found in the possession of Eugene Aram and Robert Houseman at the time. This was not evidence of murder and, in the absence of a body, both men were released. Fast forward to 1758 and the inquest's assumption and Aram, Houseman and an innkeeper named Terry were charged with murder.

Houseman turned King's Evidence (a scam, along with the later American pleading the Fifth Amendment and the even later British 'no comment' response to police, designed to deny any involvement and escape punishment). Aram told the authorities (under what duress we are not told) that Clark's body had been hidden at St Robert's Cave, a considerable distance from Thistle Hill. There seems to have been no attempt to corroborate his version of events.

Aram, despite his humble beginnings, was a gifted linguist, having taught himself Latin, Greek and Gaelic, and he defended himself at York Assizes in July 1759. He pointed out correctly that the bones found could not be proved to be Clark's but the jury did not buy it – he was hanged at Knavesmire in York and his body hung in chains at Knaresborough. His skull is still on display at the Royal College of Surgeons Museum in London.

But there was light at the end of the criminal tunnel. After centuries of hocus-pocus, guesswork and sheer nonsense, during which thousands of miscarriages of justice must have taken place, sanity began to prevail. The tithing of Saxon England, by which every male over the age of 14 was collectively responsible for law and order, was replaced by a system of policing which we vaguely recognize. The jury system changed from locals who knew the accused personally providing what today we would call character references, to 'twelve men and true' who had nothing to do with either victim or accused in court.

In 1533, the Holy Roman Emperor, Charles V, established *Constitutio Criminalis Carolina* (the Caroline Code) based on earlier experience, that a medical expert must be called into court in cases of murder, wounding, poisoning, hanging, drowning, infanticide and abortion. In this way, over half of Europe was covered by statute, although it did not yet apply to Britain. Here, the coroner (originally crowner, a royal servant) was a magistrate responsible for the initial investigation of suspicious deaths.

Science lagged behind, if only because the Catholic Church in particular had moral objections to anatomy, and curious investigators, such as Leonardo da Vinci, had to tread carefully to obtain specimens. In Britain, this became an acute problem in the 1820s. The law said that only the bodies of hanged felons could be used for dissection purposes, but the number of medical schools was growing rapidly (there were twenty-six of them in Great Windmill Street London alone!). The result was the Resurrectionists, unscrupulous grave-robbers, like London's Ben Crouch and Edinburgh's Burke and Hare, who dug up fresh corpses to sell to anatomists like Dr Robert Knox of Edinburgh. A change in the law in 1831 meant that other 'subjects' became available and the day of the Resurrection men was over.

The first known autopsy (post-mortem) carried out on a human being took place at the extraordinarily progressive University of Bologna in 1200. It would be another three centuries before the French surgeon Ambroise Paré wrote his thesis on gunshot and other battle wounds, advocating gentle remedies like honey rather than amputation. In 1591, Zacharias Janssen produced the first working microscope, improved considerably by Anthony van Leeuwenhoek's ninety years later. It was not until 1773 that Carl Scheele devised a system for detecting arsenic in the body, improved by Valentine Rose in 1806.

In 1770, the Scottish surgeon William Hunter set up a school of anatomy in London with his brother John. By the time of the French Revolution, medical treatises in forensic medicine were beginning to appear, most notable *The Complete System of Police Medicine* by Johann Franck in what was not yet Germany.

With an arrow from a bow, the arrow being barbed with an iron head 3in long and 2in broad and the fletch [flight] of the arrow three quarters of an ell long [about 33in] and 1in thick, the fletch being feathered with peacock feathers and the bow being of yew and the bowstring of hemp, the length of the bow being one ell and a half [67in] and in gross circumference 6in thick ... with that arrow gave him a blow to the left side of the breast, 3in [from the centre] descending 2in and the depth 6in so that he immediately died of the blow.

This is a contemporary account of the murder of Simon de Skeffington in 1298 and is as detailed as anything found in the nineteenth century or even today. It gives us the accurate facts of the murder weapons (bow and arrow), the size of the wound and the cause of death. Without fingerprint technology that was 600 years in the future, no one could be accused of the crime, but it was a start.

A similar piece of forensic excellence took place with a more satisfactory outcome in 1784 when Edward Culshaw was found dead in Lancaster. The cause of death was clearly a gunshot, but the doctor examining the fatal wound found a piece of paper wadding in the gaping hole. Carefully wiped of blood, this proved to be a fragment of a printed musical ballad which had been used by the killer to ram into the pistol barrel to keep ball and powder in place. The rest of the music was found in the pocket of John Toms, an acquaintance of the dead man. It was enough to lead Toms to the gallows.

Out of the scientific and even legal ignorance of the past, medicine and law enforcement were at last coming together. It was to be a rocky road, with mistakes and injustices on the way, but the direction was the right one.

Chapter 3

The Midnight Murderers

John Murray was a pawnbroker, the three balls which were the emblem of his calling hanging over his shop at 31 Ratcliffe Highway. It was the early hours of Sunday, 8 December 1811 and all hell had broken loose in the house next door. Murray and his family were still at the table, eating a late supper, when they heard a loud noise from their neighbours, the Marrs, as of a chair being scraped back on the floorboards. There had been a single scream, from a woman or a child. The Murrays thought little of it – perhaps Mr Marr was laying about his servant, Margaret Jewell, for some transgression. Normal, routine stuff.

But the noise went on, spilling out into the street. Murray looked out. There was the maid and the night watchman, George Olney, hammering on the door of the darkened Marr house. While this went on, Murray went around the back to see if he could get in that way. There was a glimmer of light here and he called 'Mr Marr' several times. The back door was open and the light came from a solitary candle on the first-floor landing. Murray took it up and climbed the stairs. The Marrs' bedroom was in darkness. 'Marr,' Murray said quietly, 'your window shutters are not fastened.' Not liking to invade the couple's privacy, Murray went downstairs into the mercer's shop that was Timothy Marr's livelihood.

Inside the door lay the first body. It was that of the apprentice, James Gowen. His head had been pounded to a bloody mess by repeated blows, the spatter of blood and brains over the walls and counter. Murray was transfixed, unable for a moment to move or cry out. He could hear Olney still pounding on the door, the man's voice calm and reassuring as he had not seen what Murray had seen.

The pawnbroker half turned and nearly trod on the body of Celia Marr, the draper's wife. She was lying face down, her head, like Gowen's, shattered and bloody. Murray got to the front door and hauled it open. 'Murder!' he shouted at Olney. 'Come and see what murder is here!' A small crowd had gathered in the Highway, roused by the commotion, and most of them followed Olney into the house. Margaret Jewell screamed.

Behind the counter, the body of Timothy Marr was lying face down, his skull demolished like the others. Some of the crowd drew back, horrified and vomiting. Others went down into the basement, looking for the Marrs' baby. They found little Timothy still in his cot, but the left side of his face had been battered and his throat cut.

In the late twentieth century, the Americans invented phrases for murders like this; home invasion and family annihilation. In 1811, it was just plain murder but there was nothing plain about it. The Ratcliffe Highway and its environs have vanished today, part of the glittering homage to big business that is Canary Wharf with its monolithic buildings, its chrome and its glass. In 1811, Ratcliffe was one of the most squalid and dangerous streets in the world, leading, as it did, to London Docks, then the largest anywhere. The place was rife with crime – the 'light' and 'heavy' horsemen – who pilfered cargo from the Indiamen riding at anchor behind the huge high walls and moved along the wharves of the Thames. Vast amounts of money changed hands here, not all of it legally, and a miniscule, badly run police force was almost powerless to stop it. Thieves, drunks and prostitutes were everywhere, anxious to fleece well-paid foreign sailors who had just come in from every port in the world. Violence was commonplace, but the murder of the Marr family was on a whole different level.

News of the atrocity reached the River Police headquarters at Wapping along the Thames. This organization, one of far too many that policed the metropolis, would later morph into T Division of the Met. Its responsibility remained the same as it had been at its formation in 1795, however: to handle crime on the Thames, from theft and piracy to murder and suicide. The Wapping building was slightly superior to the rat-infested rookeries in the river mud – it was made of brick and had a slipway for police barges. The duty officer was Charles Horton, who fought his way through the crowd of ghouls outside No. 29 Ratcliffe Highway and searched the premises with the aid of his bullseye lantern. The only thing (apart from the bodies) out of place was a carpenter's or builder's ripping chisel which was lying on Marr's counter. It had no blood on it. There was small change in the till and £5 in Marr's pocket. In the bedroom was £152 in cash (about £13,000 today) hinting that robbery was not the motive for murder. The young couple's bed was undisturbed but resting against a chair near it was a mallet, known as a maul, the kind of tool used by ship's carpenters. Its anvil-shaped head was covered in blood and matted hair. Significantly, the tapered iron point had broken at the tip, although such vital evidence would never be mentioned in the weeks of investigation ahead.

Two sets of footprints lay in the mud behind Marr's house. The mercer was having building work done on the house and it was not possible to say whose prints they were. At no point in the subsequent enquiries were any attempts made to find the wearers of those shoes. A local from nearby Pennington Street told the police he had seen ten or twelve men rushing out of the Marr house, down Old Church Lane, towards the river.

By the time Horton had got back to Wapping with the maul, three Greek sailors were already in custody; one had blood spots on his trousers. It was a pattern that would be depressingly repeated in the following weeks – foreigners of any nationality were far more likely to be guilty of these appalling murders than the native Britons; *and* there was a war on. Wellington's army was fighting in Spain but the navy was on high alert across the globe. The specific enemy was the French under Napoleon Bonaparte, but he had allies – and foreigners could *never* be trusted, according to the mindset of the day. The Thames police magistrate, John Harriot, let the three go when they provided an alibi.

Murders like that of the Marrs caused hysteria, much of it xenophobic and was meat and drink to the newspapers, local and national. The system of policing in London, despite the constant urging of politicians like Sir Francis Burdett and Sir Samuel Romilly, was chaotic. Today, we are very used to television fiction set in the States where various police forces clash and vie with each other for jurisdiction. London was like that in 1811. The front line for Ratcliffe Highway were the churchwardens, overseers and trustees of the parish vestry of St George's-in-the-East, in whose mortuary Ripper victim Liz Stride would be examined in 1888. In 1811, it had no mortuary at all. Despite highfalutin titles like High Constable, the actual work of policing was carried out by unpaid deputies (constantly on the take from a variety of criminals) and thirty-five night watchmen under a Beadle, whose collective age would threaten Methuselah. These 'Charlies' were well into their sixties or older, armed with a lantern and club and were totally inadequate when it came to maintaining law and order or catching criminals. They spent most of their shifts sheltering from the weather in wooden watch-boxes. The *Examiner* spoke of them as 'poor, superannuated creatures', but the old men were chosen as being less susceptible to the wiles of local prostitutes than younger men.

Scattered over London were seven Police Offices set up in 1792. The local one was at Shadwell, but they were nowhere near the efficiency of Henry Fielding's Bow Street office, then sixty years old, with its team of keen young 'runners' who could take on roughs and crooks and beat them at their own game. The chances of finding the killer(s) of the Marr family were remote. The three Shadwell magistrates, George Strong, Edward Markland and Robert Capper, spent the coming weeks chasing shadows and making fools of themselves. The River Police had what was likely to be the murder weapon – and a distinctive one at that – but because of the lack of scientific forensic knowledge, could make little use of it. The confusing and overlapping defenders of the peace made it a point of honour not to share information with anyone else – a disaster in terms of crime-solving.

The churchwardens viewed the Marr household's bodies, which of course told them nothing and they printed a reward poster. The issue of rewards haunted nineteenth-century crime. Because various policemen were poorly paid or not paid at all (crime prevention being seen as everybody's civic duty) it was expected that all such officers would claim rewards or take on other jobs. They also, of course, took bribes to look elsewhere when a crime was being committed. As far as the public were concerned, paying someone for information was asking for trouble, encouraging lies and splitting families and communities.

John Clement, the Vestry Clerk, put his name to the document, printed by local printer Skirven. It is not known how many could actually read the notice that appeared on walls and lampposts in the coming days, but word, nevertheless, got around:

> The Dwelling House of Mr Timothy Marr, 29 Ratcliffe Highway, Man's Mercer, was entered this morning between the hours of Twelve and Two o'Clock, by some persons unknown when the said Mr Marr, Mrs Celia Marr, his wife, Timothy their Infant Child in the cradle and James Biggs, a servant lad, were all of them most inhumanely and barbarously Murdered!!

Having managed to get James Gowen's surname and status wrong, the churchwardens described the maul and the ripping chisel found at the crime scene and proceeded to offer £50 (around £4,000 today) for information leading to a conviction. Mr Magistrate Markland, depressingly, wrote in his report that, 'We have no clue which promises to lead to a discovery.' All this was sixty years before fingerprint evidence was available, but the authorities did have the maul, the chisel and the footprints, as well as an eyewitness account of the men seen leaving the premises.

The bodies of the murder victims were laid out in the house with a Shadwell policeman on duty, but the crowd were allowed to enter to gawp, destroying or stealing any other potential evidence that the killer(s) may have left behind. The laying out of corpses for wakes was common, especially among the area's large Irish community and no one found this remotely odd.

The inquest took place on Tuesday, 10 December at the Jolly Sailor pub along Ratcliffe Highway. The coroner, John Unwin, took the jury across the road to the murder scene to view the corpses. For the first time we have a glimpse of a medical man and we know very little about him. He was Dr Walter Salter, like most doctors of the time classed as a surgeon and *The Times* reported his evidence. The 14-week-old baby's left artery of the neck was divided by a 3-inch wound that led from the mouth to the throat. Celia Marr's cranium had been smashed on the left, the temple shattered and she had two wounds on either side of the left ear. Marr's nose was broken and his occipital bone was smashed on the right. The worst injuries seem to have been inflicted on Gowen; his forehead and nose were badly cut and his brains protruded through the shattered occiput. The head wounds had caused death in all cases.

The only other witnesses were the maid, Jewell; the neighbour, Murray; and the St George's watchman, Olney. The girl had been sent out by Marr shortly before midnight to buy oysters. Unlike today, this was cheap food collected locally and it was not unusual to find shops open that late. In fact, Jewell had found none still operating and was back within twenty minutes to find the Marr house in darkness and that she was locked out. Olney testified that the bodies were still warm when he arrived. In the absence of any other evidence, all the jury could do was to deliver the usual verdict of 'murder by person or persons unknown'.

How much common-sense deliberation went on behind the scenes in the various police departments, newspaper offices, pubs and lodging houses we do not know. If this was a robbery gone wrong, the burglars perhaps disturbed by Margaret Jewell hammering on the door, why not take *something* out of the Marr house? Even if they had not had time to find the money upstairs, there were probably other things (like the cash in Marr's pocket) worth taking. And why kill everybody in the house, particularly a small child who could have offered no resistance or been any kind of threat? It was this child murder that particularly horrified the East End.

At least the owner of the chisel was traced. It had been borrowed by a builder, Cornelius Hart, working on the Marr house in the pay of Mr Pugh, a Master Carpenter, who had obviously left it lying around. The fact that, unlike the maul, the chisel had no blood or hair on it, seemed to be irrelevant and it was referred to as a murder weapon by various sources in the weeks ahead.

Now, with media hysteria mounting, it was the government's turn to offer a reward. Richard Ryder, one of the least prepossessing Home Secretaries of the century, signed a document on 12 December offering £100 'to be paid on the conviction of any one or more of the offenders …' This was unprecedented; governments did not stoop to offering money in this way.

A servant girl with the surname Wilkie (forename unknown) came forward, in effect to clear her name. She had been dismissed by the Marrs six months earlier which may have given her a revenge motive, but nobody could believe that a girl could have committed such savagery, particularly as she remained on good terms with her former employers. She also told magistrates that the Marrs were a loving couple and there was no disharmony in the household.

The Marrs were buried in the churchyard of St George's-in-the-East, six days after the murders. Some family members had turned up for a routine visit, totally unaware of the disaster that had befallen their kindred. The tombstone had a long and melancholy inscription, part of which read 'Stop, mortal, stop as you pass by/And view the grave wherein doth lie/A Father, Mother and Son/Whose earthly Course was shortly run/For, lo, all in one fatal hour/O'ercome were they with ruthless power/And murdered in a cruel state/Yes, far too horrid to relate …' The grave, along with many others, has been grassed over today to make a park and the tombstone moved. John Gowen was buried elsewhere.

There was a flutter of arrests and interrogations, mostly of Portuguese sailors (such men would also be rounded up in the Whitechapel murder investigation seven decades later – see Chapter 8). Only now, having cleaned the maul, did the authorities discover the initials J.P. punched into the metal. It took weeks to follow that up, a delay that did not impress Samuel Romilly who, in the Commons on 18 January 1812, harangued the police for arresting forty or fifty people for no good reason.

It was shortly before eleven o'clock on the night of 19 December that Constable Anderson (forename not recorded) of the Watch, went out to get a pot of beer. This was from the King's Arms and although the pub was technically shut (the licensing laws at the time were very vague!) John Williamson the landlord was always flexible for his friends and Elizabeth, his wife, poured the beer for their late guest in the kitchen. Williamson insisted that his maid, Bridget Harrington, should carry the pot round to Anderson's. It took him twenty minutes to down the pint and he opened his door to fetch some more when he was virtually bowled over by a running crowd and cries of 'Murder! Murder!' A man in his nightshirt was dangling from the second-floor window of the King's Arms shouting his head off. He had made himself a rope of bedsheets and was clearly hysterical. Another watchman, Shadrick Newhall, stood ready to catch him. Anderson grabbed his staff and cutlass and saw the dangling man drop into Newhall's arms. The crowd were hammering on the pub door while Anderson and others hauled open the doors to the cellar, where the beer kegs were stored.

In the darkness, they could barely make out John Williamson's body. His legs were splayed out on the steps to the taproom and his head on the cellar floor. His throat had been cut and his right leg was broken. His head was a mass of blood and his right hand had been badly gashed, his thumb hanging off. A bloody iron bar lay next to the corpse.

Anderson led the little crowd up to the kitchen, trampling over any evidence that might have been there and they found the body of Elizabeth Williamson. Her throat had been cut too and her skull shattered. Near her, as though she had been laying the fire for the morning, was Bridget Harrington, who, half an hour earlier, had brought Anderson his beer. Her head wounds were worse than the others and the throat wound had cut through to the vertebrae.

Despite all the commotion, the Williamson's little granddaughter, Kitty Stillwell, was still fast asleep on the second floor. She was carried outside, having no idea what was going on. Somebody contacted Shadwell Police Office and two constables came running. As many policemen as could be mustered sealed off London Bridge and combed the streets. There was no such procedure as 'house-to-house' in those days, but a number of locals were quizzed and the Bow Street Runners were sent for, riding to the crime scene on horseback. In a decision that would outrage Scenes Of Crime Officers today, the bodies were moved, washed and laid out in the back parlour.

All the evidence (such as it was) pointed to the same culprits who had attacked the Marrs. The crime scenes were within five minutes' walk of each other. Both were business premises which might have held cash and other valuables. This time, however, there were two survivors. We are not told Kitty Stillwell's age but judging from her sleeping through the whole thing, she cannot have been very old and was of no help in identifying anybody. John Turner was a different matter. He was a journeyman (travelling salesman) who lodged at the King's Arms and had lowered himself with the sheets from his bedroom. On the assumption that he *was* the assailant, he had been taken into custody. There were bloodstains on a windowsill at the back of the pub and footprints in the clay below it. Someone with a claim to forensic knowledge, perhaps a local butcher, decided from the wounds that the killer was left-handed, but since qualified doctors involved in the Ripper murders of 1888 argued over issues like this, we cannot take the guesswork seriously.

Thomas Barnes, the Vestry Clerk, rushed to have more reward posters printed (Skirven was doing well out of the atrocities). The reward was 100 guineas:

Whereas, on Thursday night, 19th December, 1811, between the hours of eleven and twelve o'clock, Mr Williamson, his wife and maid servant were all of them most barbarously murdered in his house, the sign of the King's Arms, New Gravel Lane, Saint Paul, Shadwell … [the money was to be paid to convict …] the perpetrator or perpetrators of the said horrid murder …

In terms of motive, the St Paul's Vestry was at a loss. Williamson's watch had gone, but not the money in his till. Nobody in 1811 considered a sexual motive, but equally, there was no evidence to suggest any such thing. If the Marrs and the Williamsons had been the victims of the same killer(s), seven people were now dead in the space of a week. It defied belief.

John Turner was grilled as soon as he had calmed down. He had seen a tall man looming over Elizabeth Williamson's body, but since he had clearly run immediately and had had hysterics ever since, how much faith could be placed in his testimony?

But no one was coordinating the authorities' efforts. If the Marr and Williamson murders had a common culprit, there were actually several clues available. No one in 1811 could take plaster casts of footprints, so attempting to identify the owners of the shoes outside both crime scenes was a waste of time. The witness from Pennington Street had seen up to a dozen men running from the direction of Timothy Marr's house. John Turner had seen a tall man in a Flushing coat. At least three potential murder weapons had been found, but no one was putting two and two together.

Two days after the attack at the King's Arms, coroner Unwin opened the inquest at the Black Horse pub. 'Our homes are no longer our castles,' he said in words that would echo down the years, 'and we are unsafe in our beds.'

John Turner was the first witness. He arrived at the King's Arms at twenty to eleven on the night in question and a neighbour came in while he was with the Williamsons to say that a 'stout man with a very large coat on' was peering in through the windows. Williamson went outside but could see no one. Anderson of the Watch came in for a couple of minutes (since his job was to call the hour in the streets it was probably eleven o'clock) and Turner went to bed. Mrs Williamson went up to her room too, with a watch and a silver punch ladle. She locked the bedroom door and went back downstairs.

Turner had only been in bed for five minutes when he heard the front door slam and the maid, Harrington, call out 'We are all murdered' or 'shall be murdered'. Turner heard the crunch of three or four blows and Williamson calling out, 'I am a dead man.'

Tentatively, Turner, in his nightshirt even though it was December, crept downstairs to the first floor. He heard movement and three heavy sighs. It was on the landing that he saw the large man in a room lit by a candle. His Flushing coat was dark, down to his heels (the fashion at the time) and he had his back to Turner. He heard the sounds of coins being rifled and did not stay to hear more. He dashed back to his room, which had no lock, tied two sheets together and hooked them over the bedpost. He lowered himself to the ground, seeing Anderson and screaming that murder was happening. He had left Kitty Stillwell to her fate.

Dr Salter, who had given his expert testimony at the Marr inquest, was the third witness called at the Black Horse. Williamson, he said, had a wound running from the left ear to within 2 inches of the right, cutting the trachea, down to the vertebrae. The left tibia was broken a little above the ankle, as though he had fallen or been thrown downstairs. The temporal and parietal areas of his wife's skull were both fractured, probably with a poker or similar object. The throat was cut from ear to ear. In the case of the maid, Harrington, her right parietal bone was smashed open and her throat slashed in a cut 4 inches long. The doctor stressed that there were no other marks on the body, presumably to rule out any sexual motive. Salter believed that the murder weapon was a razor. The only type available in 1811 was a folding 'cut-throat' type with a steel blade. The verdict of the jury was predictable.

Three days before Christmas, the dead of the King's Arms were buried in St Paul's Churchyard, Shadwell; all the shops in the area were closed and the huge crowd behaved with decorum.

One of several men arrested in the days ahead was John Williams, a sailor who lodged at the Pear Tree pub in Old Wapping, run by Robert and Saul Vermilloe. There is no evidence as to why the police should have been interested in Williams, but perhaps someone had fingered him for reasons now lost. He was 27, 5ft 9in tall 'of an insinuating manner and pleasing countenance'. 'Insinuating' is not a word we use today in the same context; it meant 'friendly', 'eager to please' and Williams, the police learned, was something of a ladies' man and a dandy, taking great care of his clothes. He had sailed with Timothy Marr on the merchantman *Dover Castle* but his most recent posting was aboard the East Indiaman *Roxburgh Castle*, landing in the port of London in October. He kept his sailor's chest at the Pear Tree and seems to have been regarded by the Vermilloes almost as family, babysitting their young daughter and doing odd jobs around the pub. Like all sailors, he liked a drink and got into scrapes in various pubs, where his slight build did him no favours.

On Christmas Eve, *The Times* reported that Williams had been interviewed, one of several dozen people by this time. The sailor knew the Williamsons and had been to the King's Arms about seven o'clock on the evening of the murders. He did not go home (to the Pear Tree) until twelve when he told a fellow lodger to put his candle out. *The Times* said that Williams was short (at 5ft 9in he would have been regarded as quite tall among seafarers), had a gammy leg and was Irish. He was said to be strapped for cash and yet had silver on him when he was arrested.

Williams agreed that he had been to the King's Arms – he was a popular regular there. From there he had gone to a doctor in Shadwell about an old leg wound which was giving him trouble. The doctor's fees were too high, so he went to a female chirurgeon nearby for something cheaper. The distinction between chirurgeon and surgeon is not at all clear but the fact that Williams' contact was female implies that she was probably a leftover of the 'cunning women' more commonly found in the countryside, practising homeopathic remedies, attending childbirth and laying out bodies for burial. He explained his sudden acquisition of funds by the fact that he had pawned an expensive pair of shoes.

The level of competence and probity in the enquiries into the murders can best be summed up by this exchange between Magistrate Markland and Mrs Driscoll, the wife of an Irishman who lodged near the Pear Tree:

What are you?
A poor woman, your honour.
Who is your husband?
He is Cornelius Dixon.
Why, he has just told us his name is Driscoll.
Oh, it's all the same, sir.

And another between the magistrate and local John Martin:

Are you a Roman Catholic?
I have been the chief of my life in His Majesty's service.
Of what religion are you?
Yes, sir, I have been in His Majesty's service a long while.

We cannot dismiss this as the ravings of stage Irish people. Few of the witnesses interrogated could read; many of them were drunks and their evidence generally was unhelpful. Yet forensic science was not merely in its infancy; it was still wrapped in swaddling bands in its cot. The authorities had no alternative but to try to make sense of the former.

The fullest account of the Ratcliffe/Shadwell murders is still *The Maul and the Pear Tree* by James and Critchley (1971) and the authors list twelve failings of those authorities to catch a killer. The police had discovered that the maul, with its J.P. initials, belonged to Johann Petersen, a sailor from Hamburg who had lodged at the Pear Tree and left his tools in an unlocked chest. Anyone in the pub, with its frequently shifting lodger turnover, had access to it. Had the authorities focused on the Pear Tree earlier, it was conceivable that the Williamson murders might never have happened. It was ten days before the pub was searched. During this time, dozens of 'suspects' were rounded up and interrogated, usually because they were foreign sailors or Irishmen, both groups in xenophobic England likely to be murderers. There was no attempt to exchange information between the various groups of law enforcement, so each of them was, in effect, working in a vacuum. They all hung on to 'suspects' keeping them unnecessarily in custody, breaking the laws of habeas corpus, whereby an individual had to be charged with a specific crime. Having latched on to John Williams, there was no attempt to look beyond him, even though the man's happy-go-lucky nature bore no relation to whoever battered the Marrs and the Williamsons to death. No one at the Pear Tree was cross-examined in sufficient detail; their clothes and razors were not checked for bloodstains.

For all practical purposes, none of this mattered because the day before Williams was due to be committed for trial, he was found hanging in his cell at Coldbath Fields gaol. At his inquest, again under John Unwin, Dr Thomas Webb, the prison's surgeon, reported his findings. He had found Williams lying on his back on his bed where a turnkey (prison officer) had put him. The body was cold and he had been dead for some hours. The mark of a ligature was around his neck, as was a handkerchief. There were no other signs of violence (no doubt the doctor was anxious to avoid the turnkeys being accused of murder) and the cause of death was strangulation.

Williams had been cut down by turnkey Joseph Beckett and a prisoner, Francis Knott. The dead man appeared to have tied the handkerchief (this was, more probably, a scarf or cravat) around his neck and the other end to an iron rail over the bed for drying clothes. Beckett had checked on Williams at ten to four in the morning, at which time he seemed his usual cheery self.

Unwin, with all the bigotry of his class and age, referred to the sailor as 'the miserable wretch' and pointed out that his suicide made it even more likely that he was guilty of the murders. He also railed against suicide as 'self-murder'. 'It only, therefore, remains that we consign the body of this self-murderer to that infamy and disgrace which the law has prescribed and to leave the punishment of his crimes to Him that has said "Vengeance is mine and I will repay".'

But, happy to leave Williams in the frame for the murders, the magistrates could not believe that he acted alone. Both murder scenes had three floors, with plenty of spaces for the victims to run and hide, screaming blue murder to raise the hue and cry. Timothy Marr and James Gowen could be expected to put up some kind of fight. Although John Turner at the King's Arms turned out to be lily-livered, John Williamson was a big, powerful man and his hand wounds suggested that he had fought back, perhaps grabbing a razor in the process. The big intruder with the Flushing coat seen by Turner could not have been Williams. Neither could he have made both sets of footprints running away from the Marr house and the others in the clay from the Williamsons'.

James and Critchley exonerate Williams entirely, attributing his suicide to other causes or even murder by the turnkeys. The jury is still open in the case of Rudolf Hess, Hitler's deputy, who was found hanged from a window latch at Spandau prison, Berlin, in August 1987. The forensics said that an old, frail man could not possibly have hanged himself but none of his guards admitted to anything and no one was ever charged. It was enough for most people to draw a line under the last leading Nazi of the Second World War to die. And so it was with Williams.

There were a couple of men – Cornelius Hart, the carpenter working on the Marr house, and 'Long Billy' Ablass, a Danzig sailor who was an old comrade of Williams, whose behaviour and the answers to magistrates' questions were highly dodgy – who were also suspects. Did Williams form part of an unholy trinity with them or was he an unlucky 'patsy' (as twentieth-century Americans have it) who was just in the wrong place at the wrong time?

As a fascinating angle on their 1971 book, James and Critchley invited a *real* forensic pathologist, Professor Keith Simpson of Guy's Hospital, London, to examine the Ratcliffe Highway murders and offer his expertise. Simpson, was *the* Home Office expert in the years of the Second World War and afterwards, using his razor-sharp analyses to solve dozens of high-profile cases. Blood had been found *inside* the pocket of a blue jacket *believed* to be Williams'. As Simpson said, 'the assailant would be bound to have been bloodstained, mostly around the face, shoulders, arms and hands, from repeated blows. Blood and brains can be splashed for many feet by re-hitting bleeding wounds.' Yet no such blood was found on Williams – or indeed anybody – in 1811.

In the context of Williams' own death, Simpson agrees that there is no hard evidence in the reports to suggest murder, but neither is there anything to refute it.

What can we say about the Ratcliffe Highway murderer(s)? Simpson is of the opinion that one man *could* have carried out all seven killings, but that ignores the fact that the perpetrator seen by John Turner over Mrs Williamson's body was too big for Williams. It also ignores the multiplicity of footprints near the Marr house. Whoever it was knew the area like the back of his hand. He almost certainly had watched the premises for a time before the attacks, reasoning that both households were likely to have cash and small, easily fenced valuables inside. He struck in the dark at opportune moments – when Margaret Jewell was out of the way, for example. Was that because he knew her and did not want her involved? He had no such qualms about the Williamsons' maid, Bridget Harrington. What horrified contemporaries – and still shakes us today – is the *ferocity* of the killings. Knocks over the head to make somebody unconscious is one thing, but destroying skulls and cutting throats, especially of a newborn baby, is altogether in a different league. It screams psychopathy, a bloodlust which we still find difficult to understand.

But in 1811, none of this would have been understood. That 'inhuman murderer' John Williams was lashed, in death, to a specially constructed platform on a horse-drawn cart. The maul and chisel which, it was believed, he had used on his victims, were fixed on either side of his head. Police and troops were stationed along the route on Tuesday, 31 December 1811 to keep order. The body wore a shirt and blue trousers. The arms were black up to the elbows as putrefaction had begun to set in. Local dignitaries rode or walked behind the cart, and the crowd, thousands strong, fell silent as it jolted to a halt outside Marr's shop. Somebody climbed onto the cart and turned Williams' head, as if forcing the dead eyes to look at the crime scene.

It stopped again outside the Pear Tree and the King's Arms. The only violence on that surreal day was that a coachman used his whip as he passed the cart, lashing the dead man's face three times. Nobody winced and nobody was appalled by the outrage. At the turnpike gates that marked a crossroads, Williams' body was cut down and bundled into a grave 3ft long by 2ft wide, deliberately too small so that the body had to be bent to fit. One of the turnkeys used the maul to smash a wooden stake into the corpse's heart and the crowd at last roared its approval.

In the 1880s, the body of John Williams was disinterred by accident, as part of East End rebuilding. The bones were distributed among various celebrities, including the Shakespearean actor Henry Irving. The skull, according to an entry in an old ledger in the church of St George's-in-the-East, was then in possession of the landlord of a pub at the corner of Cable Street and Cannon Street Road. Where it is now is anybody's guess.

And we still have not solved the murders in the Ratcliffe Highway.

Chapter 4

Criminal Men

In an ideal world, there would be no crime. Yet, according to the Bible, by the second generation of man's existence, a murder took place – Cain slew his brother Abel. From there it was downhill all the way! In reality, crime was as old as man – it exists too in the animal kingdom, though we tend not to call it that. But what if science can be used to make accurate predictions? What if we can detect a criminal mind before a crime has been committed? Could we then start to frame an ideal society?

In 1522, the same year that Charles V produced his Criminal Code, Barthélemy Cocés wrote *Physiognomia* with woodcuts of faces showing various features and what they meant in terms of what today we would call psychology. A high forehead denoted intelligence (which is one reason why fashionable ladies of the Renaissance shaved their heads and wore high hats). But to Cocés, it denoted ignorance and laziness. Pointed ears were a sign of spite. Small foreheads were a sign of foolishness, long foreheads were owned by good, common-sense people (perhaps Cocés himself?)

We can laugh at this, but medical diagnoses for centuries – and even today – depends on outward, physical symptoms. Deciding a patient's psychology from the shape of their heads was only a step away from this – and phrenology was born.

The founder of the movement was Franz Gall, an Austrian doctor. He was ridiculed by his fellow medics to the extent that he had to leave Vienna, but the ever-gullible public bought into his theories. Gall believed that the brain had thirty-three 'organs' and porcelain busts with all this printed on the cranium were a 'must-have' ornament in any modern gentleman's study for much of the nineteenth century. The organs were divided into three: basic human characteristics; sentiments such as kindness and a cheerful disposition; and intellectual capacity (the ability to reason). All these could be discovered by the shape of the cranium and an experienced doctor feeling the 'bumps' of the skull. It was no more laughable than the concept of the Medieval four 'humours' which had been regarded as accurate medical science for 1,500 years.

Among Gall's thirty-three organs were those covering criminal activity, including theft, fraud, sex crimes and murder. His protégé, J.K. Spurtzhein, conducted lecture tours in Britain, France and America in the 1820s and phrenology became a staple of American fairs, where a variety of snake-oil salesmen promised all kinds of remedies and solutions that actual medicine could not provide. Of particular interest to students of criminology were the heads of executed felons, so the Resurrection man William Burke, as part of his own dissection process, had his 'bumps' felt by a number of people. Several of these grisly exhibits found their way into the freak shows of fairgrounds or ended up as models for Marie Tussaud at her London waxworks or the medical museum of Dr Hunter.

Cesare Lombroso took phrenology a stage further. He had served as an army surgeon in the 1860s in Italy's war for independence and was then given the post of professor of mental diseases at Padua University. His researches led him to the work of Rudolf Virchow from Pomerania. He was professor of pathology at Würzburg University in 1849 and Berlin seven years later, the year, coincidentally, when Dr William Palmer (see Chapter 5) was carrying out his poisoning spree. His work included a study of cell structures, tumours and leukaemia and he was involved in sanitation and hygiene. He also dabbled in archaeology and had such wide experience of corpses and crime scenes that the British police were still using his techniques in the Whitechapel murders of 1888 (see Chapter 8). Virchow's analysis of early man and of modern criminals led him to believe that in the shape of the skull there were common characteristics; criminal man was a barbarous and dangerous ape. While the horror writer Edgar Allan Poe could cash in on this theme in his *The Murders in the Rue Morgue* in the 1840s, the concept gripped elements of the scientific community and thoughtful policemen who were trying to solve actual murders.

Lombroso toured Italian gaols, measuring the heads of prisoners and carried out a post-mortem on a thief. When he opened the man's brain, 'I seemed to see ... lighted up as a vast plain under a flaming sky, the problem of the nature of the criminal [with] the ferocious instincts of primitive humanity and the inferior animals.' In 1876, he published *L'Uomo Deliquente* (Criminal Man) in which he listed the physiognomy of various types. Assassins had prominent jaws, widely separated cheekbones, thick dark hair, scanty beard and a pallid face. With a *lot* of leeway, we can *just about* make John Wilkes Booth, the assassin of Abraham Lincoln in 1865 fit this bill, but it comes nowhere near to Charlotte Corday who murdered the politician Jean-Paul Marat in his bath seventy-two years earlier.

Street thugs, said Lombroso, had round skulls and long hands (presumably to make picking pockets easier). Rapists, however, had short hands and narrow foreheads. Most of them were blond and they had deformations of the nose and genitals (of course). Arsonists were underweight, had small heads and long arms. Con men had large jaws and high cheekbones. Their immobile faces were one of the few characteristics that Lombroso got right – poker faces were essential in the swindling game.

Lombroso differentiated between 'occasional' criminals or spur-of-the-moment impulses and 'born criminals' who had a hereditary defect, obvious in their appearances, which meant that they had a compulsive inclination to commit crime – they did not know any other way to live. By 1895, in a second book, the Italian had studied 6,034 living criminals and his findings were accepted for years as the truth.

In 1890, Havelock Ellis published *The Criminal*, which was a round-up of current thinking on crime and its causes. Its (rather poor) illustrations show a range of male profiles which can only be called cartoons and could have been of no help to those involved in coping with crime. Britain was believed to lag behind the rest of Europe in terms of scientific criminal study and Ellis's book attempts to make up for that.

Because all intellectuals of the nineteenth century were brought up in the Classical tradition, Ellis takes us through a long history of the study of criminals, although how much of it is accurate and could be called forensic is debatable. So sure was Ellis of Lombroso's 'types' that he quotes Homer's description of an ugly man with thin hair and a pointed head, in the belief that he was talking about an actual criminal rather than a fictional character of his own imagination. Socrates, apparently, believed that murderers were pale and had dark complexions and recent studies, says Ellis, have proved him right. Aristotle advocated euthanasia for born criminals, just as scorpions and adders are killed, for the good of mankind.

Ellis praised Gall, 'a very great figure in the history of science' and 'the founder of the modern science of criminal anthropology'. Inevitably, he spends several pages on Lombroso, equating *L'Uomo Deliquente* with Charles Darwin's *Origin of Species* (1859) in terms of scientific milestones. By the mid-1880s, international congresses devoted to criminology were taking place in various European capitals. Ellis mentions the work of Richard von Krafft-Ebing, professor of psychiatry at Vienna whose later work, *Psychopathia Sexualis,* was read by at least one prominent detective in the Ripper murders – Inspector John Littlechild.

Britain, Ellis lamented, had fallen far behind other countries. The International Medical Congress in London in 1881 had no section concerned with criminology and in international terms Britain was on a par with Portugal, Serbia and Argentina; in other words, beyond the pale. While in that decade we produced the most infamous anonymous serial killer of all time, we could not match that with *any* scholarship.

In terms of criminals past, Ellis was impressed by the thief-taker Jonathan Wild, a poacher turned gamekeeper in the eighteenth century. He draws attention to Inspector Byrnes of the New York police who had failed to catch the murderer of Old Shakespeare, but whose book *Professional Criminals of America* formed a fascinating collection of photographs which, if anything, proved Lombroso wrong. Who, using the Italian's methodology, would have believed that serial killers of the later years, like Neville Heath, Ted Bundy and Jeffery Dahmer could be, as well as handsome, homicidal maniacs?

And of course, Ellis cannot help quoting another thief-taker, Eugene Vidocq, who founded the Sûreté in Paris, as saying, 'I do not need to see the whole of a criminal's face … It is enough for me to catch the eye.'

In his chapter on the treatment of criminals, Ellis mentions Alphonse Bertillon, whose system of anthropometry was gathering ground in Ellis's day in France, Russia, Japan, Spain, Italy, the United States, Germany and even in parts of Argentina! There is no mention of its impact in Britain.

In 1879, Bertillon was a junior clerk in the Paris Prefecture of Police. He cracked the problem of identification of criminals by a careful measurement of body parts – the length and breadth of the head, the distance from the elbow to the tip of the middle finger, the length of the left foot and so on. Eye and hair colour were factored in (although the latter, of course, could be altered with dye) and a 243-drawer cabinet contained the results. Bertillon calculated that given the eleven measurements of each individual, the chance of any two people being identical was 1 in 4 million.

Photography played its part too, with full face and profile 'mug shots' of criminals (still essentially police procedure today). Bertillon was among the first to popularise crime-scene photography, which is why we have photos of Mary Kelly's body in 13 Miller's Court (1888 – see Chapter 8) and those of Andrew and Abby Borden (1892 – see Chapter 11). His *portrait parlé* system, including scars and other imperfections, was the forerunner of Identikit and Videofit of our own time. 'Bertillonage' caught on and was successful, despite the odd miscarriage of justice when Adolph Beck was wrongfully imprisoned on fraud charges after being confused with the real con man, John Smith!

Advances were being made in other areas of criminology as the nineteenth century wore on. In 1813, Mathieu Orfila, from Mahon wrote *Traité de Toxicologie Generale*, becoming Professor of Medical Jurisprudence in Paris six years later. Today, Orfila is regarded as the father of toxicology. Ten years after his groundbreaking work, Jan Purkinje, professor of physiology at Breslau and later Prague, was carrying out research into sweat glands which would, sixty years later, result in fingerprint technology. James Marsh appeared to be in the wrong job in the 1830s. He worked at the Royal Arsenal in Woolwich and assisted Michael Faraday at the Military Academy for a princely 30 shillings a week. As something of a sideline, he invented a standard test for the presence of arsenic in the body, which was named after him.

In 1875, Wilhelm Röntgen, professor of physics at Strasbourg, discovered electromagnetic rays (originally named after him) which were indispensable in terms of forensics in locating evidence of wounds, especially in ballistic (gunshot) cases.

The first known example of ballistic technology pre-dates a truly scientific study and it was carried out by eye alone. In 1835, Henry Goddard of London's Bow Street Runners (not yet quite phased out despite the establishment of the Metropolitan Police six years earlier) was called in to investigate a burglary in Southampton. The Runners had a reputation far higher than any other existing forces and robbery of well-to-do homes could be 'looked into' for a fee.

A pistol had been fired at the butler (who did not get a good look at his assailant) and the ball lodged in his bedhead. Goddard dug the lead out and noticed a small notch in it. On a whim, he checked the ammunition of the butler's own pistol and found a match; the balls came from the same mould. Not only had the butler gone and staged an artificial crime scene, but a milestone had been reached in the science of ballistics.

Very often in history, someone invents a gadget which benefits mankind and some criminal invents a way to adapt it to their own purpose. In some ways, the reverse was true of firearms. Goddard was lucky that the balls were so easily identifiable because pistols in the 1830s (and rifles) were smooth bore. Already by that decade, gunsmiths were experimenting with grooved or rifled bores that had the effect of spinning the projectile (which increasingly was bullet-shaped rather than round) and increasing the range and accuracy of the gun. Such usage caused striations, scratched on the bullet's surface which came from the grooves and lands of the barrel's interior. That meant that a specific bullet could be matched to a specific weapon and the probable shooter identified.

In 1889, Alexandre Lacassagne, professor of forensic medicine at Lyon University, was able to match seven such grooves in the wounds of a body that came before him. Dr Llewellyn Hall wrote *The Missile and the Weapon* in the United States that became the standard textbook on ballistics for years.

Did this all make trigger-happy criminals think twice? Of course not!

Chapter 5

Saintly Billy

'*Primum non nocere*' are the words central to the Hippocratic Oath – 'first, do no harm'. Unfortunately, the medical profession has all too often ignored this injunction, most often through ignorance and carelessness, but sometimes through 'malice aforethought' – the legal definition of murder. In our own time, the reason that serial killer Dr Harold Shipman and baby killer nurses Beverley Allitt and Lucy Letby got away with their crimes for so long was no one could believe that a medical professional could also be a killer. Yet, the nineteenth century is awash with them.

In *They Hanged My Saintly Billy* (1957), author Robert Graves believes that Dr William Palmer was innocent. Unfortunately, the evidence proves otherwise. Palmer was born in 1824 to a con man father and a prostitute mother (she of the 'saintly Billy' phrase), not the best start in life, and by his teenaged years he was addicted to gambling, betting on the dogs and horses with money he did not actually have. He took a job as apprentice to Evans & Co, a pharmacy in Liverpool, at a time when pharmacy (and medicine itself) was still the preserve of the 'quack'. Anybody could hang out a shingle and start dispensing drugs with no qualifications whatsoever; 'snake-oil salesmen' were literally that. It was all about lies and quick profits.

Palmer's mother paid £100 to get her boy through a 'crammer' to pass his medical examinations, when he was apprenticed to Mr Tylecote, a surgeon in Haywood, near Palmer's birthplace in Rugeley, Staffordshire. Tylecote kicked him out after his student's misappropriation of funds and dalliance with women of ill repute. Undeterred, Palmer went to

London and received his surgeon's diploma from St Bartholomew's Hospital before returning home to practise medicine.

Palmer's first victim was probably his mother-in-law, Mrs Brookes, but he got away with it because the death certificate was signed by octogenarian Dr Bamford who seems to have had no medical qualifications at all. But the crime with which Palmer was charged was the murder of his gambling and drinking 'buddy', John Cook. The fact that two others – Bladen and Bly – had died in 1850 while staying with Palmer seems to have been missed by law enforcement, probably because such deaths were not that unusual at the time.

Palmer's most repellent crimes were the murders of four of his own children, all of whom died in infancy. Between January 1851 and January 1854, he smeared his fingers with honey to soothe sore throats. But the honey was mixed with antimony and they died. When his wife Ann – 'my poor dear Annie', as Palmer called her – died in September 1854, one of Palmer's colleagues, Dr Knight, diagnosed the cause of death as cholera, a water-borne disease then ravaging the country.

When John Cook died, the medical profession again tried to come to his aid. Cook had been ill, on and off, throughout most of November 1855 and the same obliging Dr Bamford called his death the result of apoplexy. Palmer managed to inveigle himself into the post-mortem where his behaviour was suspicious. On 14 December, the inquest decided that Cook had died as a result of 'wilful murder' and Palmer was arrested. The crowd around Stafford Gaol made it clear that the doctor would not get a fair trial (or indeed any trial at all) locally so the case was transferred to the Old Bailey, beginning on 14 May 1856.

The interesting point about the trial of William Palmer is the complete hash of the forensic testimony involved. It cannot have impressed anybody that Cook's family doctor, Henry Savage, at first gave him the highly dangerous mercury for his sore throat, only later modifying the remedy to tonics. On Wednesday, 14 November, Cook became ill having drunk brandy and water with Palmer at the Shrewsbury races.

His throat burned and he vomited violently, only feeling better after a local doctor recommended an emetic and purgative pills.

Over the next four days, Cook's symptoms reappeared, always after drinking a glass prepared by Palmer. At the trial, Alexander Cockburn, the Attorney General, for the prosecution, described at length the chemical properties of strychnine (nux vomica) and the effects that it has on the human body. Antimony was only the preparation for this far more dangerous poison. A half or even a quarter grain was fatal. Cockburn may have lost the jury entirely with his description of human physiognomy, nervous systems etc., but his symptomatic explanation was clear enough – convulsions leading to rigidity in all muscles, including the lungs and diaphragm. He was totally wrong, however, in referring to this as tetanus, which has causes other than strychnine. The prosecution knew that the defence would challenge the medical evidence and told the jury to pay particular attention to the details. This may have been beyond them.

Dr Bamford's regimen, when called in to attend Cook, consisted of calomel, morphia and rhubarb. It was noted that when Palmer was away, Cook began to recover. On Monday 19th, Palmer was back and obtained three grains of strychnine from a Mr Newton, assistant to Dr Salt. Since Palmer was a doctor, Newton thought nothing of it. Bamford's remedies were delivered to the Talbot Arms, where Cook was staying, and were administered by the hotel housekeeper. Palmer supervised his dosages himself. Shortly after midnight, Cook was having convulsions again, screaming 'Murder!' and calling on Christ to save his soul. Ironically, he sent for Palmer.

The next morning, Palmer went to a local pharmacy in Rugeley, run by Mr Hawkings, to buy two drachms of antimony. He also bought six grains of strychnine, almost as an afterthought, and a bottle of Battley's solution, an opium remedy. Oddly, Palmer sent for a friend of Cook, Dr W.H. Jones of Lutterworth, telling him that Cook was suffering from a bilious attack and diarrhoea (both untrue). Bringing an independent medical man into the picture seems odd in the extreme, but perhaps Palmer was hoping for some medical support from Jones (after all, he had always had it from Bamford). If that was his ploy, he had got it wrong. Jones examined Cook and doubted Palmer's diagnosis. The three doctors (Bamford had joined them) agreed that Bamford's medicine should continue. It was Palmer who actually administered the dose, however, but not before he had asked Bamford to write the dosage clearly on the pillbox lid and to sign it. In the event of any subsequent investigation, it would be Bamford's name in the spotlight.

Cook's death scene was ghastly. Even though Dr Jones was in his room, Palmer continued to administer the strychnine under the pretence that it was Bamford's ameliorative. Cook's body was 'rigid as iron' and he could not move. He died shortly afterwards. While two women laid out the body, Palmer was ransacking the room, searching behind cushions and in clothes for cash, IOUs and betting paraphernalia, which was his motivation.

The dead man's stepfather Mr Stevens, insisted on a post-mortem. Palmer suggested the surgeons to do it, just as he had urged Bamford to give apoplexy as the cause of death. At the next day's post-mortem, the ever-fussy and ever-present Palmer told the doctor that Cook was full of disease and had 'all kinds of complaints'. Dr Devonshire disagreed – the dead man's liver, lungs and kidneys were all healthy. Only Bamford noticed slight congestion of the brain; the others did not.

Cook's body was exhumed in January for a further autopsy to be carried out. During it, Palmer (present yet again) nearly knocked over a jar containing the victim's stomach and intestines. He even went so far as to remove this jar to the other door to the post-mortem room, explaining to the others that he had put it there for everybody's convenience. Two slits had been made in the jar's seals and Palmer suggested that it was not wise to allow the contents to be taken away for analysis.

Having failed so far, Palmer offered John Myatt, the post-boy driving the fly (pony and trap) with the jars to overturn it for £10 (over £10,000 today). The inquest was likely to have been a problem for the doctor, who accordingly sent presents to the coroner. He even tried to interfere with the evidence of expert doctors Taylor and Rees, of Guy's Hospital, with their findings having examined Cook's stomach contents.

The problem for the prosecution was that no trace of strychnine was found in Cook's body. Cockburn tried to explain this away by suggesting that fatality depended on the speed of absorption. Since Cook vomited so regularly over his last days, the grains had little time to take effect. Palmer himself was aware of this. In the days before Cook's last illness, he had asked the chemist Newton how much strychnine would be found in a stomach had someone taken a dose of half a grain to a grain. Newton's (quite correct) answer was 'None at all'.

The trial evidence given by the nurses and hotel-keepers at the Raven and the Talbot Arms during Cook's illness are clear and concise, but we are concerned with the forensics of the story. William Jones, the surgeon friend of the dead man, having explained in detail his last hours, told the court that Cook had died from tetanus 'or, in the ordinary English parlance, lockjaw', effectively leading everybody in the wrong direction. It did not help Jones's diagnosis, of course, that it was the early hours of the morning and the room was lit by a single candle. His description of the newly dead body 'twisted back like a bow' was, however, classic strychnine.

The post-mortem report, produced by Dr John Harland, was read out in court and the doctor was there to answer follow-up questions. He reported that Palmer, who knew him, had told him on the way to the autopsy that Cook had had an epileptic fit and there would be signs of an old disease in the heart and the head, he also told Harland 'a queer old man [William Stevens, Cook's stepfather] seemed to suspect him [Palmer]'. The post-mortem at the Talbot Arms was crowded. There were at least four doctors there, including, of course, the man who had caused the procedure in the first place.

The exhumation report from January was the work of Dr Monckton in conjunction with Harland. This ran for two solid pages of text and must, once again, have sailed completely over the heads of the jury. The bottom line, however, was that there was nothing to indicate the cause of death, any more than there had been at the post-mortem itself. Monckton remembered, after the pushing incident that nearly dropped the specimen jar, that Palmer had nudged Bamford and joked 'They will not hang us yet'. When he asked who had cut the jar's seals, Monckton was told that Palmer, Newton and Devonshire all denied responsibility.

The defence tried to rattle Harland by suggesting that he should have carried out his examinations with a magnifying glass. Harland said that was not necessary. The next doctor in the firing line was Charles Devonshire, of London University, who essentially backed up what the court had heard already. David Monckton followed, but his belief that Cook's body was no more rigid that was usual in corpses threw the strychnine argument into doubt. It would not be the last time that 'medical differences' nearly destroyed a capital case. To make matters even more confusing, Monckton then told the court that he agreed with Harland!

On the fourth day of the trial, the first of what would years later be called an expert witness appeared. Thomas Curling was a Fellow of the College of Surgeons, based at the London Hospital, Whitechapel. He was a tetanus expert and this was why he had been called by the prosecution. Cook's symptoms, he told the court, were not caused by either type of tetanus, traumatic or idiopathic. The poison nux vomica, however, did cause tetanic convulsions. Curling was followed by Dr Robert Todd of King's College Hospital who in twenty-five years of practice had never seen a case of idiopathic tetanus. It was wrong, in his opinion, to describe the effects of strychnine poisoning as being like tetanus because it gave an altogether false impression. He was sure that Cook did not die from either epilepsy or apoplexy.

The original idea was to call Dr Bamford to join the medical men quizzed (his own diagnoses, under Palmer's influence, were, in fact, woefully wide of the mark) but as he was ill with cholera, could not attend court. His deposition from the inquest was read out instead and in it, Bamford had said that the cause of Cook's death was congestion of the brain. Palmer had agreed. Having heard this, Todd rubbished Bamford's findings and pointed out that of all poisons, strychnine produces symptoms synonymous with those he had heard in Cook's case. He criticized the delay in examining the spine, however; this should have been done at the post-mortem, not in the exhumation nearly three months later. By that time, the body's decomposition would have produced confusion.

And still the doctors kept coming. Sir Benjamin Brodie of St George's Hospital agreed with the previous experts as did Henry Daniel, an experienced surgeon from Bristol Hospital. It was very telling, however, that Daniel said he had never read either Curling's or Todd's books on tetanus, almost as though bothering with another doctor's opinions was rather beneath him. Samuel Solly of St Thomas's agreed with every expert opinion so far expressed, but claimed that he had been told that Cook had screamed, fallen back in bed and died, while others present said the actual death was very quiet.

Back on the medical straight and narrow again, Glasgow doctors Robert Corbett and Ebenezer Watson testified to other, similar cases. I am amazed that the judge, Lord Chief Justice Campbell and his colleagues Cresswell and Alderson allowed this or that the defence did not object. The Glasgow doctors were followed by eight witnesses, most of them medical, who discussed other cases all over the country that had nothing to do with Cook's death. Symptoms may have been similar, but the relevance of this testimony should have been challenged and thrown out.

On the fifth day, one of the 'greats' of forensic medicine appeared for the prosecution: Dr Alfred Swaine Taylor. His work on toxicology I have quoted elsewhere because it was of groundbreaking importance in court evidence. He was a lecturer in medical jurisprudence at Guy's Hospital and an expert on strychnine. That said, he had never personally seen the effects of strychnine poisoning on humans, only on animals used in his experiments. The symptoms Taylor described in his rabbit specimens were identical to Cook's. Since his testimony runs to eight pages in the trial transcript, he must have been in the witness box for most of the day. As the whole thing was about stomach contents etc., the jury must have glazed over. Only when Taylor told the court that he had examined the contents of Cook's stomach did the evidence become relevant. The doctor had checked for the presence of well over a dozen poisons ranging from prussic acid to hemlock and white hellebore. All he could find were small traces of antimony. The carrying of the viscera by fly (and train? The information is not there) had shaken the jars' contents so that the specimens were shaken up in a chaotic mess. Taylor also examined the liver, spleen and kidneys and was clearly mildly amazed that a bottle of blood was also sent, unlabelled. All these contained antimony.

Mr Serjeant Shee for the defence tried to goad Taylor. 'You know of course that [Palmer's] life depended in a great degree on your opinion?'

Taylor's reply was excellent and put the man squarely in his place. 'No; my opinion was in reference to the death by poison; I expressed no opinion of the prisoner's guilt.'

The press had already misquoted him and he had written to his own professional platform *The Lancet* correcting the media errors. Serjeant Shee tried to muddy the medical waters by quoting Dr Christison who claimed that victims of poisoning did not show rigidity just before death. Taylor replied, 'Dr Christison speaks from his experience; I speak from my own.'

Dr George Rees, who had conducted the Cook specimen tests with Taylor agreed with his comments as did Professor Brande of the Royal Institution. Then, perhaps surprisingly bearing in mind the exchange above, Robert Christison was called. He was Professor of Materia Medica at Edinburgh University, after Taylor probably the greatest heavyweight in the case. Like Taylor, he had carried out strychnine experiments on animals, including a wild boar! He reiterated his view on the onset of rigidity *after* death and not before or during it. In cross-examination, Mr Grove QC had Christison's textbook in front of him and quoted from it, evidently trying again to undermine the official line.

On the sixth day, the last of the doctors appeared. He was John Jackson of the College of Physicians and had practised for twenty-five years in India, where idiopathic tetanus was far more common than in Britain; he had seen forty such cases, especially among children. All in all, his testimony seemed rather pointless.

After all this medical expertise, it must have been a relief for the jury to hear testimony from lawyers, bank managers, butchers, bakers and candlestick makers – people whose language they more or less understood.

What did all the medical forensics add up to? On the trial's seventh day, Shee opened his speech for the defence. One of his key arguments was that, despite the prosecution evidence, there was no trace of strychnine in Cook's body. Dr Taylor, Shee said, was a 'skilful analytical chemist'; so was his assistant, Dr Rees. But neither of them found strychnine. Cook's death by poison was only an hypothesis; it was not provable scientific fact. Certainly not by Dr Taylor – 'good, humane man' – who poisoned five rabbits twenty-five years ago. Shee intended to call his own medical experts – and the jury may have winced at the prospect – to rebut what the court had heard. We do not know exactly when Palmer scribbled a note to one of the defence team – 'I wish there was 2½ grains of strychnine in old Campbell's [the judge] accumulated draught solely because I think he acts unfairly.' This was probably during the summing up, but it tells us a great deal about Palmer's mindset.

Shee was snide about the prosecution's medical experts, along the lines of Shakespeare's 'for Brutus is an honourable man' while rousing the Roman crowd against him. 'Mr Jones gave his evidence and he is a competent, professional man.' They were all 'very learned gentlemen' … 'and Dr Todd gave his evidence in a way to command the respect of everybody …' He quoted from another expert, Dr Coupland, who effectively rebutted, in his textbook, the whole convulsion evidence of the prosecution. 'Do you believe,' Shee asked the jury, 'that if Dr Taylor had read that before he went to the inquest he would have dared to say that this man died of strychnine poisoning?'

Shee's opening speech taking up the whole day on Wednesday, was extraordinarily long – sixty-five transcript pages as opposed to the Attorney General's twenty-four – but of course he had to factor in a lot of the evidence that the court had now heard. His first witness next day was Thomas Nunneley, Professor of Surgery at the Leeds School of Medicine. The judge was not happy with the evidence Nunneley gave, based as it was on the opinions of others actually involved in the case. 'We must take it that medical men are not to be substituted for the jury.' It *could* be argued, of course, that, since Palmer was a doctor, the jury should have been composed of doctors – genuinely a jury of his peers – but this has never been the case in British trials. Nunneley went on to itemize Cook's weak constitution, his syphilis, his lung disease (emphysema), his throat problems, the 'loss of substance of his penis [?]' the fact that his parents had died young and his siblings were also 'delicate'. In explaining the convulsions that Cook underwent, Nunneley put that down to epilepsy and reminded the court that all sorts of complaints caused them – worms in children, hysteria, indigestion ... the list is laughable to modern readers but the mid-Victorians still clung to considerable mumbo-jumbo as hard science desperately tried to make its presence felt. He attacked the doctors who had not carried out tests on Cook's spinal cord immediately after death, as vital evidence was lost.

Nunneley had carried out post-mortems on two women murdered with strychnine and, like Taylor, had carried out experiments on dogs, cats, rats, mice and toads. He described the symptoms as Taylor had earlier and assured the court that rigidity was not present at the time of death. When asked specifically what might have caused Cook's ravings in his last hours, Nunneley suggested they might have been triggered by a noise in the street (implying that this was Cook's own explanation). The doctor was sure that strychnine had nothing to do with the man's death. In every animal case he had worked on, the poison was detectable in the post-mortems.

The Attorney General cross-examined Nunneley on the earlier poison cases. The doctor had described the dead woman's feet and hands as being arched and curved. That was not unusual in corpses, the doctor explained (although, of course it was). When pinned down again on the causes of Cook's convulsions, Nunneley said that many, perhaps all, the dead man's underlying illnesses could be responsible, including depression. 'There was a great deal of mental depression at Rugeley [!]' Nunneley was undoubtedly under fire during his session in the witness box and his answers became less and less convincing as time went on.

The defence's next witness was William Herepath, Professor of Chemistry and Toxicology at Bristol Medical School. He too believed the strychnine could be found in corpses up to the time of putrefaction (i.e. the body 'has become a dry powder') – 'If it was there [in Cook's body] Professor Taylor ought to have found it.'

Julian Rogers was Professor of Chemistry at St George's Medical School, London. He agreed wholeheartedly with Herepath, as did Dr Henry Letheby, Professor of Toxicology at the London Hospital. Like the others, he had heard the previous medical testimony in the court and had read the various reports by those involved in the post-mortem. In his experience, Cook could not have behaved rationally when he did, by ringing his bedside bell and calling for help, had he been given strychnine. He had asked for his hands and neck to be rubbed, but that, to a strychnine victim, would have been unbearably painful. Letheby contested Taylor's argument re the colouring tests for the presence of strychnine. He had said they were 'fallacious' – Letheby disagreed. And, in a phrase that might have caused counsel on both sides to throw their papers up in exasperation, he said, 'We are learning new facts every day.'

Robert Gay was a member of the Royal College of Surgeons. He described the symptoms of a bus conductor who died of idiopathic tetanus and they were remarkably similar to those of Cook. The conductor had a sore throat caused by exposure to bad weather and because of his 'nervous and anxious disposition' had convulsions and died. This is not that far removed from the examples quoted in Chapter 2 of this book!

On the ninth day of the trial, by which time the jury must have been heartily sick of (often irrelevant) medical testimony, John Ross, house surgeon at the London Hospital, gave evidence. He described the rapid death, in the hospital, of a labourer with the same symptoms that Gay had described. His colleague Ryners Mantell appeared to back up Ross's diagnosis, which was a classic piece of time wasting by the defence. Dr Francis Wrightson, analytical chemist at the Birmingham School of Chemistry, echoed the mantra of all the other defence expert witnesses. For reasons that are far from clear in the trial transcript, the judge singled Wrightson out. 'I cannot allow this gentleman to leave the box without expressing my high approbation of the manner in which he has given his evidence.' Since the evidence was merely a tedious repetition of what the court had already heard several times, it is difficult to know what the Chief Justice was talking about.

Richard Partridge was Professor of Anatomy at King's College, London. He too criticized the delay in examining Cook's spinal cord, saw no contradiction in the idea that he died of tetanus. The prosecution reminded Partridge that the exhumation was carried out by four medical men – would he doubt that their competence over the level of decomposition? William Shee objected, which was a pity because the cut-and-thrust of medical and forensic debate might have ended there – in 1856. Instead, it lingers on today, a ludicrous he said/she said playground spat. In the case of the death of John Cook, as with all others, supposedly intelligent men were drawing totally opposite inference and conclusions from the same evidence. Charles Dickens, in *Oliver Twist*, written sixteen years before the Palmer case, described the law, rightly, as an ass. He could have ascribed the same epithet to the medical profession.

Confusingly, *another* medical witness called Gay, this time John, a Member of the Royal College of Surgeons, appeared next. He had worked for eighteen years at the Royal Free Hospital. He described the last hours and death of an 8-year-old boy who died as a result of traumatic tetanus a week after an accident the previous week. Since the lad continued to talk, it was unusual enough to be written up in *The Lancet*. The implication was that Cook had shown similar unusual behaviour and from the same cause.

Dr William McDowell of the Edinburgh College of Surgeons had a rough ride from the Attorney General. He had posited that Cook's syphilitic symptoms led to the sore throat and that in turn could have caused convulsions. That was too much for Cockburn. 'Do you mean to stand there, as a serious man of science, and tell me that?' McDowell stood his ground but he must have known that he had lost that one.

Dr John Bainbridge was medical officer at St Martin's Workhouse. He had considerable experience of epilepsy but admitted he could not tell the difference between that and hysteria. Edward Steady, George Robinson and Benjamin Richardson followed, backing up the defence line. Richardson in particular was very far adrift in claiming that Cook's death (complete with convulsions) could have been caused by the heart condition, angina. As Eric Watson, who wrote the Introduction to the Palmer case in the *Notable British Trials Series* says, this is 'preposterous'.

Quite what the purpose was in calling Catherine Watson, of Garnkirk, Scotland, to the witness box is unclear. She had had a fit, had not been previously injured and had not been poisoned (as far as she knew). She experienced stomach cramps and cramp in the arms. Then she recovered and had not had them since. Perhaps the defence hoped to lift the (no doubt, depressed) mood of the jury by having a female, non-medical presence in the box.

On the tenth day, however, it was business as usual. Oliver Pemberton was Lecturer in Anatomy at Queen's College, Birmingham and had attended the exhumation the previous January. All he could say was that he could not form an opinion on the cause of death from what he saw. And with that rather anti-climactic squib, the forensic medicine evidence came to an end.

Policemen followed, saddlers, gaming gentlemen who had known both Cook and Palmer and the case took off in a different direction. When the Attorney General asked for permission to recall the ridiculous Dr Richardson with his angina diagnosis, the judge, no doubt to the jury's relief, refused.

The bulk of the evidence in the trial of William Palmer was taken up with medical forensics. In a sense it set the tone for most murder trials for the rest of the century and beyond. The prosecution had summoned seventeen doctors; the defence sixteen. Perhaps because Palmer himself was a medical man, who would know his way around poison, both sides pushed the boat out in this respect.

The prosecution's closing argument was clear; John Cook died from tetanus and that itself was caused by strychnine. Cockburn included the evidence of Curling, Todd, Brodie and Daniel, all of whom had expressed no doubt about the nature of Cook's cause of death. The various defence witnesses 'appear to come into that box with the determination as far as possible to misconceive every fact which they could pervert to their purpose.' Cook's family doctor, Henry Savage, assured his patient and the court that he did not have syphilis (which *might* have contributed to his death) and checked him out at regular intervals to see that all was well. The defence had 'launched into a sea of speculation and of possibilities'. The medical profession was drawn into disrespect by these wild guesses. He was scornful of prosecution scientists who quoted cases from textbooks. Most of these authors were still living – why were they not called to make the point?

Cockburn was surprised by the range of 'natural' possibilities for Cook's death as put forward by the defence. Was it general convulsions, arachritis, epilepsy, or epilepsy with tetanic complications? Most bizarrely of all, was it angina? The prosecution's argument was: none of the above. It was caused by *strychnia nux vomica* administered by William Palmer, in Cook's brandy and Cook's coffee to disguise the taste.

The rest of Cockburn's summing up went into the non-medical aspects of the case, the evidence of Palmer buying strychnine from a local pharmacy, his almost constant attendance on Cook in his last days and the links of that attendance with convulsions. In particular, the Attorney General had it in for Jeremiah Smith, Palmer's solicitor; Cockburn had never seen a lawyer behave that way in court. Smith was evasive, very much in cahoots with Palmer over betting and other financial wrongdoing and may very well have been having an affair with the doctor's mother. The Attorney General pointed out Palmer's huge debts, quoting chapter and verse on how much he owed. It was obvious that the doctor was not really in the league of the 'fancy', rich aristocrats who won – and lost – fortunes at the races. He was struggling to keep up a lifestyle he could not afford.

Palmer's behaviour during Cook's illness, his insistence of being present at the post-mortem and attempts to interfere with it aroused suspicion. What had he got to cover up? Cockburn tore into Shee for assuring the court of his client's innocence – he had never known it before and it was an insult to the jury. The defence had lamented the attacks on Palmer in the press and the opprobrium of the mob. That, said Cockburn, was irrelevant.

Because the defence had already opened with a speech, William Shee had no chance of a repetition. It was up to the senior judge to deliver a balanced summary. Campbell held forth on the eleventh day, Monday, 26 May. Because of the presence of the media and the public, Palmer's case had been rushed through to make this happen. This would become standard in various cases in the years ahead. The Lord Chief Justice spoke of medical and moral evidence, but believed the two inextricably linked in the minds of the jury. The medical evidence rested on the question whether or not deliberate poisoning was involved; the moral pointed a finger (or not) at William Palmer.

In the medical context, the judge was not impartial. He referred to the prosecution doctors as 'gentlemen of high honour and solid integrity and proved scientific knowledge, who came here only to speak the truth and assist in the administration of justice.' Others (by which he clearly meant the defence expert witnesses) had a motive 'to procure an acquittal of the prisoner'. He itemized most of them, careful to allude to their experience and integrity.

When he had finished, Shee objected. He was chancing his arm here, an advocate who had already committed a legal gaffe by expressing his client's innocence. To challenge the highest judge in the land took some nerve, but it did him no harm – he went on to become a high court judge too! He complained that Campbell had put the wrong question to the jury, whether the evidence proved that Cook had been poisoned with strychnine. The Chief Justice shot back that was '*a* question' not '*the* question' and that he had fairly covered it all.

It took the jury an hour and eighteen minutes to find William Palmer guilty and he had nothing to say in court. With the black cap on his head, Campbell told him that all three judges agreed with the verdict – 'You must prepare to die.' The decision was made to execute the doctor in Stafford rather than London in that that was essentially the scene of the crime – 'And may the Lord have mercy on your soul.'

The press had a field day. In Staffordshire in particular, the body count against Palmer ran up to ridiculous lengths. He had poisoned his mother-in-law so that her inheritance went to his wife (and, by British law, him). He had killed four of his five children, to save the expense of bringing them up (in a country with no child benefits). He had murdered his wife (having taken out an insurance policy on her). He killed his brother for the same reason. Oh, and he killed John Cook because he had forged betting slips so that the £4,000 win by Polestar at Shrewsbury Races could come his way. Throw in sundry creditors and the possible victim rate stands at 141!

While he was still rational (he became less so by 1889 – see Chapter 9) the lawyer James Stephen, who knew Palmer personally and attended the trial, wrote that the doctor had all the advantages of a solid, respectable life (despite his dodgy parentage) but that he blew it through greed and cruelty. 'The fact that the world contains an appreciable number of wretches who ought to be exterminated without mercy when an opportunity occurs, is not quite so generally understood as it ought to be – many common ways of thinking and feeling virtually deny it.'

William Palmer was hanged at Stafford gaol at 8 a.m. on Saturday, 14 June 1856, denying his guilt to the end. As for the people of Rugeley, the taint on the place led them to petition the prime minister to rename it. He agreed, on condition that, like Melbourne in Australia, it should be named after him. So Rugeley it stayed and we still have no town called Palmerston!

In the context of forensic medicine, very little was achieved. While the prosecution witnesses in effect won the day, that left a lot of assuredly competent professionals with egg on their faces. Had they been subject to school reports, they might have been told, 'Must do better!'

Chapter 6

The Labyrinth of Road

Joshuah Parsons was the first medical man on the scene. He knew what to expect because 14-year-old William Kent had called at his home in Goose Street, Beckington, a little village on the Somerset–Wiltshire border. William's little brother, 3-year-old Saville, had been found in the outside privy (toilet) with his throat cut. The doctor took the boy to the crime scene in his carriage and went into the house via the back door because, that early in the morning, William did not know whether his mother had been told of her little boy's death.

Parsons was the family doctor and knew both Road Hill House and its occupants very well. The building was large and imposing with a carriage drive at the front, a cellar, three floors and an attic. The owner was 59-year-old Samuel Kent, a sub-inspector of factories whose remit was to check all the woollen mills in the West Country to see that the constantly evolving Factory Laws were being adhered to. That alone made him unpopular. We might expect that parents would be grateful to him for freeing their children from hard labour in the 'treadmill' of the factories, but they saw it as government interference – families lost income as a result. On a personal level, Kent was autocratic and unpleasant, arguing with neighbours over minor disputes. All of this became public knowledge in the weeks after his son's murder. Mary Kent was Samuel's second wife. She had been his older children's governess and Kent's housekeeper and when the first Mrs Kent (also, confusingly, Mary) died, insane, the factory inspector married her.

In the house, the four children of the first marriage, Mary Ann, Elizabeth, Constance and William, lived cheek-by-jowl with their half-siblings of the second marriage – Mary Amelia, Saville (the murdered boy) and, as the police investigation continued, baby Eveline. There were also three live-in servants: the nursemaid Elizabeth Gough; the housemaid Sarah Cox; and the cook Sarah Kerslake.

When Dr Parsons arrived, he was shown into the library and was greeted by an obviously distraught Samuel Kent who gave him the key to the laundry room where the boy's body had been laid out. The doctor examined the child. He was stiff with rigor mortis and Parsons concluded that the murder must have happened at least five hours earlier – before three o'clock in the morning. The body was still wearing a nightdress (it was common in Victorian middle-class households for little boys to wear female clothing especially for bed) and was lying on a blanket. Both were covered in blood and excrement. 'The throat,' Parsons testified later, 'was cut to the bone by some sharp instrument, from left to right; it completely divided all the membranes, blood vessels, nerve vessels and air tubes.' There was also a single stab to the chest with little blood, that pointed to a post-mortem injury. 'The mouth of the child had a blackened appearance, with the tongue protruded through the teeth. My impression was that the blackened appearance had been produced by forcible pressure on it during life.'

Parsons was still there when the police arrived. The Wiltshire Constabulary had been set up six years earlier and, like all such units, was finding its way in both crime prevention and detection. It did not have plainclothes detectives in the modern sense – uniformed men were expected to do it all. When it was discovered that little Saville was missing from his cot in the nursery, Samuel had taken his pony and trap to Trowbridge while the servants looked for the boy. With hindsight, this seemed an odd thing to do.

Superintendent John Foley, at 64, was probably too old for effective field command, but he turned up at Road Hill House before ten o'clock and was shown the scene. Saville had been taken from his cot, so Foley inspected the nursery. He worked with Parsons, as a rudimentary pathologist at a crime scene, inspecting the clothes of the household – family and servants. Saville's bedclothes had been neatly folded back and none of the kitchen knives showed any blood traces. Parsons did not believe that such knives were the murder weapons anyway.

With Constable Henry Heritage in tow, Foley checked the boy's body and the outside privy where it had been found by two villagers drafted in to help the search for what everybody hoped would be a living child. They were shoemaker William Nutt and farmer Thomas Beyer. Suspicion would fall on Nutt in particular in the weeks ahead; 'first-finders' were almost always in the frame – they found the body because they had put it there.

Victorian toilets were gruesome places before modern flushing systems and there was a 10ft vault below the seat into which effluent fell. Foley fished out a piece of flannel from this which was later identified as a woman's 'bosom flannel', worn under a corset to cushion the chest. It was bloody.

Later that morning, 29 June 1860, two visitors turned up. One was Rowland Rodney, a solicitor friend of Kent's and the other Dr Joseph Stapleton, a certifying surgeon for Kent's factories. The doctor wrote the first book on the Road murder a year later. Professional though both of these men were, they had no right to become involved in the police enquiries, but both were present in the afternoon when Foley interviewed the nursemaid, Gough. The doctor was impressed with the woman's obvious intelligence. She had no idea who might have killed Saville.

Almost certainly on Foley's orders, local men emptied the pit under the privy and found nothing. With the same authority, Eliza Dallimore, the wife of another constable from Trowbridge, was brought in as 'searcher'. There would be no policewomen for another sixty years and in 1860, Victorian middle-class prudery was at its height. Part of the problem in solving the labyrinth of Road Hill House was the tweeness of language and behaviour of everybody involved. Polite society was playing by the rules; the murderer was not. So Dallimore searched the female servants and their clothes and only found a tiny quantity of menstrual blood on the nightdress of Mary Ann, Kent's eldest daughter. Class snobbery intruded here too; Dallimore could only look at the family's clothing – she strip-searched the servants.

The menstrual blood had been identified as such by both doctors and by five o'clock that day, the official word came from the coroner that a post-mortem should be carried out. We do not know whether either doctor had read Swaine Taylor's 1844 treatise on autopsies, but two doctors working together was the ideal, to avoid mistakes, and they co-operated. The laundry room cannot have been ideal, but it was probably no worse than the slabs on which most post-mortems were carried out for the rest of the century.

Stapleton noted that the boy's face was calm. He had almost certainly been asleep when he was murdered, which was no doubt a crumb of comfort for his parents. Saville's stomach contents included rice which was part of his dinner the day before. There was no sign of laudanum or any other drug in his system, although this could only be detected in 1860 by smell. The chest wound, an inch wide, had pushed the heart out of place and had ruptured the diaphragm. It would have been delivered with some force and was done with a knife, 'sharp-pointed, wide and strong'. The cause of death was the cut to the throat. The blackening around the mouth Stapleton attributed to suffocation, perhaps to keep the child quiet if he had woken up. Parsons could not explain the lack of blood. If Saville had been killed in the privy, why was there no blood spatter on the seat and walls? Foley stayed with the corpse all day, not out of any sense of veneration, but to watch the comings and goings of the household in that context. Of them all, only Elizabeth Gough came in and kissed the boy's hand. The next day, all the Kent girls kissed the boy and Gough came again, the only one to cry.

The inquest opened on Monday, 2 July. The coroner for Wiltshire, George Sylvester, presided. Proceedings were held at the Red Lion pub in Road, the ten jurors typical of the great, good and ordinary of any country village in the land. Samuel Kent could not bear to attend and Rodney took his place. This did the sub-inspector's already poor reputation no good at all; what had he got to hide? In such a microcosmic setting (as opposed to the macrocosm of big cities in other cases) the jury were taken to view the corpse and to tour the relevant rooms of the house.

This idea of viewing bodies dates, as we have seen, from the Medieval belief that a corpse would 'bleed anew' in the presence of the murderer and, in a small community, the probability was high that just such a miscreant would be among the jury. The *Bath Chronicle*, whose reporter was there too, said that little Saville 'presented a horrible spectacle, from its hideous, gaping wounds, which gave it a ghastly experience'. 'Orrible murder sells newspapers.

When the jury got back to the Red Lion, the place was so crowded and suffocatingly hot, that the inquest adjourned to the bigger Temperance Hall nearby. Superintendent Foley showed the dead boy's nightdress and bed clothes to the jury. An amateur pathologist, Stephen Miller, a local butcher, testified that, from what he knew of slaughtering animals, 'the child was held with his legs upwards and his head hanging down and his throat was cut in that position'.

Dr Parsons' evidence repeated what you have read already: Saville was killed before 3 a.m. with evidence of suffocation as well as the obvious knife wounds. The coroner was all for closing proceedings after that, but the jury insisted on having testimony from the Kent family, especially the teenagers Constance and William. There is no doubt that there was a great deal of animosity against the family, much of it class-biased. The Tolpuddle Martyrs, a group of farm labourers from over the county line in Dorset, had been transported to Australia twenty-four years earlier for defying their landlord bosses. There was no trade union as yet for agricultural labourers and feelings ran high. The next extension of the franchise would not happen for another seven years and even then, it gave no vote to the villagers of Road, based as it was on property ownership. The coroner reluctantly agreed, but Constance and Willian had to be interviewed at home, not in the Temperance Hall.

The siblings sang from the same hymn-sheet. Neither knew anything about the murder, but Constance in particular gave her evidence in a whisper, her gaze fixed to the ground. The result of the day? The inevitable 'murder by person or persons unknown'. But the murderers *were* known and despite rumours of a break-in from outside, Mrs Kent herself was always adamant: 'Someone in the house has done it.' The jury tended to agree, but without hard evidence, nobody was listening to them. The coroner's summing up is a classic example of the tweeness and hopelessness of crime-solving in the mid-nineteenth century. 'Although the action was concealed from the eyes of men, yet it was seen and recorded by One above.' He was also characteristically over the top with, 'I say, gentlemen, it is the most extraordinary and mysterious murder that has ever been committed.'

As police enquiries continued and it was discovered that one of the daughters' nightdresses was missing, Saville was buried in the family vault at East Coulston. The inscription on his tomb read 'Shall not God search this out? For He knoweth the secrets of the heart'. Parsons and Stapleton were among the mourners.

Eliza Dallimore searched the maids again, finding that the flannel found in the privy fitted Gough perfectly. Foley and the local force came to the conclusion that the nursemaid had killed the boy because he had seen his father in bed with her and was a notorious tell-tale. He would have told his mother and all hell would have been let loose. In a panic, she suffocated Saville – and Samuel mutilated the boy to make it look as though some maniac had done it. How such a villain could have got into a locked house with no sign of a break-in was not explained.

Accordingly, Gough was arrested on suspicion of murder (note, no action was taken against Kent) and she was kept under house arrest at the police station house (where Dallimore lived) in Trowbridge. She appeared before magistrates in the Temperance Hall on 10 July but was released without charge. The press went into overdrive, the *Morning Post* on that day stating 'a crime has just been committed which for mystery, complication of probabilities and hideous wickedness, is without parallel in our criminal records … The secret lies with someone who was within … the household collectively must be responsible for this mysterious and dreadful event.'

Four days later, a magistrate asked the Home Secretary to send a Metropolitan Police officer to investigate and on Saturday, 14 July, over two weeks after the murder, he duly turned up. His name was Jonathan Whicher.

'Calling in the Yard' became standard procedure in the decades ahead because the Metropolitan Police had more expertise than any other force in handling complex enquiries. That was not true in 1860 because the Detective Department was comparatively new. It was often a difficult line to follow in terms of relationships between the Yard and local constabularies. There was often resentment on both sides. In the Road case, the stereotypical assessment, however, was the correct one. For all the apparent painstaking work of Foley and his officers, they had produced virtually nothing in the way of hard evidence, had trodden far too lightly when it came to the Kent family and had jumped to the wrong conclusions.

By the time Whicher had arrived, the forensics of the case were essentially over and done with. Both Parsons and Stapleton had done a good and thorough job by the standards of the time, but of course they had been hampered by the glacial progress of science. The Wiltshire bobbies talked of 'footmarks', Whicher spoke of 'footprints', but none had been found in the privy where the murder had probably taken place and nobody had access to fingerprint technology which would have proved invaluable in a murder such as this. From now on, at Road, the crime could only be solved by dogged police work.

The Detective Force had been set up in August 1842 after the disbandment of the Bow Street Runners three years earlier. The Met itself had been organized in 1829 and there was still much antipathy towards them. To put plainclothesmen on the street to mingle with the crowd smacked of spying and was dismissed as 'unBritish'. The first detectives (there were only eight of them in Whicher's day) were, like all policemen, drawn from the working class and the snobbery of men like Samuel Kent undoubtedly hindered such officers from doing their job.

While Stephen Thornton earned fame in arresting the Bermondsey murderers, the Mannings and others rumbled the Great Bullion Robbery, Whicher became forever associated with the Road mystery. Three years after it, Adolphus 'Dolly' Williamson, another colleague, was promoted to lead the department and remained in post until 1889, nominally overseeing the search for Jack the Ripper in the previous year. Whicher – Jack to family and friends – was hailed as 'the prince of detectives' and became the model for Sergeant Cuff, the policeman hero of Wilkie Collins *The Moonstone*, written in 1868. Charles Dickens, who was probably over-impressed by the Yard, spent some time with him and provides one of the few descriptions we have. He was 5ft 8in tall with a solid frame and a pockmarked face. He carried out house-to-house enquiries long before that became the norm and was famous for his 'hunches', the 'nose' for spotting criminals at a glance. Such behaviour cut no ice with the courts, of course, who insisted on hard evidence.

Whicher spent days examining every aspect of Road Hill House. One of the large sash windows into the drawing room on the ground floor had been found open on the morning of the boy's disappearance and by experimentation, the inspector realized that it could only be opened from the inside. What did not add up was the apparent strength of the killer, as well as the silent expertise. For someone to remove the sleeping Saville from his cot without waking him, they would need to know the layout of the house. Then, they would have to open the window with one hand while still holding the boy with the other. As there had been no bloodstains in the house, the throat-slitting must have happened in the privy itself. Similarly, the chest wound would had been delivered by a strong hand, even if, as the doctors implied, the boy was dead by then. And whose was the flannel fragment found in the privy sink hole?

Whicher came to the conclusion that there were *two* people involved, a murderer and an accomplice. And they were not Samuel Kent and Elizabeth Gough. To that end, he travelled to the boarding school where Constance Kent was taught. Her teachers were not helpful but two of the girl's friends, Emma Moody and Louisa Hatherill, were. Moody told Whicher that Constance often teased the younger children – 'she disliked the child and pinched it' – because 'the parents showed great partiality'. It was obvious to the detective that it was actually Constance's stepmother, the 'new' Mrs Kent, who was the target of her resentment. Little Saville, the woman's favourite, was almost collateral damage. Whicher also found out that Constance was something of a tomboy, enjoying wrestling with girls in the dormitory of the boarding house.

He also discovered that Constance and William, two years her junior, had once run away to sea (their eldest brother had been in the Merchant Navy). This implied a deep unhappiness in the Kent household, to the extent that Constance had dressed in her brother's clothes and cut her hair so that she could pass as a boy. Intriguingly, they had sneaked out of the house and begun their adventure (they were soon apprehended) from the privy where Saville's body was found.

Whicher ordered the local stretch of the River Frome that ran past the house to be drained. The search revealed nothing. He searched again every inch of the grounds, sometimes with local coppers. The missing nightdress irked the inspector. Whose was it and where was it? According to the local constabulary, Constance's was clean and starched on the morning of the murder. Had she changed it before dawn to avoid detection? It did not help that the older sisters, Mary Ann and Elizabeth, were peculiar in their own right. Twice, Mary Ann became hysterical when she thought she may have to appear in court. Elizabeth insisted on doing her own washing and would not let the maids touch her clothes.

By 19 July, Samuel Kent began to agree with his wife that Constance was probably deranged. The *Devizes and Wiltshire Gazette* risked all kinds of legal action by claiming that 'Mr Kent has not hesitated to intimate … that his own daughter committed the murder! and it is alleged as a reason … that she has been guilty of freaks [hysterical outbursts] during childhood.' The media and the locals put two and two together – Constance's mother, the first Mrs Kent, had died insane. Why shouldn't this trait be carried on to her daughter? The girl had become morbidly fascinated by the Madeleine Smith murder case three years earlier, in which a Scottish jury found the charge of murder by poison 'not proven'. Thirteen-year-old Constance was deemed too young to read such stuff and Mrs Kent had hidden *The Times* from her so that she could not access it.

Whicher interviewed Constance twice, both times in the presence of magistrates. She admitted being strong enough to carry Saville 'the length of this room, easily' and that she and William had once run away 'because I was cross at being punished. I persuaded my brother William to go with me.'

On 20 July, Whicher reported to local magistrates that he believed Constance had killed her little brother. He admitted his case was circumstantial and that he would clash with the local force whose theories ran elsewhere. Nevertheless, the arrest went ahead.

'I am a police officer,' he told the girl that day (even though she knew very well who he was) 'and I hold a warrant for your apprehension, charging you with the murder of your brother, Francis Saville Kent …'

Constance burst into tears.

She was remanded for a week in Devizes gaol while all kinds of rumours flew in pubs, shops, homes and the local press. Whicher was on his own. If he had hoped to shock the girl into a confession, it had not worked. He asked the Commissioner of the Met, with whom he was regularly in touch, to send him Dolly Williamson, his protégé in the Detective Department. The pair took lodgings at the Woolpack Inn in Trowbridge and worked out their case. As with the inquest, Samuel Kent chickened out of visiting Constance in her cell and his solicitor, William Dunn (Rowley had resigned, believing Constance to be guilty) went instead. And the detectives were still looking for the missing nightdress, bloodstains and all. Constance, Whicher believed, had craftily muddied the waters here by blaming the servants who handled the laundry.

In the meantime, the Wiltshire Constabulary continued their own enquiries and tried to rubbish the Yard as far as possible. Superintendent Francis Wolfe and Captain Meredith, the county's Chief Constable, effectively went over Whicher's ground and managed to find the *opposite* of what he had. Constance, said her teachers (Miss Williams and Miss Scott), was a 'well-conducted pupil in every respect'. So that was all right, then.

And, as in every juicy murder enquiry, the fickle media swung this way and that. In the early days of the case, an Englishman's home was his castle and how dare the big-booted 'bobbies' invade the Kent's privacy? Then, Kent and the nursemaid were up to no good and the child must be silenced. One man confessed to the murder, had no links with Road at all and was quietly sectioned. Somebody else was sure that the crime was committed by a sleepwalker. Others believed in the guilt of the perennial fall guys, the gypsies or the travelling people. Now, with Constance in the frame, the press railed against bullying authorities pointing the finger at a tender innocent of only 16, much as they did in the case of Ruth Ellis (1955) and Lucy Letby (2024). It was true, of course, that throat-slitting was not a typical MO as the spectacular contemporary poisoning case of Madeleine Smith proved.

On 27 July, Constance faced magistrates to decide whether or not she should be sent for trial. Whicher had no murder weapon and no nightdress and he knew that his case was circumstantial. That said, circumstantial evidence often hanged people, as it had ten years earlier when Professor John Webster of Harvard was found guilty of killing his colleague, George Parkman. Constance played the 'little girl lost' card to perfection, ably assisted by her counsel, the bullying Peter Edlin, he of the 'glaring eye, distinct utterance and somewhat cadaverous expression of countenance'. His opposition, for the prosecution, in effect, was Henry Clarke, the unprepossessing clerk to the magistrates.

Edlin ran rings around him, pushing the envelope in a way he would not have got away with in a full trial. He accused Clarke of 'most unusual and improper' questions, when they were nothing of the sort. The leading magistrate, Henry Ludlow, did his best to keep him in check.

Dr Parsons gave evidence on the post-mortem, Constance's 'very clean' nightdress and the force used to stab the boy. He was not asked to speculate on Constance's mental state – perhaps he should have been. Edlin was talking rubbish in his closing. 'There is not a tittle of evidence against this young lady ... I say that an atrocious murder has been committed, but I am afraid that it has been followed by a judicial murder of a scarcely less atrocious character.' That may have made some sense had Constance been hanged for the murder, but the whole point of the exercise was to decide whether she should stand trial. He criticized Whicher as an obsessive who had made up his mind on Constance's guilt and may have done so for the reward. Edlin had never known a case so 'unjust, so improper, so improbable'. At the time, the mob orator had the bulk of the audience with him. I wonder what they all thought nearly five years later when the girl confessed to the murder:

> I, Constance Emilie Kent, alone and unaided, on the night of the 29th of June 1860, murdered at Road–hill–house, one Francis Saville Kent. Before the deed was done, no one knew of my intention, nor afterwards of my guilt. No one assisted me in the crime, nor in the evasion of discovery.

She made this admission at Bow Street magistrates' court, London, on 25 April 1865, having attended a high church Anglican finishing school which was actually Catholic in all but name. There were those (possibly Edlin among them) who claimed she had been coerced by her tutors and the Lady Superior into admitting guilt where there was none. Everybody bent over backwards to ensure that the confession had been made of her own free will and the girl was sent for trial.

In the police, there was a change at the top. Foley of the Wiltshire Constabulary had died and was replaced by Superintendent Harris. Jonathan Whicher had resigned from the Met, a disappointed man, and had become a private detective. And the more rational elements of the media now talked sense as most of them had not five years earlier. *The Times*, in particular, spoke of the dodgy character of some teenaged girls 'who go through a period of almost utter heartlessness'. True crime stories before and after Constance Kent bear this out – 'Constance Kent … only did what myriads of her age and sex only wish should come to pass by other agency than her own.'

In the medical area, Dr Parsons had slightly revised his views on the murder. He now believed that Saville had been partially suffocated before he was stabbed but remained adamant that the chest wound was made with a sharp-pointed knife. Congregational minister Edwin Paxton Hood wrote:

There is nothing at all wonderful about [Constance] or her crime or her five years' silence, or her confession, except that she was very cruel, very close [secretive] and very callous. And much as she was she probably is. Her confession does not exalt her; and we decline to accept her either as a model penitent or, as has been attempted, as a heroine. She is simply a very wicked young woman.

The trial was held towards the end of July 1865 and, because Constance had pleaded guilty, the result was a foregone conclusion and something of an anti-climax. Dolly Williamson was there and he had brought Jack Whicher with him. Dr Justice Willes was typical of the more humane judiciary of this period, blaming 'the Evil One' rather than Constance for the murder of her brother. As he passed the death sentence, with the black cap on his wig, he broke down in tears. After five years, nobody was crying for Saville Kent.

The broadside ballads hit the newsstands immediately with appalling doggerel to explain to the uninitiated what had happened:

His little throat I cut from ear to ear,
Wrapped him in a blanket and away did steer,
To the water closet, which soon I found,
In the dirty soil then I pushed him down.

As to motive:

My father married a second wife,
Which filled my bosom with spleen and strife …
I see the hangman before me stand,
Ready to seize me by the law's command …
Oh, what a sight it will be to see,
A maiden die on the fatal tree.

But Constance Kent did not die at Tyburn or anywhere else by the hangman's rope. For a cold-blooded murderess, she elicited a great deal of sympathy from the newspaper-reading public. Politicians, judges and lawyers pushed for mercy and her sentence was commuted to life imprisonment by the queen on 27 July. Her effigy was made in wax by Madame Tussaud's people but it was not displayed until 1873 when Samuel Kent died. It lasted for five years before being melted down to be replaced by more up-to-the-minute murderers.

In two letters written by Constance, one to Sir John Wilmot who had befriended the Kents and probably helped them financially during the trial, the other to the alienist (psychiatrist) Dr Charles Buckmill who had interviewed Constance in Salisbury gaol and found her sane and fit to stand trial. 'The only peculiarity,' he told the *Salisbury and Winchester Journal* 'was for extreme calmness – the utter absence of any symptom of emotion.'

Constance Kent applied for early release six times between 1880 and 1884. Even in Victorian England, 'life' rarely meant life and she served twenty years. She was finally released on the Home Secretary's recommendation, in July 1885. She emigrated to Australia, where her brother William had found fame as a biologist, and she reinvented herself, becoming a nurse, changing her name to Emilie Kaye and living to be 100, dying in April 1944.

The letters that Constance wrote made it clear that her motivation was jealousy. Sidelined by her stepmother, she was sent away to boarding school and, according to her, humiliated when she was back at Road Hill House. Her first instinct was to kill the woman who had taken her mother's place, both in the house and her father's affections. Then she realized that the woman's agony would be more prolonged if she killed Saville, her stepmother's favourite. Accordingly, she stole one of her father's cut-throat razors (the only type available in 1860), a candle and some matches. Shortly after midnight, she went downstairs (she and William were the only children to sleep alone) and opened the drawing-room door and the window shutters. She collected the sleeping Saville from the nursery and put on her galoshes, raised the sash window with one hand and crept out to the privy with the boy still sleeping in her arms.

Lighting the candle, she held her brother upside down in a blanket and cut his throat. She was not sure he was dead so she stabbed him in his left side with the razor and threw the boy and the blanket into the pan. The flannel she was carrying, presumably to wipe her hands of blood, was thrown in as well.

Back in her bedroom, she found only two spots of blood on her nightdress and washed these out in the overnight wash basin. Then she put on a clean nightdress and folded the other one away before eventually burning it, five or six days later, as the police enquiries continued. She cleaned the razor and slipped it back in her father's case and then proceeded to lie through her teeth about any knowledge of her brother's murder.

Jonathan Whicher had been right. There was no illicit liaison between Samuel Kent and Elizabeth Gough, certainly no wandering intruder who had happened upon the boy and decided to kill him. Yet hardly anyone credited the 'prince of detectives' with some excellent work well done. The social snobbery of mid-Victorian England would not let that happen and nobody (not even Whicher himself) understood the cold, callous motivation of Constance Kent. Today, we recognize the symptoms of the sociopath – the lack of empathy, the unawareness of cruelty. In her silences, in her lowered eyelids, in her bald lies, the 16-year-old showed all the outwards signs of a killer who cared for nobody except her own obsession, that of jealousy. This was barely understood in 1860 and it led to Kent escaping the hangman's noose.

Yet even Constance's confession did not fully meet with Whicher's approval. Saville Kent was a big, healthy child and strong as she was, how could his sister have managed him, the galoshes, the window and the matches on her own? Most importantly of all, as Doctors Parsons and Stapleton had agreed, how could a blunt-ended razor have caused the stab wound to Saville's chest? Whicher *knew* that there had to be a knife and that Constance had had help on that ghastly summer's night. Several times in her original confession, she stressed that she had acted alone, before, during and after the murder. Why? Because she was covering up for someone and that someone had to be her brother William. They were only two years apart in age. She was the elder and was clearly the senior partner in their relationship. It was Constance who had persuaded him to run away to sea. It was only Constance and William who slept alone, enabling them to roam the house at night. How easy it must have been to drip the poison of jealousy into the lad's ear, that the second Mrs Kent had it coming. Perhaps the strong Constance held the boy while William used the razor. Perhaps it was William who used the knife, the one that was never found and which could so easily have been tossed into the Frome that ran close to the house. Either of them could have kept Saville quiet with Constance's flannel over his mouth.

But William, like Constance, said nothing. As far as medical forensics went, both doctors had done a good job, but in 1860 forensics could only go so far. Whicher did a much better job but because of the social obstacles and niceties of the time, he could not prove his case.

So Constance Kent never kept her date with the hangman. And neither did her brother William. Both of them effectively got away with murder.

Chapter 7

The River of Death

The Thames always had a macabre reputation. While it was home to the largest docks in the world in the nineteenth century and while the beautiful people of their day punted and boated upstream at Henley, the river held secrets dark and unfathomable. The winds that rippled its surface and the contrary eddies and whirls of its tides played havoc with the senses and tested the skills of those tasked with investigating the work of the man who was arguably the world's first serial killer.

Countless people died in the water because of boating accidents. On 3 September 1878 a pleasure steamer, the *Princess Alice*, collided with a steam-collier, the *Bywell Castle*, with a loss of over 700 lives, many of them as a result of poisoning (the sewage outlets into the Victorian Thames made the river lethal).

Suicides were common, especially below London Bridge and much of the work of the River Police when they were instituted in 1795, was fishing bodies out of the water. Tower Bridge, opened in 1894, had a small room in one of its towers for storing such corpses until they could be identified and buried. One high-profile suicide was Montague John Druitt, a barrister and teacher who was found floating on the afternoon of Monday, 31 December 1888 by a waterman. Today, Druitt is infamous as a potential suspect in the Ripper murders that convulsed the East End in that 'autumn of terror'. Charles Dickens described the grisly work of dredgermen who fished out bodies in *Our Mutual Friend*, and the social commentator Henry Mayhew notes acidly that no corpse in the Thames was ever found with money on them, hinting at the lack of integrity and even decency of the dredgers

By the 1890s, such corpses were routinely photographed at mortuaries along the river bank, such as St George's-in-the-East, where Ripper victim Elizabeth Stride ended up (see Chapter 8). The river was also a highway of crime. Patrick Colquhoun's River Police (later called Thames Division with the letter T in white metal on their collars) was set up to cope with all of this.

Body One – Battersea – 5 September 1873

Because the identity of only one of the Thames victims could be ascertained, I have no option but to give them numbers. This seems heartless in the extreme but for reasons of clarity it has to be done.

On 5 September, a galley rowed by River Police on a routine patrol saw an object floating on the water near Battersea. They hauled it onto their boat and saw at once that it was the left quarter of a female. Two days later, two more parts turned up, the right thigh floating off Woolwich and the right shoulder at Greenwich. The arm was covered in tar, almost certainly from contact with ropes and boat keels along the river.

Those who knew the Thames's idiosyncrasies deducted that the body parts (all from the same corpse) had been dropped in the water upstream, where the Wandle tributary ran into the Thames, near Wandsworth Bridge. When the parts were assembled, a post-mortem was carried out by Dr William Henry Kempster, of Battersea Bridge Road, a police surgeon attached to V Division, based in Wandsworth. Police surgeons were doctors used to violent crime and had the unenviable task of examining corpses, often in situ at murder sites, and of patching up victims of brutality who had survived attacks, including the police themselves.

Little is known about Kempster, but in the case of the 'Battersea Horror' as it was known, he was the nearest thing to a forensic pathologist. He became a member of the Royal College of Surgeons in 1862 but spent much of the decade in Scotland where he became MD at St Andrew's University. At the time of the Battersea find, he was also Medical Officer of Health for the area at a time when public health was becoming a serious issue under Disraeli's Conservative Government.

The media were not allowed to report grisly details of crime, but the medical journal, *The Lancet*, told things as they were. Death was caused by severe blows to the right side of the head, but of that, only the skin remained, the skull itself was missing. The carotid arteries had been cut and Kempster believed that the murder had happened recently (on or just before 5 September) because of the fresh appearance of the neck muscles. The scalp and face had been removed by horizontal and vertical cuts, the skin peeled off – which effectively made recognition impossible. The upper part of the nose was missing, as was part of the right cheek, chin and lower lip. This kind of 'surgery' would have taken time.

The dismemberment was neat, even the complicated joints of the ankles and elbow. Only at hips and shoulders had the bones been cut. Kempster carried out his post-mortem in the mortuary of the Clapham and Wandsworth Union Workhouse. Independent mortuaries, and those associated with hospitals, did not exist, at least for anonymous murder victims. Kempster believed that the body had been in the water for about twelve hours and this, of course, had an effect on the appearance of the body.

The body part that had been found first had been taken to the police ship *Royalist*, moored on the Embankment, the new structure recently completed by the architect Joseph Bazalgette. This ship was known as 'the Abode of Bliss', Inspector 'Daddy' Bliss being the man in charge. From there it had been taken to Kempster. That same day, Henry Locke, a visiting policeman, saw another body part floating in the water at Brunswick Wharf, Nine Elms. Constable 349W, Henry Turner, took possession of it and passed it to Inspector Starkey of the River Police.

The head, or what was left of it, came to light on Sunday, 7 September at Duke's Shore, Limehouse – 'the head of a woman with the brain cut out' as the police described it. The ears and eyelashes were still there but no eyes. Interestingly, in the context of modern forensic science, the police were castigated by the coroner at the inquest, W. Carter, who complained that too many officers had handled the body parts. This was undoubtedly true, although in an age before DNA evidence, or even fingerprints, it is debatable how much damage these men had done. It did not help everybody's case that river debris presumed to be the dead woman's lungs, turned out to be those of a sheep!

Kempster was able to conclude that the victim was about 40 years old and 'very stout'. A knife and a fine-toothed saw had been used and the dismemberment had occurred shortly after death. Moles on breast and neck, and an old burn scar on the chest was held in high hopes of identification. The hair was dark and thin and the skin olive coloured. There was a little moustache – 'the feminine moustache, as we call it'. The nose had been round and fat, and the ears had been pierced at some time and the wounds to the head had almost certainly caused death. The woman had given birth.

What happened next is sadly typical of the ghouls of any and every generation. People referred to as 'dealers in horror' turned up in large numbers to view the body parts in the mortuary. One man believed that the corpse was that of his daughter, but she had had smallpox and there were no traces on the torso. *The Times* spared nobody in its account of this – 'If morbid curiosity had led the old man to travel this distance [from Hoxton] he had all the horrors he could have desired. He was taken to the dead house where the severed breasts were taken from a shell [coffin] and put together and the ghastly face having the scarred nose with the scalp, thinly covered with hair, was taken from a jar of spirits and laid before him.' The man could not remember any moles or burns to the chest and he left, at once relieved and disgusted; his 39-year-old daughter had been missing for three weeks.

On 11 September, a foot was found floating off Hammersmith Docks. The police by now believed that the Wandle was not the dumping ground, but that the various parts had been dropped at high tide in the early hours of the previous Friday morning. By that date,

Kempster was still lacking the skull, both hands, both legs, the left shoulder and most of the internal organs. He had no clothes on the torso either. While the police concentrated on bargees, many of whom were gypsies with a poor reputation, the old man referred to above had found his daughter very much alive in the Waterloo Road.

The inquest resumed on 15 September, the coroner having given the police time to investigate. By that time, missing body parts had turned up at various points along the river – Blackwell Point, Woolwich, Albert Bridge, White Hart Docks near Vauxhall and Eastern's Wharf, Lambeth. Kempster could now say, having examined an ovary and part of a uterus, that the victim had never given birth, but she may have miscarried (very common in Victorian England). One arm and one thigh carried old scars. The blistering on the skin was probably caused by the sun on the parts bobbing for two weeks on the river. Both Kempster and Dr Edmund Hayden, the Workhouse Medical Officer, now believed that the dismemberment may have begun while the woman was still alive.

One idea in circulation was that this was the work of a prankster, a medical student. The body was real enough, but where had it come from? *The Lancet* leaped to a defence, regretting the fact that such nonsense got in the way of justice. The medical schools (there were several in London), were all closed at this time of year and the Inspector of Anatomy assured everybody that no corpses had been given out for dissection purposes.

Kempster and Hayden undertook a bizarre reconstruction. They pulled the skin of scalp and face over a wooden butcher's block and photographed it. On 20 September, *The Times* was sure that this would result in instant identification. The photograph has not survived, but it yielded results. The face had been disfigured, the skin was waterlogged and the block itself was arguably the wrong shape for the dead woman's skull. Only those with a viable reason to view the photograph had access to it. This did not stop the irresponsibly ghoulish *Illustrated Police News* (20 September) publishing a drawing of the head, lifted by an officer from the water. The *Police News* was the equivalent of graphic comics today or the video 'nasties' that hit the High Streets in the 1980s; they sold/sell widely but have no basis in reality.

People were still coming to view the corpse by 25th with a plethora of ever more unlikely stories that the police were obliged to follow up. The inquest verdict was, inevitably, 'murder by person or persons unknown'.

Body Two – Tottenham Court Road, October 1884

There is no doubt that whoever murdered the Thames victims, also killed the girl with the rose tattoo found on 23 October 1884. The MO is startingly similar. What caused the eleven-year gap between Battersea and the Tottenham Court Road is unknown. Perhaps the killer was out of the country or in prison; perhaps (and this is shakier ground) the impulse to kill for some reason receded.

In October 1884, the job of trying to piece together a person, as well as her life, fell to Dr Samuel Lloyd. Unlike the medical men who appeared in the Whitechapel series of murder four years later, whose every word was reported in the media, men like Lloyd fell under the radar. So too, in fact, do the Torso Murders. And such is the Ripper's hold on the true crime fraternity today, that many people blithely assume that both sets of murders were carried out by the same man. As we shall see, nothing could be further from the truth.

There was a delay in starting the proceedings because of the confusion over body parts. It did not help that the press routinely used banner headlines such as 'shocking case' and 'extraordinary outrage' to sell newspapers, so that *real* atrocities were often consigned to the small print. Bones had been found in the Ornamental Gardens at Mornington Crescent, almost a mile, as the crow flies, from the Thames. Parts of a woman had turned up in Alfred Mews, a cul-de-sac off Tottenham Court Road. A parcel containing a human arm had been thrown over railings in Bedford Square. The police located more. All those gruesome finds were taken to St Giles mortuary.

The finds in Mornington Crescent were initially dismissed as a medical student's prank – à la *The Lancet* of eleven years earlier. There was a left arm, a hand and two feet, enough to convince the police surgeon that the victim was young and female. On 11 November, coroner Dr Danford Thomas opened the inquest at St Giles Court and began questioning his list of witnesses.

Dr Lloyd testified that the body parts from Alfred Mews, Fitzroy Square and King's Cross Station, all came from the same cadaver. The nails were well manicured, the arms and hands delicate, the hair long and fair. He regarded her as a gentlewoman in the class-obsessed language of the time; and yet, no one came forward to report such a woman missing. About the only potentially useful clue was the tattoo on an arm. Such things were rare, especially on women in the 1880s and the suggestion was that this was a street-walker, an 'unfortunate' from the prostitute class. It was in this decade that 'General' William Booth of the Salvation Army was preparing his *In Darkest England*, a social survey of poverty to mirror Mayhew's work thirty years earlier. Sex and prostitution were taboo subjects to most people – Mayhew and Booth were exceptions – and coyness, at least in print, was the order of the day.

Dr Lloyd believed the tattooed woman to be between 25 and 50 years old, a large window it is true, but he had little to go on. Dissection had been carried out by 'someone skilled, but certainly not for the purposes of anatomy'. He believed that two different bodies were involved, but the Mornington Crescent remains had already been buried and the doctor wanted an exhumation. He then decided it was one body only, the murder having taken place in April.

Both these finds and those of 1873 appeared to have been crushed at some point, possibly by being piled up in a container. And there, unsatisfactorily, the matter lay until the next time.

Body Three: Rainham, May 1887

Three years passed before the next dismembered corpse turned up and once again, the killer had used the Thames as his dumping ground. Rainham was a long way downstream, the furthest of all the body parts found, and the victim was spotted floating by a lighterman, Edmund Hughes, who dragged it ashore. Inside a rough canvas sack was a woman's torso, minus arms, legs and head. Part of both breasts had been cut off. Initially, the press of the day dubbed this latter atrocity 'The Rainham Mystery' but it had nothing to do with Rainham at all; it was merely the body's penultimate resting place on its way from further upstream. Rainham was a small village with no mortuary or coroner's court and the body was placed in a shed next to the Phoenix Hotel where an inquest was held the next day, Saturday, 14 May.

The coroner was C.C. Lewis who presided over the South Essex district and his first witness was Dr Edward Galloway, R Division's police surgeon from nearby Barking. The post-mortem he had performed almost certainly took place the previous day and Galloway gave his opinion that the legs had been cut at the thigh tops with a very sharp saw, leaving two bones of the lumbar vertebrae. Tendons and muscles had been cut with a sharp knife. The legs had been cleanly taken out of their pelvic socket by oblique cuts. They were the work of an expert. There were no signs of bruising so the actual cause of death was impossible to determine.

The doctor believed that the woman had been dead for two weeks, some time around the beginning of May. The victim would have been 5ft 3in to 5ft 4in tall (average for the time) and he guessed that her hair was brown (although none was found on the body). She was perhaps in her late twenties, but could have been as old as 35. Perhaps to allay any more press speculation on medical school pranks, he was convinced that the body had never been used as a 'hospital subject' and that such things were contrary to the Anatomy Act of 1831 which legislated over bodies made available to science for dissection. Galloway was forced to concede, when pressed by the coroner, that the killer had 'a thorough knowledge of surgery'. Perhaps because of the three-year gap since Tottenham Court Road and the very different locale, the media do not seem to have made a connection. The last river dismemberment, after all, had happened fourteen years earlier. But two days later, more body parts turned up. The mutilated remains of a female were found floating near Temple Pier, half way between Blackfriars and Waterloo Bridges. The 'large parcel' reported in the newspapers turned out to contain a human thigh, wrapped in sacking and cord. More was found later in the day, on the river's south bank by Battersea Park along Chelsea Reach. This was the 'upper portion of a human body'.

The medical expert here was Assistant Police Surgeon, Dr Hamerton, who agreed with Galloway that the removal of the thigh from its socket was expertly done. But Galloway went further. He was convinced that the thigh came from the Rainham torso. The Temple and Battersea finds had not been in the water very long (the skin was not waterlogged or even wrinkled) and it was clear that the body parts had been placed in the river at different points and on different dates. Someone was able to store such parts until he chose to distribute them.

A top-level conference was held on Saturday, 11 June at Battersea. Coroner A. Braxton Hicks presided and two Scotland Yard Officers were present along with Dr Kempster of V Division. Perhaps because of this, the Home Secretary, Henry Matthews, ordered the Rainham body to be exhumed, along with the Ilford thigh. The items were preserved in spirits of wine, the usual method at the time and hermetically sealed in case more parts turned up.

And turn up, they did. More body parts were found (the media is unclear whether this was off Battersea or Rainham, but more likely is off Waterloo Pier, upstream from Temple Stairs).

There was a further twist to the Rainham story. A week later, labourer William Gate saw a bundle floating, not in the Thames this time, but in Regent's Canal, near St Pancras Lock. The sack contained two human legs and had been in the water for some time. Unlike the river, the Canal had no tide and no current and the unblemished skin suggested an older woman. Yet they fitted the preserved Rainham torso, as Dr Galloway proved. On 19 July, he spoke to the press to explain that the entire body, minus head and upper part of chest was in the hands of the police. He explained that the collarbone and breasts had been taken off and the canvas in which the parts had been wrapped was the same.

The Rainham inquest came to a close at Crowhale Hall in Camden Town on 13 August. The coroner was the highly experienced Danford Thomas and as well as Galloway, another high-profile medical man was in attendance. He was Dr Thomas Bond, a graduate of King's College Hospital whom we shall meet again investigating the Ripper murder of Mary Kelly in November of the following year. He was there at the request of James Monro, Assistant Commissioner of the CID, as having more experience than Galloway.

Bond's conclusions were that the Rainham victim was between 25 and 40 years old, 5ft 2in to 5ft 4ins tall and had never given birth. Her killer had a knowledge of anatomy. 'The removal of the head,' Bond said, 'was not for the study of anatomy, but was done for the purpose of covering up a murder.' On 1 July, he had examined the eleven separate body parts of the Rainham victim along with Dr Charles Hebbert. He began with the sex organs. The ovaries were small and the ridges of the vagina proved the woman's virginity. Dismemberment was done quickly and soon after death. The skin was fair and the hair initially black. There was no ring indentation on the fingers, and the arms had been removed by the same oblique cuts as the thighs. The Canal bones were more decomposed than those from the river, riddled with water-worm holes. The feet were not deformed, indicating that this was not one of the very poor whose badly fitting shoes often led to malformation of the toes. That said, the toe-bones themselves were missing along with the nails. The skin indicated that the victim was white, but in 1880s London, that hardly cut down the field. The woman had recently menstruated and tell-tale grooves below the knees implied the wearing of garters (a working-class fashion in this position).

Hebbert may have been anxious to distance the torso killer from his own medical profession – 'I do not think that any surgeon or anatomist could have done the work as well, as they are not *constantly* operating, while a butcher is about daily cutting up carcasses.' He may have been right, but the argument seems extremely weak.

Body 4: Scotland Yard, September 1888

What happened next is like something out of a modern psycho–drama, where a deranged killer taunts the police. In the real world, such things *do* happen. When the Ripper struck in the 'autumn of terror' (1888) over 2,000 letters and postcards were sent to the police and media, several of them purporting to be written by the Whitechapel murderer.

On the face of it, the body discovered on 11 September 1888 was the most brazen taunt of all because it was found in the foundations of Norman Shaw's opera house, which, from 1885, had been designated the new Scotland Yard because the old headquarters of the Metropolitan Police was overcrowded and inadequate. Three days before the body was found, a prostitute named Annie Chapman had been found in a yard behind 29 Hanbury Street, Whitechapel, with her throat cut and her bowels ripped out. In the previous week, Mary Ann Nichols had suffered a similar fate. The hideous work of the Whitechapel killer (see Chapter 8) quickly dominated the headlines to the extent that other cases were put on the back burner. Although the media believed that the torso killer and Jack were one and the same (and some writers still do today), the police knew differently. Even so, the way police resources were taken up with the East End atrocities, including drafting in officers from other divisions, meant that the torso killings faded to an extent into the background.

In fact, the first body part, a woman's arm, was found near the sluice of Ebury Bridge Road by labourer Frederick Moore. This was B Division's patch, making this the third Met unit to be included in the Torso murders. The police passed the find to Dr Nevill, their divisional surgeon, and Drs Bond and Hebbert, examined it on the 16th. Seven, neat, clean cuts had been used to release the arm from its torso, and even with so little evidence, the doctors concluded that the owner was almost 20 years old with a dark complexion. She had been about 5ft 9in, tall for a woman at that time. Once again, there was clear anatomical knowledge in the dissection and a ligature had been used to prevent blood from draining from the cuts. Hebbert thought the strap had at some point been wrapped in newspaper, but does not explain why.

On 1 October, a Monday, carpenter Frederick Windborn, working in the basement of what would become Scotland Yard, collected his tools from the space where had left them, hidden behind some boards, for safekeeping. He found a parcel of paper, 2½ft by 2ft, wrapped in string and inside was the maggot-infested torso of a woman. It looked like 'old bacon', he told the inquest later. The remains were taken to Millbank mortuary which, like most such establishments, was lacking in almost every respect. A contemporary account says: 'it is almost devoid of proper modern appliances. Four wooden partitions have been run up, but there is neither antecedent room to conduct post-mortem examinations, nor means of ensuring the most ordinary sanitation and assisting in the ready and sage identification of the dead.'

The smell of putrefaction must have been horrible, but the Scotland Yard basement was very near the river, which had its own smell because of pollution. When the *Princess Alice* went down in 1878, several deaths were caused by inhaling toxic water. Perhaps because of the inadequacy of Millbank, the torso was taken to the much better-equipped Westminster mortuary where it was immersed in an alcohol solution to kill the maggots. Bond and Hebbert again officiated. The torso was female, the breasts intact. The head had been severed at the sixth vertebra and the pelvis and lower abdomen at the fourth lumbar. The torso was measured, with a waist of 28½in. The breasts were large with small nipples. There were no marks or scars anywhere to aid identification. Two clean lateral cuts had taken off the head with jagged incisions from front and back. Heart and lungs were healthy.

There was partly digested food in the stomach, but it was no longer possible to say what that was. The woman had not been alcoholic, as many working-class females were in London. She was brunette, still with armpit hairs in the days before modern fashion sensibilities made this unusual. The arm from Pimlico was a perfect fit.

Death, the doctors believed, had occurred two months earlier (early August) and decomposition had taken place in the open, which meant that the torso must have been exposed somewhere potentially visible to passers-by.

Bloodhounds were brought in (they would be needed in the Ripper's case too), although details are scant and they appear to have achieved nothing.

The *Times* described the murder scene. Today, SOCO teams in specialist clothing would have been all over this, photographing, measuring, taking samples. In 1888, both doctors and policemen trampled all over the place with hob-nailed boots, blissfully unaware of the potential evidence they were destroying. Steps led down from the Embankment and a slope beyond that went further into the bowels of the building. The place was dark, a mess of building debris, and workmen's boot prints must have been all over it. The media presumed that the body had been dumped there in daylight (because of the lack of light) by someone who knew the layout. The site gates, from Cannon Row, were high and locked and the likelihood of anyone climbing then, complete with torso, was not great.

Far more likely was access from the river, perhaps via the plethora of craft delivering and unloading building materials.

It was on 5 October that the letter arrived. Ever since late September, anonymous postcards and letters had been arriving, either at Scotland Yard or other police stations, or at various news outlets relating to the Whitechapel killings. It was from these that the brilliant moniker 'Jack the Ripper' came. But the 5 October letter referred to 'the Whitehall Mystery', the torso at the Yard. It was sent to the Central News Agency in New Bridge Street who in turn forwarded it to Chief Constable Adolphus 'Dolly' Williamson.

Dear Friend,
In the name of God hear me I swear I did not kill the female whose body was found at Whitehall. If she was an honest woman I will hunt down and destroy her murderer. If she was a whore God bless the hand that slew her, for the women of Moab and Midian shall die and their blood shall mingle with the dust.

Also on 5 October, Inspector Marshall of A Division handed over remains found at Guildford Station in Surrey to Bond and Hebbert. The specimen had been boiled and the doctors agreed that the bones were those of a bear! The contents of the letter that reached Williamson had nothing to do with the pathology of the case, although today forensic graphologists would learn from it. What it does point up, however, is the misogyny of the Victorians – actually very widespread – and the obsession with the Bible. Moab and Midian were yet more examples of the 'wicked cities' of the Old Testament, like Sodom and Gomorrah, and clearly the writer had no problem with murdering women of the prostitute class.

The inquest was held in the Sessions House in Broad Sanctuary Street, Westminster on Monday, 8 October. The jury were taken to view the remains in the Millbank mortuary before Coroner John Troutbeck opened proceedings. Dr Bond's testimony after lunch revealed that one lung showed signs of severe pleurisy at some stage, but of course this did nothing to help with identification. The deceased had not been drowned or suffocated, but Bond speculated that a wound to the missing head might have caused death (the heart was pale and free from clots which led him to this conclusion). Dr Hebbert believed that the blood on newspaper wrappings of the arm was animal, but not from a bird or reptile. He was in fact, making this up; not until Dr Paul Uhlenhuth's researches of 1901 could experts tell animal blood from human.

On 17 October, a journalist, Jasper Waring, got police to allow him into the murder scene and his Russian terrier dog, Smoker, almost immediately dug up a left leg and foot. This bizarre situation begs all sorts of questions, but it does illustrate how lax the police were at scenes of crime. The animal was brought back later that day and found a left arm under where the leg had been. What this meant was that because the limbs were found below, and separate from, the torso, the killer had visited the site at least twice to make his deposits. The question also arose – why bury the limbs and not the trunk?

In the light of these new finds, the inquest was resumed on 22nd. Dr Bond believed that the leg had been in the place in which it was found for some weeks. It was Hebbert who wrote up Bond's conclusions, following the protocol that two medical men should be involved in post-mortem work. Dismemberment of the leg had been carried out cleanly and with professionalism, the date of the operation about six to eight weeks previously, which took the crime back to late August or early September. The body parts all belonged to the same victim, but dispersal methods had been different. The torso was exposed, at some point to the air and was badly wrapped in paper. The arm had been immersed in the Thames. The leg had been buried. No wonder the press used the term 'Mystery' to describe this one!

But this was Victorian England, with all the bizarre behaviour patterns of a society so unlike our own. Coroner Troutbeck gave his jury the option of 'wilful murder' by the ubiquitous 'person or persons unknown', or 'found dead'. They opted for 'found dead'!

Elizabeth Jackson, Horsleydown, June 1889

John Ryan saw some boys throwing stones at an object floating in the river near St George's Stairs, Bermondsey on 4 June 1889. With their help, he dragged the object out of the water. It was part of a woman's body and was taken to the Assistant Divisional Surgeon of the River Police, Dr McCoy.

Half a mile from Ryan, a 15-year-old wood cutter, Isaac Brett, was swimming under Albert Bridge and saw a parcel tied with a bootlace. He took it to the nearest police station, V Division, and the thigh inside could, for the first time, help with identification. The leg came complete with a section of an Ulster (overcoat) and a pair of drawers (underwear), the latter with the name L.E. Fisher written in black ink on the waistband. Could this be some sort of laundry mark or the kind of naming that schools used? Thames Division called in Dr Kempster who had worked the Rainham case, and Thomas Bond.

Kempster believed that the body parts had not been in the water long, perhaps twenty-four hours, which put the date of the murder as 3 June. The bruises on the thigh were caused by fingers while the victim was still alive. There was no doubt that the Horsleydown and Battersea finds came from the same body.

The coroner presiding on 6 June was Wynne E. Baxter, who had 'previous' in the case of Dr Bond: prostitute Rose Mylett had been murdered on 20 December of the previous year, whilst certainly *not* by Jack the Ripper and, bizarrely, Baxter refuted Bond's assertion that the woman had died accidentally, claiming that intoxication and the tightness of her stays had caused her death.

The inquest was very short, to give police more time to investigate and later on that same day, gardener Joseph Davis was working in Battersea Park when he literally stumbled on a collection of body parts tied in a package with white Venetian blind cord. Inside was a torso, wrapped in a burgundy-coloured skirt.

At Battersea mortuary, Kempster gave his opinion. The spleen, kidneys and part of the intestines were still present, as were the lower six dorsal vertebrae, but the lower five ribs were missing, sawn off. Death had occurred four or five days earlier, taking the date of the murder to 2 June.

But the finds had not ended there. Charles Marlowe was working at Copington's Wharf near Temple Pier where a Rainham body part had been found two years earlier. He saw a body part floating and reported it to the Thames Division. Engineer David Keen found yet more parts near Palace Wharf. Everything belonged to the same body. Solomon Hearne was one of the gypsy community living along the embankment and he found a woman's leg on the foreshore at Lammar Hard, near Wandsworth Bridge. It was wrapped in the same chequered Ulster cloth as that found earlier near Albert Bridge.

Yet more sections turned up the next day; a piece of human flesh at Palace Wharf, Nine Elms; at Limehouse was a right leg and foot with the same Ulster wrapping. A left arm was found the next day at Bankside, Southwark, wrapped in brown paper. Kempster reported that the hand was small and well manicured. Yet again, the dismemberment was skilful.

It was the police themselves who found the next body part, unwrapped, floating between Battersea Park Pier and Albert Suspension Bridge. But all this faded into insignificance on 8 June when journalist Claude Miller, assigned as a freelance to the torso story, found a body section thrown over a hedge along Chelsea Embankment. The garden where it had landed was the property of the Shelley family, whose ancestor, Mary, had created the famous *Prometheus Unbound*, known today as Frankenstein's monster, a creature made from body parts.

In his report for *The Lancet* Dr Hebbert refers to these finds as the Thames Case. All that was missing, as with all the other cases, was the head. The chest had been opened by a clean cut through the sternum and the lungs and heart had been removed. All remaining organs, despite decomposition in the water, were healthy. The vagina showed no signs of either childbirth or rape. The skin was fair and the pubic hair a light sandy colour. For the first time it was possible to confirm that the victim had been pregnant, between six and seven months and the foetus had been removed by her killer. The arms gave the best clues – the indentation of what was probably a wedding ring on the relevant finger and signs of recent vaccination. There was a long, tell–tale scar on the lower forearm.

There was no sign in the victim of hard, manual work and no obvious cause of death. Once again, the doctors veered away from the suggestion of a medical killer in favour of a butcher or horse-knacker.

In 1889, the doctors did not concern themselves with other evidence; that was, quite properly, the job of the police who went to work on the wrappings and clothes fragments. All these were made available for public viewing but there was nothing unusual about any of them. The Ulster, the string, the Venetian blind cord, the bootlaces, were cheap and available everywhere. Only the name L.E. Fisher stood out. And here, red herrings abounded. Constable Fisher of the Hertfordshire police reported his sister missing. She was 25 years old and had left her husband and child in May 1888 to live with another man. Another L.E. Fisher was a barmaid at the Old Dock Tavern along the Thames. According to the census of 1881, the only L.E. Fisher would have been 9 at the time of the Horsleydown find. As for the barmaid, she was found alive and well in Ramsgate.

The inquest resumed on 16 June with more discussion on the use of dogs. Jasper Waring's terrier was sent sniffing around Battersea Park and 'came up with nothing'. The search was on for 'L.E. Fisher's' missing head, but it was never recovered. The first witness at the inquest in the Star and Garter pub in Battersea was Thomas Bond. He believed that the Rainham and Whitehall murders were the work of the same man. Coroner Hicks pressed the idea of a back-street abortionist, since the victim had clearly been pregnant. Abortions were illegal in Britain until 1968 and there were various people, often midwives, who carried out such operations for money. As with the Ripper inquests, which had been going on for months by now, the issue was raised of the use of drugs, although it is not clear why this was raised at all. There was no drug culture in Britain in the 1880s, although such was the slackness of pharmacists that various poisons were available over the counter.

The inquest was adjourned again, at the request of the police, until 1 July. Before that, perhaps the only breakthrough in the Thames Torso case had occurred. Catherine Jackson had viewed the body in Battersea mortuary and could tell by the scar on her arm, that 'L.E. Fisher' was actually her daughter, Elizabeth. The dead woman had been 24, 5ft 5in tall and rather plump. She had reddish-gold hair, lovely teeth and well-shaped hands. The Ulster was hers, given to her by a friend, Mary Minter. The L.E. Fisher label was the result of Elizabeth buying a job lot of clothing with that name attached in what was a thriving second-hand clothing trade. She was the youngest of the daughters, born in Chelsea in 1865. She worked as a domestic servant from 1881 to November 1888 when she lost her job and her home. The last time her family saw her alive was in Turk's Row, Chelsea, when she had a row with her sister Annie about Elizabeth 'picking up men for immoral purposes'.

It is only 300 yards from Turk's Row to where her body parts were found and the police were now able to put together the pieces of a shattered life. Forensic science could achieve a great deal, even in Victorian England, but it could not fill in the background to a murder, any more than it can today. Jackson had lived with a pimp ('protector' was the euphemism) called Charlie and since November had moved in with a miller and former soldier, John Faircloth. He was violent towards her and she had bought the Fisher clothing during their brief time in Colchester. On 28 April, five months pregnant, Jackson and Faircloth parted company for good. Her intention was probably to move back home, but her mother was in the workhouse and her father probably dead. She slept rough – 'carrying the banner' as it was known – on the Thames Embankment, still owing her former landlady, Mrs Paine of Millwall, a week's rent.

George Sims, the journalist who wrote a great deal about London life, describes the down-and-outs who haunted the Embankment:

> there the homeless vagabond and the prowler in search of prey herd together ... There are some desperate men along the Embankment 'dossers' – men who would not hesitate to fling their stunned and despoiled victims into the Thames. But not all

these children of the night are criminals or roughs. Some are the sons and daughters of despair.

Jackson drifted back to Chelsea, gratefully accepting Miss Minter's Ulster. She refused to go into the workhouse, always an option, because her mother was there and clearly the family had issues with their wayward girl. She was seen in the company of various men in the days before her death. The last time that Catherine saw her daughter was on 31 May. She was wearing a cheap brass ring on her wedding finger.

So much research has been carried out on the victims of Jack the Ripper, that we almost expect all Victorian prostitutes to be 'bag ladies' who hawked their wares in the streets and provided sex in the open, in courts and alleyways of the East End. In fact, there was a whole hierarchy of 'scarlet sisters' from the upper-class 'demi-monde' who were the kept mistresses of the aristocracy and even royalty (think Edward, Prince of Wales, and Elizabeth Walters, known as 'Skittles') to the street walkers and camp followers of the army, considered the lowest of the low.

Today, Turk's Row is an elegant street of fashionable houses, but the buildings themselves are Victorian or Regency and it is possible that Jackson was a bordello girl, operating from one of them; she certainly followed the pattern, however. 'She was poor but she was honest' was not just at Music Hall song, but a statement of sociological fact.

'The profession of a prostitute,' General Booth wrote, 'is the only career in which the maximum income is paid to the newest apprentice.' Superintendent Joseph Dunlap of C Division, covering Chelsea, told a House of Lords inquiry in 1881 that there was a great deal of child prostitution in his manor; until 1885, the age of consent was 12. Pornographic photographs of 7–10-year-olds were widely available – 'like grown up ladies', the advertising ran, 'these little girls indulge in all debauchery.'

If Elizabeth Jackson was a prostitute, can we assume that the other torso victims were as well? Generalisations are dangerous, but the answer, in all probability, is yes; 'Unfortunates' were particularly vulnerable because of their availability.

In the context of the torso murders, one piece of advertising is particularly pertinent – and revolting. Madame Audrey of Church Street, Soho ran a brothel there and lured her punters in with:

This abbess [Audrey] has just put the Kipehook [kibosh] on all other purveyors of the French flesh market. She does not keep her meat too long on the hooks, though she will have her price, but nothing is allowed to get stale here. You may have your meat dressed to your own liking and there is no need of cutting twice from one joint; and if it suits your taste, you may kill your own lamb or mutton for her flock is in prime condition and always ready for the sticking.

How could the torso killer resist?

Body 6: Pinchin Street, Whitechapel, September 1889

Dr Percy Clark should not have been directly involved at all, but his boss, Dr George Bagster Phillips, *the* dominant personality in most of the Ripper inquests, was on holiday and Clark did the honours. He had been sent for by Superintendent Thomas Arnold of H Division (a new unit in terms of the torso killings, but one at the epicentre of the Whitechapel murders) and his field officers, Inspector Edmund Reid and Charles Pinhorn (see Chapter 8). We do not know who asked Charles Hebbert to join Clark at the crime scene but we know from his treatise *Exercise in Forensic Medicine* that he was there.

Constable 239H William Pennett, had been routinely patrolling his beat at five o'clock on the morning of Tuesday, 10 September, walking past the archways of the Tilbury and Southend Railway Company, in Pinchin Street when his bullseye lantern picked up something lying in the end archway, the only one not boarded up. It was a female torso, with a thin chemise (petticoat) draped over a shoulder. Pennett fought down the urge to vomit over the smell, and turned the half corpse over. He saw bowels protruding through a gash to the abdomen.

From there, H Division had cranked into action. What I believe was the Ripper's last victim, 'Clay Pipe' Alice McKenzie, had been found in Castle Alley two months before, but no one could be sure where and when the Whitechapel fiend would strike next. Surely, this latest find was too much of a coincidence; the killer *had* to be Jack. And, as far as the media was concerned, the Ripper sold newspapers.

Clark and Hebbert agreed that the victim was plump and well-formed with full breasts and dark pubic hair. The hands were small and well kept, like Elizabeth Jackson's. Rigor mortis had come and gone and the flesh was turning green. The internal organs were examined and weighed and found to be healthy. The stomach contained plums. The dead woman would have been about 5ft 3½in tall, between 25 and 40 years old, and had never borne children. Her distended vagina proved that she was not a virgin. Her right little finger had hardened skin which *may* have been caused by frequent writing. There was no sign of a wedding ring and the cause of death was attributed to blood loss. All cuts had been made after death with a very sharp knife. As always, Hebbert debated whether a medical man could have been responsible, despite the obvious anatomical skill involved in the dissection.

There were signs of a rope having been tied around the wrist and both elbows were discoloured from habitual leaning. The police believed – and it is unique in the torso killings – that the dump took place between five and five thirty, on the morning of 10 September. In all other cases, the timings are much more vague, or non-existent.

James Monro, new Commissioner of the Met, reasoned that the murder had taken place on the night of Sunday, 8 September. The body must have been kept somewhere throughout Monday until early Tuesday morning. So the murderer had room to stash the corpse or its component parts and he also had to move it when he did, perhaps to avoid discovery. Monro also reasoned that it was only the location that gave the Pinchin Street torso *any* links with the Ripper. Everything will else pointed to a different kind of killer altogether, although he speculated that a wound to the vagina may have been an attempt to *simulate* Jack's MO.

No other body parts turned up, despite extensive police searches in the surrounding streets, railway yards and the nearest stretch of river. The inquest opened in the Vestry Hall, Cable St, St George's-in-the-East, with Wynne Baxter in the chair again. Since Dr Clark was busy with another case at the Old Bailey, and Phillips, now back from holiday, was still catching up, Baxter adjourned until 24 September.

The resumed inquest let Clark testify that the murder had probably taken place early on Sunday morning, 9 September. The body had been recently washed and the bruises to the back were caused in life. The 'rope' mark was that made by ordinary clothing. There was a vaccination mark on the left upper arm and the hands and forearms were badly bruised.

Dr Phillips testified that Dr Frederick Brown, of the City force, who had done such sterling work in the Ripper murder of Kate Eddowes the previous October (see Chapter 8), had also attended the Pinchin Street post-mortem. Phillips believed the disembowelling weapon to be at least 8 inches long and it was possible that the cause of death was a cut to the throat, hidden by the subsequent decapitation. The doctor was also asked to comment on any similarities with the murder of Mary Kelly the previous November, and Phillips explained that the Dorset Street murder showed signs of demented frenzy, while the Pinchin Street torso was methodical and was carried out in a calculated – and, as it turned out – successful way to avoid capture.

The torso was preserved in alcohol and buried. Inspector Moore attended and reported that the body was placed in grave No. 16185 in the East London Cemetery, Plaistow. A small plaque read, 'This case contains [the] body of a woman (unknown) found in Pinchin Street, St George's-in-the-East, 10 September/89.' The point of preserving remains in alcohol was that further tests could be carried out in an age of more advanced technology. But, to date, no one has taken up the challenge.

When I wrote *Jack the Ripper: Quest for a Killer* in 2009, I named a potential suspect. I cannot do the same for the torso murderer because the records are too vague. But I can narrow the field.

While the majority of policemen, and the public, believed that such ghastly crimes could only be committed by a raving lunatic (and Britain's asylums were full of them), some of the more enlightened police surgeons – for example, Bond and Hebbert – had almost certainly absorbed the work of Professor Rudolf Virchow of the Berlin Pathological Institute. He had wise words to say about post-mortems and had studied some 6,000 criminals over twenty years, relying on the soon-to-be-outmoded 'science' of phrenology. Murderers, Virchow believed, had small crania and pronounced eyebrow bridges and muzzles. They were still, mentally at least, Stone Age animals. With orthodox views such as these dominating 'the science', how likely was it that the torso killer would be caught?

The initial problem with finding him was a lack of crime scene. While the Ripper killed his victims where he found them and left their bodies (in all but one case), in the open, the torso killer's known link with his victims is the dump site. At first, this seems random, but it is not. Despite the observations of the body parts in the Tottenham Court Road area, it is the *river* that drew the killer time after time. Just as we can draw conclusions on murder patterns via geoprofiling, so can we via dump sites. Today's psychiatrists know that a serial killer's first strike will be closer to his home or place of work. Later killings take place further afield as he grows in confidence. If we look at the geographical locations of the body parts, of the nearly forty found, half are clustered along the Battersea and Chelsea stretches of the Thames. We have to factor in the tides and currents of the river, which adds to the problem, but essentially, the notion at the time of the first murder in 1873, that the actual murder site was near the river

Wandle, a tributary that flows into the Thames between Putney and Wandsworth bridges, is correct.

By and large, the doctors carrying out post-mortems on the various victims did an excellent job. They matched body parts accurately, gauged heights and weights of the complete body had it been present and even made intelligent guesses as to the social class of the victims. This, despite the effect of the water on the skin and the post-mortem damage done by boats and ropes along the river's reaches. It was ironic, of course, that fingerprint evidence, which might have helped, was 'just around the corner' – we will look at this in a later chapter.

Doctors, especially Hebbert, were anxious to point out that the medical profession does not behave in this way. Doctors kill – a surprisingly high number of them – but they tend to use poison as a simpler, less messy MO. But if not a doctor, then the spotlight must fall on a butcher. There were, course, thousands of these all over London and fingers were pointed at them too in the Ripper case. Various letters referred specifically to the torso killings. 'Goodbye ta ta' wrote, 'One of the two women I told you about is a Chelsea girl and the other is a Battersea girl …' 'H.I.O. Battersea' told police that the Whitehall leg 'does not belong to the trunk you found there'. In January 1889, 'Jack Bane' wrote, 'I chucked some old wo[man] in the Thames because [she] began to squeal …'

How could a killer distribute the body parts where he did? At night, obviously, where darkness would mask a multitude of sins. All areas of London, especially along the river, were busy day and night. Street markets opened at five o'clock and stayed open until dark or their produce ran out. Workshops opened in the early hours. Many people lived over their shops and were literally 'open all hours'. The concept of our nine to five working day did not exist.

So we are looking for a travelling butcher rather than one who had fixed premises. And that points directly to the Cat's Meat Man. One of the jobs that has long disappeared, Cat's Meat Men wheeled hand-carts around the streets, belting out 'Cat Mee-att' for the great and good of all classes to feed their pets. Some had ponies and traps. Most of them wore leather aprons. In 1837, there were believed to be about 2,000 in London, which had fallen to perhaps 300 by 1851 when Henry Mayhew carried out his social survey.

Such a man would be welcome in the squares of Chelsea and Battersea; useful in coping with the stray cats that littered a building site like Scotland Yard. Their animals in turn helped keep down the rat population. Underneath the layers of animal off-cuts on his cart, were the packaged bundles of what remained of people.

In modern psychological terms, the torso killer was an organized, highly efficient murderer. He would almost certainly have been of average or above average intelligence. He had to be able to deal with the public, cat owners and servants and not give anything away. He was also, more darkly, able to strike up conversations with prostitutes to the extent that they felt safe with him. He was a skilled dismemberer – all the doctors agree on that and, of course, he had enough time and light at the murder site to carry this out effectively. This was no slash and run in the shadows like Jack.

What was the actual cause of death? I believe it was the same in all cases. It was a blow to the head delivered with a heavy hammer, or axe. This was why the torso killer's victims were all headless – the murder method would have pointed straight to a horse slaughterer, because this was the usual method used. The first victim in 1873 still had the skin of the scalp present and the wounds – two of them – were evident. The murderer must have realized this and took pains to eliminate the skulls in future.

One of the least well-documented traits of modern serial killers is the propensity to change jobs or domicile after a murder. Is this why the mid-1880s, killing took place in Bedford and Fitzroy squares and Mornington Crescent, land-locked areas well away from the river? And had he moved back to the Thames, for the same reason, by 1887?

Brian Innes in *Profile of a Criminal Mind* (2003), wrote:

> Such a crime is premeditated not committed on the spur of the moment. The planning forms part of the offender's fantasies, which have probably been dwelled on for years … The victims are mostly strangers, of a particular type that the offender has in mind and that he has been hunting for … the offender will have found out ways to approach the victim … gain control over them.

Most of the horse-slaughtering establishments in London were in the East End and Smithfield, which had been a meat market since the Middle Ages. But this is too far from the greater concentration of dumping of body parts in the West. Think back to *The Times* Wandle theory of 1873, later (wrongly) dismissed by most people. 'In Garratt Lane, Wandsworth,' wrote William Gordon in 1893, 'is the largest horse-slaughtering yard in London.' It was the premises of Harrison Barber Ltd.

In a country heavily reliant on horses (the combustion engine, like fingerprint technology, lay in the near future), animals too old and ill to work were routinely butchered. Famous horses like the Duke of Wellington's Copenhagen and Lord Cardigan's Ronald, were given honourable graves or were stuffed in glass cases as a reminder of their fame. Others, like the cab horses in Anna Sewell's tear-jerker novel, *Black Beauty* (1877), met the slaughterer's axe in a cold, draughty yard.

Harrison Barber was huge, on the east bank of the Wandle, with fields at the front and giving off virtually no smell, despite the blood and bones inside. The actual killing took two seconds. The horse, shaved of mane and tail stood, tethered, with a shade over its eyes. A single swing of the axe and 'he falls heavy and dead on the flags of a spacious kitchen.' Hide, hoofs, bones and flesh were all separated with saws and knives and put aside to be used for different purposes. Oil was needed in lubrication and leather dressing; bones went to manure merchants and were ground to mix with sulphuric acid to make fertilizer. Skin and hoofs made buttons, hides became carriage roofs or the leather inserts of cavalrymen's overalls (trousers).

The horse meat was boiled in coppers, tripe used as dog food (dogs being less fastidious than cats), and the slaughter went on day and night. There was a cold storage in the Garratt Lane branch, capable of storing 250 carcases. This, I believe, was the murder scene for up to six women who were all floated down the Wandle or along nearby reaches of the Thames. This was Elizabeth Jackson's patch and quite possibly the area walked by the others too, in Superintendent Dunlap's sexually busy C Division. The killer knew these streets well and he knew the river. He could not know exactly where the body parts he had created would end up but he knew it would be a reasonable distance from his own territory. Perhaps, like Dr Neill Cream (see Chapter 10) he took his victims for a drink at one of the myriad pubs he also knew well. A business deal was struck and he took her to the premises across the fields from the river. He must have been relatively senior, with his own key to enable him to come and go as he pleased. Like the horses, the murder was over in two seconds; like them, his victim fell 'heavy and dead on the flags of a spacious kitchen.'

There was no sign of mutilation of the genitals or anything like Jack's grotesque handiwork. Two of the murders were probably committed on a Sunday, when the premises would be empty. Using his saw and his knife, he went to work, wrapping the parts in anything that came to hand – the canvas bags used to store flour and sawdust, the string that was so ubiquitous throughout the capital. Twice he used parts of the victim's clothing, but we do not know why and once a piece of old newspaper, probably the *London Echo*.

As for the head, did the torso killer have an isolated, secret corner of the abattoir where he could display the heads, the ultimate trophies? Or did he crush them in the huge grinding machine at Harrison &Barber's? If so, why not destroy the bodies entirely this way? Because there was another aspect to the Thames torso murderer. He was a show-off, someone who loved to tease and shock. Many serial killers pose their victims for the maximum effect, knowing that members of the public and the police will be horrified by what they see. Why else put *floatable* packages in the river? Why choose Scotland Yard as a dump site? Why place the Pinchin Street torso in the very heart of Ripper territory, if not to titillate newspaper readers and confuse the police?

And that is as far as I can go in the search for the Thames torso murderer. He was not Jack the Ripper. He was not a bargeman or a lighterman. In 1887, the year of the Rainham mystery, Harrison Barber bought up the slaughter premises of Henry A. Curnell in Braden Road, King's Cross. Curnell's was fifteen minutes' walk from the dump site in Alfred Mews. Was the murderer of the Wandle along Garratt's Lane transferred there when the take-over happened? And is that why he abandoned the river for a short time?

We have no idea whether the police investigated Harrison Barber or any other horse slaughterer. Detailed minutes of the investigation have not survived. Neither have the names of personnel who worked for the company.

It was odd that, of the eight victims, only Elizabeth Jackson should be identified. But then, of the 700 plus dead in the *Princess Alice* disaster, 160 have no names either. If these anonymous seven were prostitutes (and it is a fair bet that they were), no punter was going to come forward with information. But such women had parents, siblings, husbands who could simply have said something.

And, of course, the man who killed them is just as anonymous as they are.

Chapter 8

Jack or Have You Seen the Devil?

While the Thames Torso murderer was still sporadically leaving body parts along the river's embankment and elsewhere in London, another serial killer hit the capital. This time, the killing fields were the adjacent parishes of Whitechapel and Spitalfields, a notoriously deprived area that the journalist Jack London called 'the Abyss'.

In the five years before 1888, Whitechapel had become home to a large influx of Ashkenazi Jews from Eastern Europe, driven out of their homelands by antisemitic pogroms of the government of the Tsars of Russia. As the Jews moved in, the Irish moved out and the locals were now an alien people with limited English, chronic poverty and often a natural mistrust and even hatred of authority. This was an area where casual violence, drunkenness and prostitution were the norm. In the 'city that never slept', there was never a time when the dingy courts and alleyways were truly deserted, with drunks staggering home, rubbing shoulders with labourers on their way to work in the largest docks in the world. There too were the 'unfortunates', the 'ladies of the night' (Victorian Britain was full of euphemisms) who pestered both groups to earn the cost of a bed (usually 4d) in a flea-infested doss house.

And there, anonymous and unfindable was the most famous blitz serial murderer in history, the 'Whitechapel fiend' whom the journalists of Fleet Street christened 'Jack the Ripper'.

Much is made in Ripper folklore, of the 'canonical five', traditionally the body count of Jack's handiwork. In fact, five victims was merely the guesswork of Assistant Chief Constable Melville Macnaghten, who listed the victims in his famous Memorandum. He claimed to have inside information, which he (illegally) destroyed. Bearing in mind how little the motivation and impulses of serial killers were understood at the time, the five victim 'fact' is actually just an assumption.

I believe the Memorandum should be amended to read:

(i)   7th August 1888. Martha Tabram, George Yard. Mutilation to stomach and chest.

(ii)   31st August 1888. Mary Ann Nichols at Buck's Row, who was found with her throat cut and with (slight) stomach mutilation.

(iii)   8th September 1888. Annie Chapman, Hanbury Street; throat cut, and stomach and private parts badly mutilated, and some of the entrails placed around the neck.

(iv)   30th September 1888. Elizabeth Stride, Berner Street; throat cut, but nothing in the shape of mutilation attempted.

(v)   And on the same date Catherine Eddowes, Mitre Square; throat cut and very bad mutilation of face and stomach.

(vi)   9th November 1888. Mary Jane Kelly, Miller's Court; throat cut and the whole of the body mutilated in the most ghastly manner.

(vii)   17 July 1889. Alice McKenzie, Old Castle Street; throat cut, stomach mutilated.

In my amended list, Martha Tabram and Alice McKenzie were also victims of the Whitechapel murderer, which takes his list to seven.

Martha Tabram

The first 'pathologist' to investigate a Ripper murder was Dr Timothy Robert Killeen. His name was misspelt 'Keeling' by Chief Inspector Donald Swanson of the Met, (not to mention, several witnesses) which hardly inspires confidence in Scotland Yard's paperwork. He lived at 68 Brick Lane, almost certainly sharing a medical practice with Dr Septimus Sawyer. He was only 24 and had recently moved to London from County Clare, Ireland. He was summoned by a uniformed constable with the information that a woman's body had been found on the concrete landing of a stairwell at George Yard Building, along George Yard, known as 'Shit Alley' to locals because of the amount of debris that often blocked the narrow passageway.

Killeen, not a police surgeon, was probably not used to the ghastly pieces of crime evidence in the area. The dimly powered gas lamps gave very little light (the Queen herself was to demand improvement in this context in the weeks ahead) and in the precise spot where the body was found there was no lighting at all after eleven o'clock. Killeen would have entered the Yard from the south, passing under the words that ran, ironically, 'St George's Residence, Board and Lodgings for Respectable Girls'.

The body he saw on the landing did not look respectable at all. Two days later, he presented his report to George Collier, Deputy Coroner, for the South-Eastern Division of Middlesex at the Working Lads' Institute, 137 Whitechapel Road. Killeen's original report has not survived, but its essence was reported in *The Times* on Friday, 10 August. The doctor believed that the woman had been dead for about three hours. Since it was 5.30 a.m. when he arrived, the time of death (always a guessing game) would have been around 2.30 a.m. Killeen estimated her age to be about 36 and that she was 'well nourished'. In fact, Martha Tabram was 39 and the mortuary photograph, the body completely covered with a blanket up to her chin, shows her to be positively stout.

Killeen's post-mortem (the word necropsy was more common at the time) showed that she had been stabbed thirty-nine times. The left lung was penetrated in five places and the right lung twice. The liver was healthy, apart from its five penetrations and the spleen carried two wounds. The stomach had been penetrated six times. It was the wound to the sternum that Killeen found to be the fatal one, and that was inflicted with 'some kind of dagger', all the other wounds being more superficial and could have been inflicted with a pen knife. All would have been carried out while the woman was still alive.

Before the inquest was adjourned for a fortnight for the police to carry out further investigations, the coroner expressed the hope that the body would be identified as soon as possible. Three women had come forward with different names already. 'It was one of the most dreadful murders,' wrote *The Times*, 'anyone could imagine. The man must have been a perfect savage ...'

From the subsequent police enquiries, we can now construct what may have happened on that black landing in the early hours of 7 August. The dead woman's name was Martha Tabram, née White, although she often called herself Turner, having lived on and off with William Turner who had last seen her three days before her murder. Tabram was a heavy drinker and most of her relationships collapsed because of this. Like many East End women, she had turned to prostitution and on 6 August, a cold, wet Bank Holiday, had gone to various pubs with another prostitute, Mary 'Pearly Poll' Ann Connolly. The pair met up with a couple of soldiers (she was unsure which regiment they were from) and had almost certainly drunk at the White Swan and the White Hart just along the street from George Yard.

It was here, in the early hours of Tuesday, that the women parted company. Tabram went up George Yard with her private; Connolly took her corporal up the equally dingy (and narrower) Angel Alley, which ran parallel off Whitechapel High Street. In the 1880s, other ranks in the army had no civilian clothes, only their scarlet 'walking out' dress. That was how Connolly knew she had gone with a corporal, he wore his stripes on his sleeve. It was also standard for soldiers to carry a bayonet in a leather frog at their belts.

The police investigation pressed this, hoping to force Connolly to tell the truth (apparently a rarity for her) and identify the men's regiment. Inquiries held at Wellington Barracks and the Tower and spearheaded by the larger-than-life opera singer and balloonist, Inspector Edmund Reid, got nowhere. Soldiers, in a spirit of camaraderie, lie for each other habitually when under suspicion, and Reid could not break the alibis of a man likely to be responsible.

The medical evidence, as opposed to the vague and often contradictory ramblings of eyewitnesses, makes it clear that Martha Tabram was attacked by two men that night. The deep wound to the chest, which penetrated the heart as well as the sternum, was delivered by the guardsman who went with her for sex, using his bayonet. This was not a final *coup de grâs* intended to finish her off, but the only wound the soldier inflicted. Perhaps they quarrelled over the price of Martha's services. Perhaps he was annoyed by her drunken antics. One stab to the chest was enough to kill her. Then he had gone to join his mate, ready to concoct a lie to alibi them both should the need arise.

Then, Martha Tabram met the Whitechapel murderer. He was not yet Jack the Ripper. If all the modern research into serial killers is correct, he was from the same social class as Tabram. He knew the streets as well as she did. He was anonymous, a nobody who could melt into the crowd. Eyewitnesses remembered seeing soldiers, upright in their scarlet. Nobody remembered seeing Jack. The compulsion to kill had been growing in his confused, contorted brain for weeks. And here was a woman, bleeding, her clothes disarranged, staggering on the landing overhead. It was the work of seconds to scuttle up the stairs to reach her, then to knock her off balance, haul up her skirts, as the soldier had done earlier, and thrust and stab with the penknife he habitually carried in his pocket. She was dying anyway, too weak to scream, too weak to fight. Technically, the Whitechapel murderer did not kill Martha Tabram; a Guardsman did. But it gave 'Jack' a taste for blood. And the next time, he would be responsible for *all* the wounds he inflicted. Next time, he would become legend.

Dr Timothy Killeen had no further interest in the Ripper case. He did not see the later murders, the escalation of violence and the mutilation. And by 1889 he had gone home to Ireland, away from the Whitechapel killing fields forever. And Martha Tabram? A verdict of wilful murder, the inquest jury decided, against some person or persons unknown.

Mary Ann (Polly) Nichols

Although commentators have pointed out Dr Killeen's relative youth and inexperience, his performance in the context of Martha Tabram seems to have been competent and professional. The same cannot be said of Rees Ralph Llewellyn, the doctor who attended the crime scene of Polly Nichols in the early hours of 31 August.

Constable 96J John Thain was patrolling at the customary 2½ miles an hour along Brady Street when he saw the flash of a lantern from Buck's Row that led to it. This was the 'bullseye' of Constable 97J John Neill who had found a murdered woman lying on the pavement outside the locked stable doors of Brown's Yard. He could see that her throat had been cut and blood was still oozing from the gash. He called out to Thain, 'There's a woman has cut her throat. Run at once for Dr Llewellyn.'

It was perhaps an odd choice of words from Thain, implying that he was looking at a suicide, but bloody corpses in the street can unnerve anybody, even experienced policemen. Llewellyn was not a police surgeon, but probably the nearest medical man, with a practice he had inherited from his father at 152 Whitechapel Road. He was 38 in August 1888 and had lived in Whitechapel (in fact in the house attached to the surgery) all his life. Clearly both Thain and Neil (and probably most of J Division) knew Llewellyn and he was the natural 'go to' choice.

The doctor got to the murder scene at about four o'clock and a little crowd had gathered. Neil had been joined by Constable 55H, Thomas Mizen, who was soon dispatched to get an ambulance and what today would be called 'back up' from Bethnal Green police station. There too were the workers at Barber's Horse Slaughterers' yard, in adjacent Winthrop Street, who had been working the night shift. Unaccountably, Thain had left his cape there earlier and had retrieved it on his way to Llewellyn's.

'Scene of crime' in the modern sense did not exist in 1888. There was no police tape, no special overalls, no photography. Policemen and passers-by trampled over evidence with complete abandon, unaware of the damage they were causing. Llewellyn would only have had police lanterns to examine the corpse by, but even so, his report was cursory to say the least. The dead woman's hands were cold, but her legs still warm. He believed death had occurred about half an hour earlier, but saw no sign of wounds other than to the throat, and ordered the body to be wheeled away to the mortuary.

The ambulance was a hand cart, often used to wheel drunks off the streets, and the mortuary to which Nichols was taken was unbelievably squalid by any standards. It was the Whitechapel Workhouse mortuary in Eagle Place off Old Montague Street and had once been attached to the Workhouse but now stood alone. A drawing of it in the contemporary press shows a single-storey brick shed next to a terraced housing row. Washing hangs from lines strung across the access point, and ragged children are playing outside it.

The mortuary keeper, Mr Edwards, was not sent for; 54-year-old, pauper inmate of the Workhouse, Robert Mann, who handled the newly arrived dead, was present when Inspector Spratling of J Division, who seems to have been more in charge than Llewellyn, helped Thain and Mizen lift the dead woman onto the cart. Spratling saw nothing wrong with the son of Emma Green, who lived in the nearest house to Brown's Yard, using a bucket and mop to get rid of the bloodstains on the pavement. Today's SOCOs would have apoplexy! The body was left on the cart outside the mortuary until Mann arrived with the keys and unlocked the door. Spratling was waiting for him and it was he who carried out an initial examination of the corpse and sent an officer to fetch Llewellyn back.

By 6.30 a.m., Mann and his assistant James Hatfield stripped and washed the body, doing their bit (like everybody else) to destroy evidence. We still have Spratling's report which is very detailed. In it he incorporated Llewellyn's observations. The woman had been disembowelled and her throat had been cut from left to right, with two distinct cuts on the left. The windpipe, gullet and spinal cord had been cut through and there was bruising around the jaw. The abdomen had been ripped open with two small stabs to the private parts made by a strong-bladed knife. Llewellyn believed that death was almost instantaneous and that the killer was left-handed. Spratling also meticulously listed the victim's clothing and belongings. She was about 45 (Nichols was 44), 5ft 2in tall with dark, greying hair. She had a missing tooth and lacerations to the tongue. She wore a brown Ulster with seven brass buttons engraved with a horse and rider. She wore a grey linsey woollen petticoat and a second one of flannel, as well as a white chest flannel, brown stays, a white chemise [petticoat], black woollen stockings, a pair of men's boots and a straw bonnet trimmed with black velvet.

The multi-layers of clothing were typical of the poorest working women of the East End who might end up 'carrying the banner' (sleeping rough) in the alleyways and courtyards of the Abyss. The dead woman's dress bore the marks of Lambeth Workhouse and it was assumed that she was an inmate. By the time Inspector Joseph Helson of J Division wrote his report, four days later, the police knew that the victim was Mary Ann Nichols and were putting together a picture of her life. In strictly forensic pathology terms, the murder had been committed where the body had been found, but there was no sign of any weapon. Spratling and Helson visited the mortuary again, noting a broken comb and a piece of a magnifying glass among the clothes. The murder weapon, they believed, was a 'dagger or a long, sharp knife'. At that stage, the police were concentrating their enquiries into local gangs who regularly threatened and abused prostitutes.

By 19 October, when Chief Inspector Donald Swanson wrote a further report, Llewellyn had changed his mind about the left-handedness of the killer. The doctor's full autopsy was carried out on 1 September, the day of the inquest, again at the Working Lads' Institute. The jury were taken to view the body at the Eagle Place mortuary and local and national newspapers carried detailed reports of the proceedings. The police had changed their minds on the gang issue, both Helson and Detective Inspector Frederick Abberline of Scotland Yard being of the opinion that one man was responsible for the murder of Nichols. The coroner was Wynne E. Baxter of the South-Eastern Division of Middlesex, whose name would be all over the press in the weeks that followed. *The Times* got it wrong on 3 September, listing the doctor as Mr Henry Llewellyn.

Interestingly, Inspector Spratling's evidence included the fact that one of his men, Sergeant Patrick Enright, had given explicit instructions to the mortuary keepers *not* to wash the body, but they had done it anyway. Neither Mann nor Hatfield remembered these instructions, but since the coroner told the jury that Mann was subject to fits and that his evidence could not be relied on, we are entitled to wonder why he was called in the first place. At some point, a police photographer had taken a photograph of Nichols, lying in her coffin, in which her eyes and mouth are slightly open and only her head is visible. As photographic evidence, such exhibits are pointless and were only taken to aid identification.

Llewellyn was happy to talk to the press and media coverage was already going into overdrive by this time. He acknowledged that he had never seen anything like this level of violence before, and told *Reynold's Newspaper*, 'she was ripped open just as you see a dead calf at the butcher's.' He believed that the attack took between four and five minutes to carry out and introduced the idea that has plagued Ripper enquiries ever since. The murderer, he believed, 'must have had some rough anatomical knowledge, for he had attacked all the vital parts'.

Because Llewellyn's original report no longer exists, all we can do is to piece together his views from contemporary police reports and newspaper articles. Both are unreliable, especially the latter. What does emerge, however, is that Nichols had at least three, and possibly five, teeth missing, not the *one* that Spratling alludes to. Her spinal cord was not severed.

One of the most telling contemporary articles was that written by a journalist of the *East London Observer* on 1 September. 'Yellow journalism' was a scandal at the time and a problem for modern researchers. Newshounds trailed around police stations and murder scenes, recording any piece of trivia that seemed vaguely relevant. If they had no story, they simply made one up. The 'In the Dead House' article rings true, however. When the reporter arrived, there was already a crowd in the yard outside the mortuary. Nichols' clothes lay in a heap on the flagstones where Mann and Hatfield had dropped them. The reporter was allowed in by Edwards, the keeper, to view the body. He saw what we cannot because of the coyness of the photograph, the naked body of the victim. In particular, he noted the terrible gash from the pubis to the sternum, with bowels protruding from it. Llewellyn does not mention this. Was that carelessness, or did he believe, like many of the medical fraternity, that such details were fit only for the medical journal, *The Lancet*, and not even for evidence at an inquest? Intriguingly, the reporter also noted Nichols' straw bonnet. There was no black velvet trim. Was that because Mann and Hatfield had helped themselves to such trinkets, either as gruesome souvenirs or to sell on the clothes–hungry markets of the East End?

I believe that the Whitechapel killer preferred to kill in small, confined spaces. This was why Martha Tabram was perfect for him on the landing of a darkened stairway. In the case of Nichols, he was trying to get her inside Brown's Stable Yard, but the gates were locked and he was forced to kill her in the open, chancing his luck as all driven murderers do. In fact, luck was the hallmark of Jack the Ripper. The police beats around Buck's Row involved officers patrolling every half an hour. But Jack knew that ...

'Dark Annie' Chapman

George Bagster Phillips emerges as the medical heavyweight in the Ripper case, largely because he was involved in all the later murders and because he took a principled (if wrongheaded) stand against the coroner in the inquest into the death of Annie Chapman. A uniformed constable arrived at Phillips' address, 2 Spital Square at 6.20 on that Saturday morning, 8 September. Unlike Killeen and Llewellyn, Phillips was a Divisional police surgeon with twenty-three years' experience and was probably used to the knock of a constable at unsocial hours. The pair went to 29 Hanbury Street, one of a row of terraced houses with two front doors. One led to a shop run by Harriet Hardiman, who sold cats' meat, and the other to a 25ft passage that led to a rear door. This opened onto the two steps going down to a yard, about 13ft square, which had a privy in one corner and a workshop for basket weaving in another. To the left of these steps was the body of a woman, lying on her back. By the time Phillips arrived, 6.30 a.m., it was fully daylight and he had a clear view of the corpse. Because so much unverified nonsense has been written about this murder, it is vital to look at Phillips' original report in detail.

The dead woman lay with her head near the step and her feet towards the shed at the bottom of the yard. Her legs were drawn up, her feet on the ground, and her knees spread. The face was bruised and swollen, and the tongue protruded slightly through the teeth. In fact, Phillips was impressed by the 'fineness' of the teeth. The stiffness of *rigor mortis* was just beginning. The throat had been cut in a jagged line virtually all the way around the neck.

What is noticeable in this case is that Phillips examined the crime scene minutely, which had not been done by either Killeen or Llewellyn, although, to be fair, the enclosed space of the yard was a gift to what today we would call a Scene of Crime Officer. The doctor found a piece of coarse muslin material and a pocket comb in a paper case. He believed – and this gave rise to ever more fanciful theories in the weeks ahead – that these had been placed near the body deliberately. He also found a leather apron which was to assume huge import in the following days. Phillips noted the blood spatter on the wooden fence, the first example I have come across of attention to a phenomenon now crucial at murder scenes. On the wall of Number 29 were six patches of blood about 18 inches from the ground. There were blood smears 4 inches lower on the fence panels. Either Phillips' testimony (the above is taken from the inquest on Wednesday, 12 September) is a summary, or he missed scene of crime clues. The police found these and it may be they had removed them before the doctor arrived. As well as the comb and muslin referred to, there was a small envelope near the victim's head which contained two pills. The envelope carried the crest of the Surrey Regiment (the lamb and flag) and the letters 'M' and 'Sp', perhaps of an address. As a result of this murder, press and public were whipped into a state of panic and similarities were noted with the Tabram and Nichols murders. Soldiers had been involved with Tabram and here was another army link. The postmark read 'London Aug 23 1888'. In the Scotland Yard files, the regiment is wrongly referred to as the Sussex Regiment but on 14 September, Inspector Chandler visited the depot of the 1st Battalion, The Surreys, at North Camp, Farnborough. All enquiries there drew a blank.

For accuracy in scene of crime items, we must look at Inspector Chandler's account. He saw the body before Phillips and noted the small intestine and flap of the abdomen lay on the victim's right side, with much blood on the left shoulder. There is no mention of coins or rings being found at the crime scene, which destroys at once the nonsense of the Freemason theory, that a row of coins was left neatly laid out between the dead woman's feet in a ritualistic post supposedly linked to Masonic murder over centuries.

The victim was taken to the same workhouse mortuary where Polly Nichols had ended up, and both Chandler and Phillips were able to examine the body there. Phillips used his time in the dock of the inquest to complain about the inadequacy of this mortuary. He was surprised to find that the body had been stripped and washed (à la Nichols) and it transpired that this had been done, not by Mann and Hatfield, but by the nurses from the Workhouse Infirmary. Post-mortems could not properly be carried out and at certain times (high summer?) the conditions were actually dangerous to the operator.

The coroner grudgingly conceded that there were no public mortuaries in the City of London before Bow in the east (although technically, the Eagle Place mortuary and the murder scene were not in the City's jurisdiction anyway).

At the mortuary, Phillips could see a variety of bruises to the face. Rigor mortis was now far more advanced and there were abrasions on the fingers, as if rings had been forcibly removed. The throat cut had been made from the left, with two distinct cuts. There appeared to have been an attempt to separate the neck vertebrae. The mutilations on the body were made after death and it was now that Phillips refused to go into further details, which could only be painful to the feelings of the jury and the public. The coroner accepted this but both men seem to have been wildly ignorant of the public's attitude; 'Orrible murder' sold newspapers.

Phillips explained that the cause of death was syncope, failure of the heart to cope with the blood loss from the throat. He believed that the murder weapon, which had not been found, was a 'very sharp' knife, 6–8 inches long. Clearly with reference to the Tabram murder, there was no suggestion of a bayonet being involved here. They (the wounds) could have been done by such an instrument as a medical man used for post-mortem purposes. A slaughterman's knife was another possibility, although those used in the latter trade (a clear reference to the apron found at Hanbury Street) were too short in the blade. There were signs that the killer had some anatomical knowledge. He thought that the victim had been dead for about four hours by the time he saw her, which would take the killing window to about 4.30 a.m. This was to confuse the police enquiries who, by this time, had two witnesses who had seen the woman alive at this time. Her stomach contained a little food but no alcohol, and some of the bruising on the face at least had been made days earlier. The killer, Phillips believed, had grabbed his victim by the chin and slashed her throat from left to right. The swollen face and protruding tongue pointed perhaps to a gag of some sort being used, but he could speculate no further on that.

By the time of the inquest, the police had identified the Hanbury Street victim. She was Annie Chapman, born Eliza Anne Smith in

Paddington, in 1841, which made her 47 at the time of her death. The mortuary photograph, again covered up to the chin, shows a plain woman with curly hair. Police descriptions call it brown but there is little to explain Annie's sobriquet of 'dark'. Her mouth is slightly open and her eyes are closed. This contrasts sharply with a wedding photograph discovered by researchers years later, which shows Annie in a pretty floral dress in 1869, sitting alongside her husband, John, whom she married in May of that year. They moved several times and had three children, one of whom was crippled from birth and another who died of meningitis six years before the Ripper struck.

Annie's drinking led to the collapse of the marriage and by 1886 she had taken up with a sieve-maker. Many of her contemporaries knew her as Annie Sievey. Police enquiries discovered that Annie was a frequent inmate of Crossingham's, a common lodging or 'doss house' along Dorset Street. The bruises on her face were the result of a fist fight she had with another inmate days before she died. The pills in the envelope were Annie's, issued to her by the Whitechapel Workhouse infirmary, hoping to alleviate the headaches she had after the altercation.

While Phillips had refused to describe the mutilations to the court, he did so in *The Lancet* on 29 September. The abdomen had been entirely laid open; the intestines, severed from their mesenteric attachments, had been lifted out of the body and placed by the shoulder of the corpse, whilst from the pelvis, the uterus and its appendages, with the upper portion of the vagina and the posterior two-thirds of the bladder had been entirely removed. The incisions were clearly cut, avoiding the rectum and dividing the vagina low enough to avoid injury to the cervix interior. This information explains why Phillips assumed a degree of anatomical skill; the mutilations were carried out (as was the case in all but one of the Ripper murders) in a hurry and in the dark.

The continuation of the Chapman inquest on 19 September saw the clash between Coroner Wynne Baxter and Dr Phillips (*The Lancet* had yet to publish). The doctor was clearly annoyed that Baxter had changed his mind and was now demanding full disclosure – 'We are here to decide the cause of death and therefore have a right to hear all particulars. I have never before heard of any evidence being kept back from a coroner.'

Phillips supposed that the gruesome mutilations were carried out after death and had no bearing on the cause itself. 'That is a matter of opinion,' Baxter said and, in a line that sums up the whole problem of forensic medicine, 'You know that medical men often differ.'

Baxter cleared the court of women and children before Phillips began. This, according to *The Times*, was 'totally unfit for publication'. The doctor said that he could not carry out those mutilations in less than fifteen minutes and would probably need at least an hour.

Jurymen asked Phillips his opinion on the generally held belief that photographing the victim's eyes would produce an image of the last thing she saw, i.e. her killer. He was also asked about the use of bloodhounds. The farcical introduction of Barnaby and Burgho, the dogs of breeder Edwin Brough of Scarborough, did not take place until 9 October. In the event, the animals proved useless and Brough withdrew them, fearing for their safety because they were not insured. It is a good example of the lack of understanding of the average juryman that they thought Phillips was qualified to offer an opinion on the idea.

Wynne Baxter summed up the inquest on Thursday, 27 September. Chapman had drifted from doss house to doss house, 'where such as she herded like cattle'. She was badly fed and typical of some 5,000 inhabitants who nightly paid their 4d for a bed. She was last seen in the company of a man near Number 29 Hanbury Street and a passer-by, Elizabeth Darrell, heard him ask Annie, 'Will you?' and Darrell saw her nod. The man was described as about 5ft 4in, dark, a 'foreigner' (a euphemism for 'Jew') and over 40. If this was Jack, he had probably agreed a price for Chapman's services and she led him along the corridor frequently used by prostitutes, to the yard at the back. They would probably have had sex standing up (many prostitutes believed pregnancy was less likely that way) against the fence of the wall. But that was not what Jack had in mind ...

Chapman's rings had gone. Were those stolen by the mortuary attendants, Mann and Hatfield, or even the nurses who had washed the body? Or were they the killer's trophies in an unknown world of madness that nobody yet understood? More alarmingly, the dead woman's uterus had been taken away. This followed the same pattern. A serial killer's trophy? Or a macabre object offered for sale in various medical quarters? 'For it was clear,' Baxter said cryptically, 'there was a market for missing organs.' The coroner had been contacted by a doctor from 'one of our great medical schools', who told him that the curator of the Pathological Museum had been approached by an American who wanted to buy uteri, or as Baxter euphemistically put it, 'a number of specimens of the organ that was missing in the deceased'. The American was prepared to pay £20 each for these. All this was for the purposes of research and he wanted them preserved in glycerine (spirits of wine was the usual medium) and shipped directly to the States. The curator had refused but the information was passed to Scotland Yard.

Out of this 'missing organ' came one of the great red herrings of Ripperology. Researchers Stuart Evans and Richard Gainey came across the Littlechild letter, a missive written in 1912 by Chief Inspector John Littlechild, which named Dr Francis Tumblety as the Whitechapel murderer. By the time Littlechild wrote, the Ripper case was well and truly over, but the Ripper 'industry' had not yet started. Tumblety was not a qualified doctor, but a quack, snake-oil salesman with delusions of grandeur. He was certainly in London during the 'autumn of terror', but his arrest (on charges of outraging public decency with men) did not take place until 7 November. *Nothing* points to Tumblety being the Whitechapel killer, nor to the fact that he was the American looking for wombs. He had no history of violence, no known links with the East End, had no surgical (or even medical) experience. Tumblety was a con man and a liar of epic proportions (he once claimed to have been President Lincoln's doctor) but why he should want uteri for research remains a mystery. Above all, Tumblety was a flamboyant dresser, with a huge waxed moustache, and, at 6ft 4in, would have towered over anybody in the East End. Yet, there are no reports of anyone like this, either to the police or the media.

The last point about the Chapman murder is the curious case of the apron in the daytime. Crime scenes are notoriously complex places, often providing 'evidence' which has nothing to do with a case at all. The problem was that 'leather apron' had, in more recent police parlance, 'previous'. On page 6 of the Met's report on the Nichols murder is the entry 'John Pizer alias, "Leather Apron".' On 19 October, as the Nichols inquiries continued, Chief Inspector Swanson outlined the case against the suspect – 'on account of his alleged levying blackmail on prostitutes and assaulting them if they did not comply with his request, as detailed to police by women in the common lodging houses'. The police tracked him down on 10 September and took his statement. He claimed that on the night in question (31 August) he had slept in a doss house along Holloway Road. This was confirmed by the proprietor. On 8 September (the Chapman murder) he was in another doss at 22 Mulberry Street, confirmed by a number of people. Until police found him, he had been in hiding because of the press furore over the apron found in the back yard of Number 29 Hanbury Street.

It was true that Pizer carried knives and that he wore a leather apron because he was a shoemaker by trade. As the inquest into Annie Chapman began, Pizer was giving evidence at Leman Street police station. Things looked bad for him when Inspector William Causely and Sergeant William Thick put him in an identity parade and he was picked out by the unlikely named Emmanuel Delbast Violenia as a man threatening Chapman with a knife. Violenia was later charged by police for wasting their time. But the media had got their teeth into Pizer. On Wednesday, 5 September, *The Star*'s headlines screamed 'Leather Apron – a noiseless midnight terror. The Strange Character who Prowls About Whitechapel After Midnight – Universal Fear Among the Women – Slippered Feet and a Sharp Leather Knife.' The capital letters say it all!

The article itself goes on with more of the same. Pizer had kicked, bruised and terrified a hundred women, all of whom could testify to the outrages. He was responsible for the murders of three women (probably Emma Smith, Amie Millward – who was not actually murdered – and Martha Tabram). With his 'ugly grin', 'malignant eyes' and 'razor-like knife' he had been terrorizing the East End for years, the 'ghoulish and devilish brute'. *The Star* demanded his arrest. Sergeant Thick – 'Johnny Upright' to the Underworld – did the honours because he knew Pizer well.

The bootmaker-turned-serial-killer gave evidence at the adjourned Chapman inquest so that, according to the coroner, he could clear his name. The police had released him, but the fact that Pizer was Jewish left a nagging doubt in some people's minds. It is ironic that in one of the most cosmopolitan cities in the world, it is universally assumed that the 'Whitechapel fiend' *had* to be a foreigner; he was not 'one of us'.

As for the leather apron in the yard at Hanbury Street, it belonged to one of the seventeen residents of Number 29, and had been washed and put out to dry overnight.

'Long Liz' Stride

The movements of Jack's next victim shortly before her death are confused and contradictory, but the medical involvement was more straightforward. That said, there is confusion at the outset. The first medical man to be informed of a murder in Dutfield's Yard, Berner Street, was Dr Frederick William Blackwell of 100 Commercial Road. While he was dressing, he sent his assistant, Edward Johnston, to accompany the officer who had knocked them up. This is where the confusion lies. At the inquest that followed, Johnston reported that the constable's collar badges were 436H. The problem is that the officer who was sent from the crime scene was Reserve Constable 12HR Albert Collins, and he had been sent by Constable 252H Henry Lamb. Presumably, Johnston had misremembered Collins' number, but this is typical of the problems involved in investigating the Ripper case; it is full of such inconsistencies.

There are two eye-witness accounts of the murder of Becket in Canterbury Cathedral in 1170. This depiction follows those accurately.

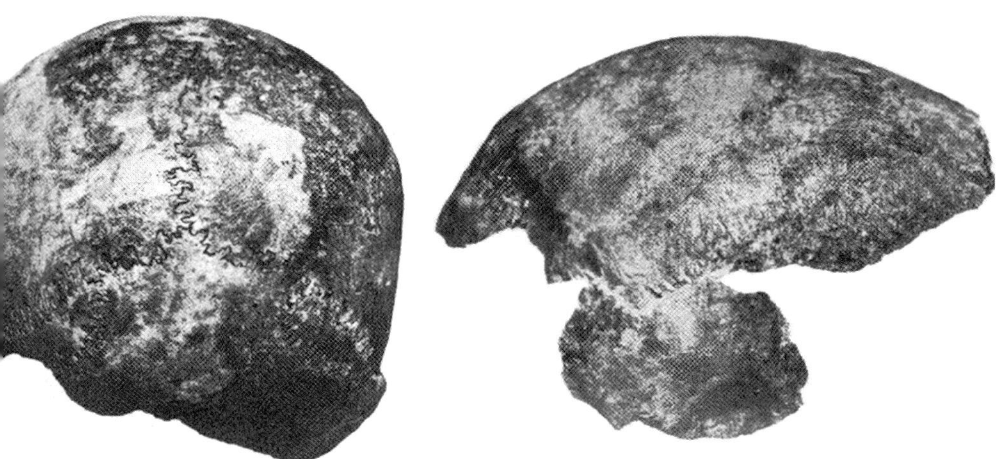

Above left and above right: Parts of the skulls of the bodies disinterred in 1933 believed to be those of Edward V and his brother Richard of York. Technology at the time meant that identification of these boys was pure guesswork.

Above left: Henry Irving as Eugene Aram who was hanged on very flimsy evidence fourteen years after the supposed crime had been committed.

Above right: Dr William Palmer was hanged for poisoning a number of people including his own children in 1856. Only his mother called him 'Saintly Billy'.

Below: The sailor John Williams committed suicide in his cell. His body was taken on a cart past the Ratcliffe Highway where he was alleged to have murdered two families in 1811.

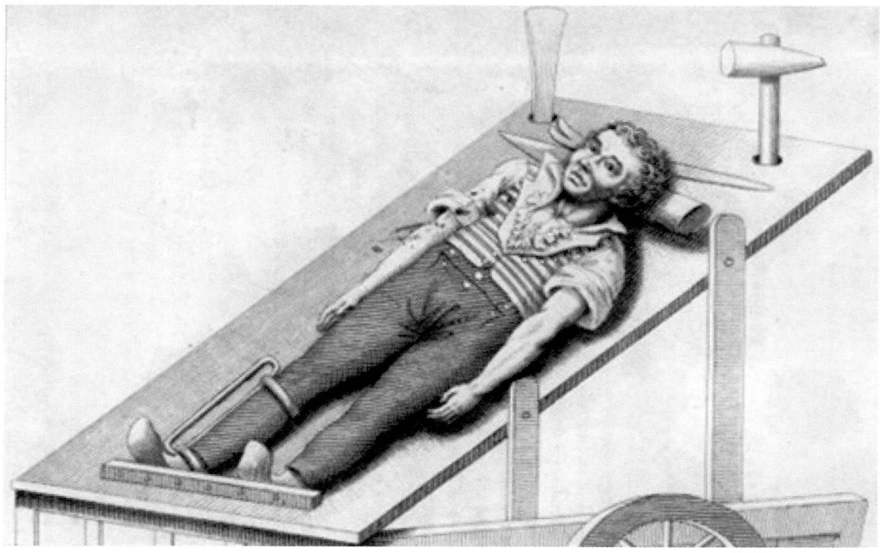

Above left: Constance Kent, aged 16, confessed to murdering her little brother. Despite the excellent police work of Inspector Jonathan Whicher, most people could not believe that a nice middle-class girl could commit such a crime.

Above right: Cesare Lombroso believed that it was possible to tell a criminal by his/her physical features. He was wrong.

Below: Alphonse Bertillon perfected the technique of criminal photography. In this image we see a prisoner with his head 'in the frame' to keep it still. The idea of the mugshot which all police forces now use comes from Bertillon.

The mortuary of St George's in the East. This is the only building still standing with direct links to the Whitechapel murders of 1888. Two of Jack's victims were examined here.

Kate Eddowes' body in Mitre Square. The original of this drawing, taken from contemporary newspapers, shows Dr Phillips examining the body. In fact this was done by Dr Brown, attached to the City Police. Note there is no attempt at securing the crime scene and the doctor is wearing his everyday clothes. (Redrafted by Author)

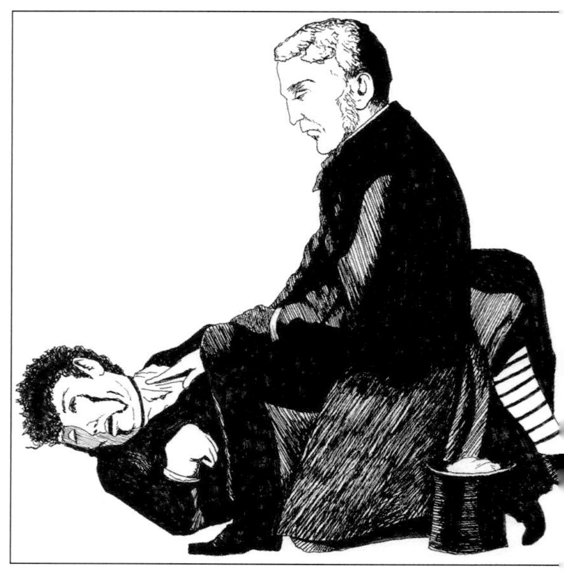

Mary Kelly was the only Ripper victim to be photographed at the murder scene. She is seen here on her bed in her room at 13 Miller's Court. At least one other photograph was taken but it is unknown who requested these.

This was one of nearly 200 letters and postcards sent to the police or the media during the Ripper scare. What is unusual about this one is that it was sent with half a human kidney. Graphologists today can deduce a great deal from the handwriting but this was not possible in 1888.

It is easy to fake a diary. Paper, ink and pen are all genuine but no one can prove, even today, when all three were put together. (Author)

Above left: The American girl who married a monster – or so some would have us believe. She was convicted of murdering her husband James who some people contend was also Jack the Ripper.

Above right: Dr Neill Cream confessed to being Jack the Ripper on the gallows. He was not but he did use poison to murder at least four women in 1891-2.

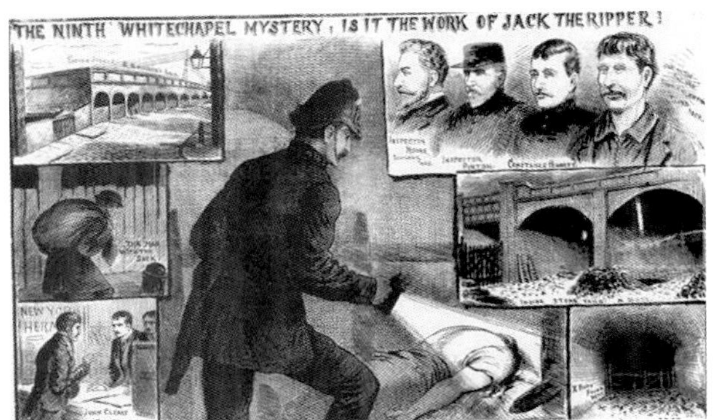

The discovery of a female torso under the arches at Pinchin Street in London's East End. The media believed that this was another Ripper victim, but the police – correctly – tied it to the Thames Torso Murders.

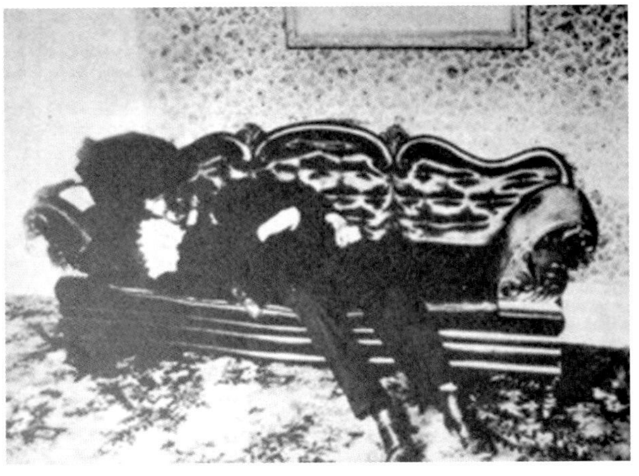

Andrew Borden was a well-known figure in Fall River Massachusetts in 1892. He and his wife Abbie were axed to death, almost certainly by their daughter Lizzie. Unaccountably, she was acquitted.

George Chapman (real name Severin Klosowsi) ran several pubs in the East End. Here he is with Bessie Taylor, who worked as his barmaid.

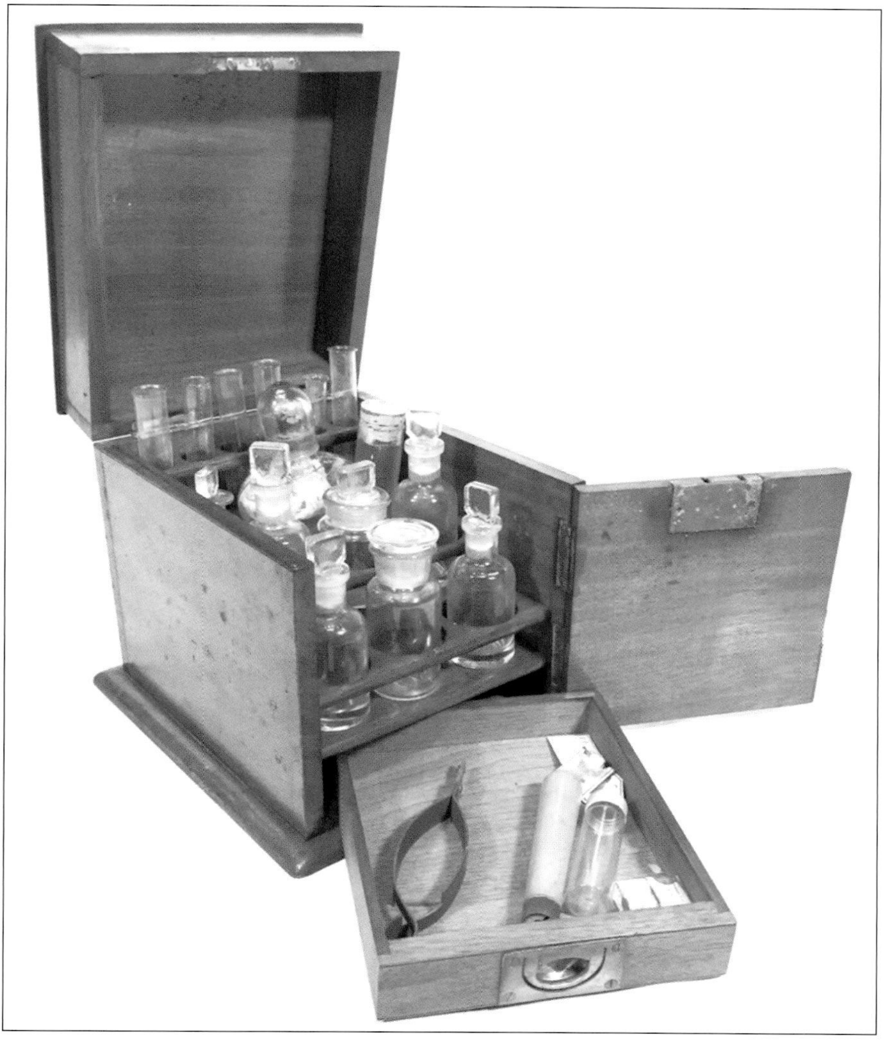

Potentially lethal poisons were available over a pharmacist's counter for most of Victoria's reign. Some families had medicine chests like this one.

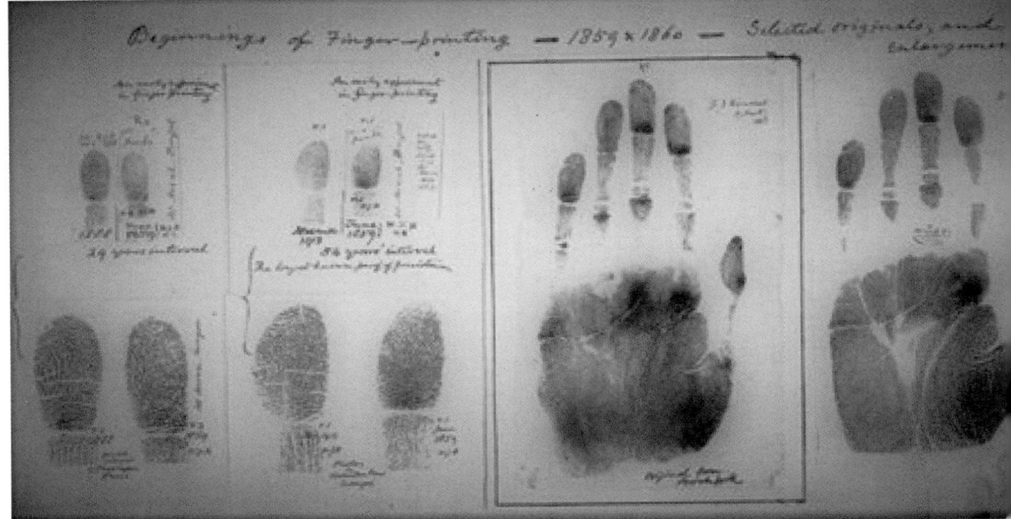

Above: Originally used in Indian bureaucracy, it was discovered that no two people had identical patterns on the ends of their fingers. It was not until 1905 that a murder conviction rested on fingerprint evidence.

Left: The Spy cartoon of Edward Henry, Assistant Commissioner at Scotland Yard. With his background in the Indian Civil Service, he brought fingerprint technology to the forefront of crime solving.

Johnston opened the door between 1.05 and 1.10 a.m., woke Blackwell and accompanied Collins to the crime scene. They got there at 1.13. Dutfield's Yard was a narrow thoroughfare enclosed by a large gate. To the right was the International Working Men's Educational Club, set up three years earlier which housed offices that printed *Der Arbeter Fraint* (The Worker's Friend). As a potential hotbed of both Jewry and Socialism, it was a place of interest to the police, although there was no trouble there until 1889 when a mob attacked the premises. The murder that Johnston had come to investigate had no relevance to this.

Johnston found a crowd of people, including policemen, blocking the yard. The only light available was from police 'bullseyes'. A woman's body lay alongside the Club wall, her blood trickling into a gutter. Johnston felt the hands, which were cold and the rest of the body which was warm. At the inquest, the coroner asked him if he had seen any footprints in the blood. Johnston admitted he had not looked and was no doubt happy to pass jurisdiction to Dr Blackwell when he arrived at 1.10 by his watch (another unexplained anomaly).

Blackwell, whose sketch appeared in the press days later, complete with huge beard and top hat, was born in Brighton in 1851 and was married with one son. He was clearly not a police surgeon but was presumably called because of his geographical proximity to Dutfield's Yard. He saw what Johnston did, a woman with her legs drawn up, her feet against the Club's wall, not 3 yards from the gate. The right hand lay on the chest, smeared on both sides with blood. The left hand contained a packet of cachous (sweets) wrapped in tissue paper. The face was placid, the mouth slightly open. This is entirely consistent with the mortuary photograph taken the next day. There was a silk scarf wound tightly around the neck, above an incision which began on the left side, 2½in below the angle of the jaw. The neck vessels on the left were severed and the windpipe cut through.

In response to the coroner's questions, Blackwell noted that a number of feet had distributed the blood pattern. Because of the yard's darkness, it was impossible to see any blood spatter on the wall. The victim's clothes were dry (it had been raining earlier) and her dress was undone at the top. (This was most certainly Johnston's work to test the temperature of the body.) She had a bunch of flowers in her jacket. Blackwell believed she had been dead for between twenty or thirty minutes before his arrival, which would make the time of the murder about quarter to twelve. We have learned over the years to be wary of 'accurate' times of death, but doctors' views in 1888 were usually considered sacrosanct. It was unlikely that the deceased could have cried out, given the injuries to the throat, and she effectively bled to death.

Blackwell believed the killer had grabbed the victim's scarf, jerking her head backwards while still standing. He could not tell if the throat had been cut in an upright or supine position.

George Bagster Phillips, as Divisional police surgeon, was summoned at 1.20 that Sunday morning and went with a constable to Leman Street police station. From there he was escorted to Dutfield's Yard. There he found two detectives 'in possession of the body' as the parlance of the day had it, Chief Inspector (actually, Acting Superintendent) John West and Inspector Charles Pinhorn who would go on to investigate the Pinchin Street torso later. Phillips' description of the body chimed with Blackwell's and he picked up the spilled cachous and gave them to Blackwell.

Because the murder had taken place in Berner Street, the mortuary to which the body was taken was not Eagle Place but St George's-in-the-East, at a corner of the churchyard. It is one of the few Ripper-related sites still standing, although it has gone through a number of changes (and purposes) since 1888. The post-mortem took place there at 3 p.m. on Monday, 3 October in the presence of Drs Blackwell and Rygate. One of the seminal treatises in forensic medicine, *A Manual of Medical Jurisprudence* by Alfred Swaine Taylor (1844), had recommended that two doctors be present at an autopsy, in case anything was missed. It also made sense in that one doctor could carry out the dissections (in this case, Blackwell), while the other took notes. Dr Rygate was probably

John Jones Rygate, but since all of his sons joined the profession, we cannot be sure.

Once again, the mortuary was barely adequate. It had glass skylights in the roof to allow natural light, but a body and four doctors would have made it all very cramped. This must have been almost impossible when the coroner brought the inquest jury to view the corpse, still wearing the clothes in which she died.

Rigor mortis had not yet faded on that Monday afternoon and the doctors themselves removed the clothing (clearly, she was redressed for the jury visit). Phillips noted a blue discoloration on the shoulders which he had seen on the other occasions. This cannot have been lividity as, surely, he would have seen that regularly. He does not explain what it was. The throat gash was 6 inches long and very clean. As there were no other wounds, the doctors focused on other issues. The woman's right leg was not straight and she carried old scars. All her lower jaw teeth were missing, her heart was unusually small, her lungs pale. There is no comment on the most obvious deformity, clearly visible in the mortuary photograph, of a damaged mouth (which, again, had no links to the murder).

The next day, Phillips went back to the mortuary and found, in an underskirt pocket, a pencil, the two combs, a spoon and some buttons and hooks. There was talk of the handkerchief, but Phillips did not see it. At the inquest, he attributed the cause of death to a cutting of the windpipe and the slashing of the left carotid artery. Like Blackwell, he saw no blood spatter on the wall next to the body.

The inquest continued on Friday, 5 October in the Vestry Hall in Cable Street. Phillips was in the witness box again, but this time he testified that his later visits to the mortuary were in the presence of Dr Brown. This impressive medic had officiated in the second murder of the night of the 'double event', that of Catherine Eddowes in Mitre Square. By now, Phillips had examined the handkerchief and found no blood traces. By this time, the fruiterer Matthew Packer had come forward, telling the police that he had seen the victim talking to a man outside Dutfield's Yard on the night in question and that they had bought grapes from him. Modern readers might find it odd that a fruiterer/greengrocer's shop should be open that late at night, but this was the East End in the 'city that never sleeps' and it was standard for the time. Packer was a time-wasting self-publicist who delighted in telling embroidered stories to anybody who would listen. Phillips was able to say categorically that the dead woman had not eaten grapes for many hours before her death.

The doctor had been shown a knife given to him by Constable 282H. This is perhaps a typo error for 252H, Henry Lamb, although where he found the knife is unclear. It had blood on the blade, although in 1888 no doctor could say that it was human or animal. The blade had been blunted and Phillips could not say it was the murder weapon. He was, however, able to speculate on the killer's MO. He believed the dead woman was knocked to the ground and her assailant, on her right side, cut her throat. He could not explain why her right hand was covered in blood. The attack would only have taken seconds.

Inevitably, the coroner asked Phillips whether there were any similarities between this murder and that of Annie Chapman. By this time, the media was sure that these – and others – were linked and that a maniac was prowling the streets of Whitechapel (which was more or less true!). The doctor pointed out the obvious dissimilarities – there were no mutilations to the Dutfield's Yard victim. He also pointed out – and this was largely ignored by police and press at the time, and by far too many researchers since – that the killer would not necessarily have blood on him. Bobbies patrolling the streets looking for a blood-soaked fiend were in for a disappointment.

When Blackwell was recalled, he introduced a red herring, almost certainly as a result of press stories now in circulation. The weapon used was sharp-pointed, not round-ended like a slaughterer's knife. As the coroner pointed out, no one had said a slaughterer was involved. Blackwell and others had missed the point. At least in the case of horses and cattle, slaughterers killed with a hammer blow to the head as we have seen. That was the cause of death and the kind of knife used afterwards was irrelevant. None of Jack's victims suffered a blow of this kind.

The inquest revealed what the police already knew by this time. The dead woman was Elizabeth Gustafsdottir, a Swedish prostitute from Torslander and she was 35. She had moved to London in 1866 and three years later married John Stride (her nickname of 'Long Liz' was connected with this, although at 5ft 7in, she was the tallest of Jack's victims). The marriage did not last long and she lived in doss houses and Poplar Union Workhouse before taking up with labourer Michael Kidney some months before she was murdered. She claimed that the damage to her mouth, loss of teeth and deformed leg were as a result of the *Princess Alice* disaster in September 1878 when a pleasure streamer collided with a barge in the Thames. There was a huge loss of life – 527 – but the family of Liz Stride was not among them, as she claimed. John Stride died in the Workhouse in October 1884.

Catherine Eddowes

Some forty-five minutes after the murder of Liz Stride, Jack struck again, the speed and ferocity of the attack sending press and public into something approaching hysteria. At 1.55 a.m. on that Sunday morning, while Drs Phillips and Blackwell were officiating in Dutfield's Yard, a constable knocked on the door of Dr George William Sequeira, the nearest medical man to the second murder site of the night, who lived at 34 Jewry Street in the parish of St Katherine Cree, Aldgate. The latest outrage had happened in Mitre Square in the jurisdiction of the City Police, not the Met.

Sequeira was one of a medical family of Portuguese Sephardic Jews although he himself had been born in London and knew the murder scene well. There were three ways in to Mitre Square and it is not certain which one the doctor and the constable took. The square itself had only two gas lights so it was very dark at night, particularly in the corner where the body lay. Most of the existing police reports, by both the City and Met forces, ignore Sequeira altogether, as, since the Met had been alerted to the murder, he was soon joined by Dr Frederick Brown, Surgeon to the City, and the ubiquitous Phillips. He nevertheless gave evidence at the inquest into the murder of the woman by then identified as Kate Eddowes. He told Coroner Samuel Langham that he agreed with Dr Brown about the position of the body (on the pavement in what is often called today 'Ripper's Corner'). He believed there would have been enough light for the killer to be able to carry out his mutilations, but 'I do not think he was possessed of any great anatomical skill; neither did he appear to be searching for any particular organ.' After the Chapman murder, the press had speculated wildly on the medical skills of the murderer. If not a slaughterman, could he have been a doctor? Sequeira explained the lack of noise by the suddenness of the attack and the slashing of the blood vessels of the throat and severing of the windpipe had caused death. Once again, the killer would not have been heavily bloodstained and Eddowes had died less than an hour before he arrived, but he did not examine the body in detail, waiting instead for the arrival of Dr Brown.

It was shortly after 2 a.m. that Brown had heard the knock on his door at 17 Finsbury Circus and he was at the Square eighteen minutes later. The body was on its back, the head turned to the left towards the brick wall of the rear of a shop owned by a Mr Taylor. Eddowes' arms lay at her sides, palms uppermost with a thimble next to her right hand. The killer had pushed his victim's skirts above her waist and her legs were bare, the left straight and the right bent at the knee. Alone of the Ripper doctors, Brown made detailed sketches (which he improved later) of the position of the body, indicating the pools of blood to either side. He also drew the woman's bonnet, still attached to her hair and a rough sketch of the face. The intestines were drawn out and placed over the right shoulder, smeared with faeces. A 2ft length was separated from the body and placed, Brown believed, in a deliberate position between body and arm. The body was still warm when the doctor arrived and there was no sign yet of rigor. There was no sign of bruising and no blood on the front of the clothes. Neither had Eddowes had sex recently.

What was entirely new in the Mitre Square murder was the mutilations to the face. Brown was able to see those more clearly at the post-mortem and the sketch he made is clearer than the subsequent photographs. The lobes of both ears had been cut and the tip of the nose removed. Both eyelids had been nicked and there were 'V' shapes carved into the cheeks. No doctor at the time speculated on this, but today, experts agree that it is possible that Eddowes knew her killer and the savagery of the slash from nose to mouth was an attempt at overkill to silence her forever. There was also the idea of the eyes recording their last vital sight (see above) which might explain the cutting of the eyelids.

I can find no accurate description of the Golden Lane mortuary to which Kate Eddowes was taken, but it was clearly larger and more impressive than either Eagle Place or St George's-in-the-East, because the room above it, high and airy, was used for her inquest, as altogether more appropriate than some pub where 'fumes of bad tobacco and stale beer were not calculated to impress the public with the majesty of the law'. Alfred Swaine Taylor had written this in 1844 and only now, over forty years later, was *some* notice taken.

The post-mortem began shortly after 2 p.m. on Sunday afternoon, Brown doing the honours, accompanied by Sequeira, Phillips and William Sedgwick Sanders of 13 Queen Street, Cheapside, who was not only a doctor and surgeon, but Public Analyst for the City. Brown's report at the inquest is one of the most detailed and perceptive of all the medical contributions to the Ripper case. In modern editions, it runs to four pages of solid text. Rigor mortis had set in by the afternoon and the body was washed. There were bruises on the hands, but most of these pre-dated the attack. Brown describes the facial injuries first, complete with measurements, depth of cuts and so on. He then worked his way down the body. The throat slash was 6 or 7 inches long, with vocal cords divided and the larynx severed. There was a great deal of clotted blood around the carotid artery and the jugular vein, all wounds caused by a sharp, pointed knife. Death (caused by carotid blood loss) would have been nearly instantaneous. All mutilations were carried out after death.

The walls of the abdomen were laid open from breast bone to pubes. The liver was stabbed and slit and a deep cut ran round the navel to the right side of the vagina and rectum, with cuts to the groin and upper thighs. Like Sequeira, Brown believed the murderer would not have much blood on him because the wounds were post-mortem. The killer was kneeling to the right of the body (à la Stride) if only because there was so little room to the left because of the proximity of the wall. The stomach contents were recovered and put in a jar for Dr Sanders to examine in his laboratory.

Two feet of the colon had been cut away and the liver was healthy. The right kidney was pale and bloodless but the left had gone, the renal artery cut through – 'I should say,' Brown said, 'that someone who knew the position of the kidney must have done it.' In this, of course, he differed in his opinion from Sequeira, who believed the killer had no anatomical skill. Much of the womb had been taken away, too (raising again the spectre of specimens for sale in some macabre black market). The throat wound was inflicted first, while Eddowes was lying on the ground. The knife involved in the body mutilations was about 6 inches long and its wielder had 'considerable knowledge of the position of the organs … and the way of removing them'. Intriguingly, Brown made the point that such organs would be of no use for any medical purpose. More intriguingly, in his report the word 'medical' has been crossed out, perhaps because Brown realized that he was, in effect, pointing a finger at one of his own profession. He quickly veered away in the direction of 'one in the habit of cutting up animals'. The mutilations would have taken at least five minutes (Jack had a fifteen-minute 'window' between police patrols in Mitre Square, and this was an area he almost certainly did not know well). Brown could see no reason why the body parts would be taken away because no one at the time had any inkling of a serial killer's predilection for trophies. The final wounds had been made 'to disfigure the corpse' but the doctor said no more about this.

Dr Sanders testified at the inquest that he had examined Kate Eddowes' stomach contents which tested negative for any poison. There had been various lines in the press that the reason that no sounds were heard in any of the murders is that some sort of drug had been used. We have to understand that there was no drug culture in Britain in the 1880s. Laudanum was used for pain relief but it was expensive and beyond the pockets of the East End's working girls. Alcohol, of course (considerably cheaper and very plentiful) was an alternative, although neither woman killed in the double event had been drinking recently. Bizarrely, Sanders said he agreed with Sequeira and Brown that the Mitre Square murderer had no anatomical skill. It was only Sequeira, of course, who had said that; Brown said the opposite. The coroner should have intervened to correct that; Wynne Baxter certainly would have done.

Most of the questions fired at Brown came from Mr Crawford, the City Solicitor, who also told the inquest that the Lord Mayor had suggested a reward of £500 for the detection and conviction of the murderer. The money, of course, was never claimed.

So, what happened on the night of the 'double event'? The phrase comes from one of the evermore lurid – and distracting – letters and postcards sent either to the media or the police. In all there were over 2,000 of these, fewer than 200 of which survive today. They range from 'confessions' to taunts to genuinely meant offers of help from appalled citizens. On 1 October, 'Saucy Jacky' wrote to the Central News Agency – 'You'll hear about Saucy Jacky's work tomorrow double event this time number one squealed a bit couldn't finish straight off. Had not got time to get ears for police …' I personally believe that this (like 99.9 per cent of the correspondence) was a hoax.

I believe that Jack met Liz Stride in Berner Street where she had ended up after an altercation with an unknown man. She went into

Dutfield's Yard with Jack for sex and he attacked her from behind, probably grabbing her scarf (at 5ft 7in, her height may have caused him problems he had not encountered before) and he forced her down and cut her throat. What happened next was one of those quirky things that happened in the 'city that never sleeps'. Travelling salesman Louis Diemschutz, having been on the road all day, turned his pony and trap into the yard as Jack ducked behind the gate. The animal shied, either at the killer's movement or the body on the ground, and Diemschutz dismounted and struck a lucifer. As soon as he saw the trickling blood he dashed up the stairs to his right to the Working Men's Club of which he was a member, to raise the alarm.

Jack saw his opportunity and got out into Berner Street. He had killed but the mutilations that were an essential impulse-driven part of his MO were denied him. He had to find another victim, as far away from Dutfield's Yard as possible. The murders of Tabram, Nichols and Chapman meant that extra police patrolled the streets and he had to be careful. He was carrying his bloodstained knife in his pocket and could have been stopped at any minute. He went west, into relatively unknown territory, out of his comfort zone and he came to Mitre Square. Here, waiting for business on her usual patch, was Kate Eddowes. Jack struck up the usual brief 'business' conversation and the pair melted into the shadows of the Square's darkest corner.

There are three tantalising 'P.S.'s' in the story of Kate Eddowes, all of which have muddied the waters of Ripperology and are still irritating us today. In the flurry of police activity after the discovery of the Mitre Square body, Constable 254A Alfred Long made a startling find in Goulston Street, east of the square. The fact that he was from A Division is proof that by now, officers were being drafted into Whitechapel and Spitalfields from all over the Metropolis. At 2.55 a.m., Long found a piece of bloody apron which had been dumped in the drain of a standpipe. These pipes could be found everywhere, providing cold water for the city. Asked about this apron at the inquest, Dr Brown opined that the bloodstains were recent, 'as if a hand or a knife had been wiped on it.' It fitted exactly the torn portion of apron still on Kate Eddowes' body. What Brown, and science, could not say at the time was whether the blood was animal or human, but everybody, from the coroner down, drew their own conclusions.

It was the other piece of evidence that has caused controversy. Above the standpipe, in white chalk on the black bricks of the entrance to the stairway of 108–119 Wentworth Model Dwellings (essentially a block of flats) were the words 'The Jewes are the men that will not be Blamed for nothing.' *Everything* about this phrase is problematic and has led to endless speculation. Today SOCO would have photographed it, taken scrapings of the chalk and analysed every aspect of it. In 1888, feeling that the words would lead to the assumption that a Jew was responsible for Eddowes' death, Sir Charles Warren, Commissioner of the Met, ordered the Goulston Street graffito to be washed away. The lad Green had done the same with Polly Nichols' blood in Buck's Row and only half an hour before the writing was found, Constable Collins had done the same with Liz Stride's. Detective Constable Daniel Halse, on plainclothes duty in the area that night, contended that the writing should be left to be examined further, but he was ignored.

Consequently, the *precise* wording of the Goulston Street phrase is unclear. The double-negative is odd, because it implies that the Jews are *not* to blame. The capital letters are a meaningless jumble. The spelling of Jews (either Jewes or Juews) while almost certainly the product of poor elementary education (it would be another six years before school attendance was made compulsory), has come to have sinister implications, especially in the hands of journalist Stephen Knight in his *Jack the Ripper: the Final Solution (1976)* who wove a ludicrous fantasy around the Masons and the 'highest in the land' to explain why Jack was never caught. There are at least seven slightly different versions of the words from senior policemen at the time, only one of whom (Warren) had actually seen the message. The bottom line about Goulston Street is that it cannot be proved to be Ripper-related at all. In many quarters, the newly arrived Jews were deeply unpopular and they were blamed for taking the jobs and lodgings of local gentiles. Like the leather apron found at the back of Hanbury Street, the writing may have nothing whatever to do with Jack.

One thing we can say with some certainty is that because the apron belonged to Eddowes, her killer travelled east after the crime. I believe he was going home, to Whitechapel.

The second ongoing problem in relation to Kate Eddowes, is the missing kidney. On the evening of Tuesday, 15 October, George Lusk, chairman of the self-appointed Whitechapel Vigilance Committee, received a parcel at his home. There was nothing odd about this – there were up to eight postal deliveries a day in London, in the good old days! But the parcel's contents were shocking. Half a kidney was surrounded by a badly written letter. The address was 'From Hell' which has spawned innumerable books and a movie and read:

> Sor, Mr. Lusk, I send you half a Kidne I took from one woman prasavved it for you tother piece I fried and ate it was very nise I may send you the bloody knif that took it out if you only wate a whil longer
> Signed. Catch me when you can
> Mishter Lusk

As we have seen this was one of a number of letters and postcards in circulation purporting to have been written by the Whitechapel killer (even though he does not use the 'Jack' moniker). It was the presence of the kidney that set it apart. A graphologist today would find the letter disturbed, its jagged, spiky letters the sign of anger and frustration, but forensic science could make no comment on that in 1888. On the face of it, the writer was Irish – 'Sor', 'prasavved' and 'Mishter' are all Irishisms – but the Irish were under suspicion in London at the time because of nationalist Fenian bombings carried out, even at Scotland Yard. Was this a deliberate attempt to stir up trouble as the Goulston Street graffito might have been against the Jews? On the other hand, the 'k' in 'knif' implied literacy in disguise, with the final 'e' missing and 'nise' The implication that Jack was something of a cannibal adds a whole new dimension to the murders and few people took this seriously. Lusk himself regarded it as a sick practical joke but took it to his next committee meeting at the Crown pub in Mile End Road, showed it to his local doctor and eventually to Dr Thomas Openshaw, curator of pathology at the London Hospital. He pronounced it human rather than animal, although his words were distorted by the press in what was (relatively) a quiet month as far as outrages were concerned.

The letter was sent to Scotland Yard and the kidney to the City Police office in Old Jewry. Here, Dr Brown examined it and agreed with Openshaw – it was human. Both doctors believed that the kidney had been taken from an autopsied body because, unlike medical specimens, it contained no formalin (despite the letter's mention of preservation).

A myth (one of many) emerged from Commissioner Henry Smith of the City Police in his autobiography written in 1910. He claimed that the renal artery was from Eddowes' body, with the 2 inches left in the body and the other inch attached to the Lusk kidney. He also said that the kidney was 'ginny' showing syptoms of Bright's disease from which Eddowes suffered. He was wrong on both counts. The kidney removed from Eddowes was cut clearly with no renal artery dangling and she did not have Bright's disease. Dr Sanders told the *Manchester Evening News* three days after Lusk received his parcel, that there was 'no indication that the woman drank' … it was 'a student's antic'.

Openshaw had not told the press that the kidney was female or the left kidney, even though the *Telegraph* reported that he had. The informal opinion of all medical men involved was that the kidney had no links with the Mitre Square victim at all.

But Openshaw had received a letter too. It was signed 'Jack the Ripper' and the writing was nearly as dystrophic as that sent to Lusk. It began 'Old boss' (the American term had been used on several earlier letters, reproduced in the press) 'You was rite it was the left kidney, and it ended with a macabre little ditty – 'O have you seen the devle with his mikerscope and scalpel a looking at a kidney with a slide cocked up.' While devil, microscope and scalpel are all mis-spelled, the address on the envelope is immaculate – 'Dr Openshaw, Pathological Curator, London Hospital, Whitechapel'. A medical student would be able to spell 'pathological' and only a medical man would know what a slide was in the context of laboratory work.

The final forensic link to the murder of Kate Eddowes is the ongoing nonsense concerning her shawl. In 2007, Russell Edwards, an amateur Ripperologist, bought a shawl from auctioneers Messrs. Lacy, Scott and Knight, allegedly for £2.9 million (this is unconfirmed). The shawl was said to have been taken from Mitre Square by a policeman and was subsequently handed down through the generations. To put it mildly, the provenance of this garment is highly dodgy. We have an incredibly detailed list of items found on Kate Eddowes' body and I quote them here for the sake of accuracy. She had: a black straw bonnet, a black cloth jacket, a chintz skirt, a brown linsey dress bodice, a grey stiff petticoat, a green Alpaca skirt, a ragged blue skirt, a white cambric chemise, a man's vest, no drawers or stays, a pair of men's lace-up boots. The rest of the items were found in her pockets – tea, sugar, soap, spoon, knife, clay pipes, match box, a ball of hemp and a piece of cloth holding pins and needles. Like Annie Chapman, she was dressed for sleeping rough, with several layers of clothing.

The disputed shawl is dark, but of good quality, fringed and woven with a floral design. It does not at all match the scruffy, torn items listed above. It *is* possible that she had acquired it recently and wore it flamboyantly to attract punters. It is also possible that a policeman helped himself to a souvenir from what by now was a spectacular series of murders and that it had already gone by the time the above list was made at the Golden Lane Mortuary. Except that the policeman in question was Acting Sergeant Amos Simpson, stationed in North London who was not known to have any links with the Ripper case, nor to have been in the jurisdiction of another force on the night in question.

Having bought the shawl, Edwards had it tested for DNA, hoping that the cloth would carry blood and perhaps semen stains. The tests were inconclusive but *the* expert on DNA, Sir Alec Jeffreys, pointed out that the DNA variant found – 315 1C – was actually present in over 99 per cent of sequences. Archaeological geneticists claim that the techniques used by Edwards' team are not accurate, especially as they relate to the evidentially weak mitochondrial DNA. In 2007, two of the descendants of Edwards' 'Jack' were in the same room as the shawl for three days, no doubt handled it and therefore rendered the 2014 tests inadmissible. As one scientific critic wrote 'If I examined that shawl, I'd probably find links to 150 other men from the area'.

So, who does Russell Edwards finger? 'Seven years after I bought the shawl,' he told the media, 'we had nailed Aaron Kosminski.' Kosminski has been in the record since 1894 with the emergence of the Macnaghten Memoranda (three versions of the same document). He is Number 2 of three (the others are the lawyer/teacher Montague Druitt and the con man Michael Ostrog):

Kosminski, a Polish Jew who lived in the very heart of the district where the murders were committed. He had become insane owing to many years indulgence in solitary vices. He had a great hatred of women, with strong homicidal tendencies. He was (and I believe, still is), detained in a lunatic asylum about March 1889. This man, in appearance, strongly resembled the individual seen by the City PC near Mitre Square.

A number of eminent Ripper experts, such as Paul Begg, Martin Fido and Philip Sugden, have researched Kosminski with a fine-tooth comb. To begin with, as we have seen already, it is most unusual for a serial killer to choose victims out of their class, race or religion.

None of the seven on Jack's list was Polish or Jewish. There are always exceptions, of course, so let us give Kosminski the benefit of the doubt. Robert Anderson, Assistant Commissioner of the Met from the end of August 1888 wrote his memoirs, called, bizarrely, *The Lighter Side of My Official Life*. Like far too many senior policemen, he claimed to know who the Ripper was and 'In saying that he was a Polish Jew, I am merely stating a definitely ascertained fact.' This was some twenty years after the killings and is definitely ascertained tosh.

There is no doubt that Kosminski was an oddball, one of the many 'men behaving madly' in the East End at the time. He rarely worked, never washed, ate all his food from scraps found in the gutter and drank water from stand-pipes. But we can dismiss Macnaghten's explanation for his insanity – masturbation does not cause mental problems, even though virtually all Victorians thought it did. Are we seriously to assume that such a shambling wreck could carry out seven murders in one small area and elude police patrols and prowling vigilantes? It defies belief. As Hallie Rubenhold says in her recent work *The Five*, 'This is history at its worst.'

What was new in the case of the double event was the pictorial record in the Eddowes' murder. Not only were Dr Brown's drawings clear and excellent, but City Surveyor Frederick Forster provided a superb plan of Mitre Square with the body in situ for the inquest. While the photographs of the earlier victims were of heads only, Eddowes is shown naked in her coffin with the throat and facial wounds obvious. Two other photographs are even more gruesome. Both of these were discovered by researcher Don Rumbelow in Snow Hill police station in the 1960s. One shows the head and upper body, complete with Dr Brown's post-mortem suture cut. This is not yet the 'Y' incision of pathologists today, but a vertical wound from the sternum to the crotch. In the second, whole body photograph, Eddowes has clearly been pegged upright against a wall, a common process being adopted in the United States at the same time. Perhaps oddly, Frederick Forster produced a drawing of the body on Sunday, 30 September before the post-mortem.

As with all the Ripper victims, we now know a great deal more about Kate Eddowes than anyone did at the time. She was born in

Wolverhampton in April 1842, making her 46 when she died. Bounced from family member to family member after her mother's death, she ended up living on and off with Thomas Conway, whose initials were tattooed on her arm. They had three children. By 1881, she had taken up with labourer John Kelly and they dossed at Cooney's Lodging House in Flower and Dean Street. Much of the summer of 1888 had been spent hop picking in Kent, which was both a means of making money and enjoying some fresh air away from the East End slums.

On the night before her murder, she had been warned to stay off the streets – 'Don't you fear for me,' she had said, 'I'll take care of myself and I shan't fall into his hands.'

But she did.

Mary Jane Kelly

'A much more rational and workable theory,' wrote Melville Macnaghten in his Memorandum, 'is that the "ripper's" brain gave way altogether after his awful glut in Miller's Court and that he committed suicide …'

This line of thinking has dogged Ripper research for far too long and has led us into a dead end. Serial killers very rarely commit suicide and I believe that the murder of Mary Kelly was not the last in the series.

George Bagster Phillips was once again in the thick of it. The police had called at 2 Spital Square at about 11 o'clock on what was a holiday in London – Lord Mayor's Day, Saturday, 9 November. He accompanied the officer to Miller's Court off Dorset Street, called 'Dosset' by locals because of the number of doss houses along its length.

The Court itself was reached by a narrow passage to the right of which was Number 13, a single room, 12ft square which was the scene of the crime. In all the Ripper attacks so far, the victim had at first been anonymous, but that was not the case here. The corpse belonged to Mary Jane Kelly, who rented the room and it had been discovered by Thomas 'Indian Harry' Bowyer who had called to collect the overdue rent. He, in turn, had dashed to find his employer, landlord John McCarthy, and the pair had hurried to Commercial Street police station and had spoken to Detective Inspector Walter Beck and Detective Walter Dew, the latter going on to a kind of immortality years later by arresting Dr H.H. Crippen for murder.

Phillips arrived at 11.15 and found the door to Number 13 locked (as Bowyer had), but could see Jack's handiwork through the window, two panes of which were broken. He saw no one else in the room and knew at once that Kelly was dead, so, rather bizarrely, hung around until 1.30 when Superintendent Arnold authorized McCarthy to break the door in. Thomas Arnold was head of H Division and not, by all accounts, a very good copper. He had actually ordered the destruction of the Goulston Street writing and went on to give a very garbled account of the Ripper murders to the *Eastern Post* in February 1893. The delay was caused by everybody waiting for the use of bloodhounds (Phillips himself thought this a good idea), but Charles Warren, the Commissioner, had resigned the previous day under pressure from the media over his ineffectual leadership and there was no one in charge. Detective Inspector Abberline, who got to the murder scene fifteen minutes after Phillips, was seething, and presumably, wandering about with the doctor as the crowds grew in Dorset Street. Technically, Beck was in charge of the scene until Arnold arrived.

Phillips examined Kelly's body lying flat on the bed. The room was so small that the door banged against a table under the window. He believed that the body had been moved because the injury that had caused her death was on her right side. Judging by the amount of blood on the bedclothes and mattress, the killer would not have had room to carry out the mutilations from that side. The cause of death was severance of the right carotid artery. At that point, in Phillips' testimony to the inquest under Dr Roderick MacDonald at Shoreditch Town Hall three days later, the coroner halted proceedings and went on to another witness, Phillips to be heard again later.

The body was butchered in a way that had not been seen in previous murders but what was immediately apparent, to the police and no doubt

Phillips, was that Mary Kelly's murder was the first to occur indoors and that she herself, it transpired, was only 24, half the age of the other victims. There could be no doubt, however, that this was another outrage by the 'Whitechapel fiend'.

Abberline undertook an inventory of the crime scene, noting that a large fire had burned in the grate (it was a cold and wet November) so fierce that it melted the spout of a kettle on the hearth. In the ashes, the inspector found items of women's clothing which he believed had been used to give a bright enough fire to light the murderer's work. The only other source of light was a solitary candle. The pipe that Abberline found belonged to Joseph Barnett, Kelly's on-off lover. The room key, Abberline told the inquest, had been missing for some time, but the door could be opened by operating the latch – via the broken window. This last evidence came from Barnett.

It seems to have been Phillips who ordered the photographs to be taken and they are the first – in fact, the *only* – examples taken in situ of any Ripper murder site. Crime scene photography would become standard in the years ahead, but it was a radical idea in 1888. The external photograph taken of Kelly's room from the Court looking towards Dorset Street, clearly shows the four-paned window and the door on the adjacent wall. This was discovered by the indefatigable researcher Don Rumbelow in the Old Jewry headquarters of the City Police in 1967. Why a case squarely in the Met's jurisdiction should end up in the City archives is not clear. It was here too, that the ghastly photograph of the body on her bed was found. Kelly is lying with her head to the left, facing the camera. Her left hand is lying across her stomach (rather as Stride's was across her chest) and her legs are open. She is clearly wearing a chemise which has been torn open. The third photograph causes all kinds of problems. It was taken from the right side of Kelly's body (the left arm can be seen clearly) but this was an impossibly cramped position for a cameraman to arrange his tripod and take a shot. It shows the bloody body, and on the table beyond it, body parts that have been hacked away and spread over the sparse furniture. This one is doubly problematic because it was in an album (also containing the mortuary photographs of Nichols, Chapman, Eddowes and Stride) returned to Scotland Yard in 1988 by the Miller family. Ernest Miller was Deputy Assistant Commissioner of the Met in the 1970s and should never have had these photographs in his personal possession. It is a reminder that archives have been routinely ransacked over the years – God knows what we will now never know about the Ripper or any other criminal case as a result. As Don Rumbelow himself remarked in *Jack the Ripper: Scotland Yard Investigates (2006)*, 'All police forces should be compelled to have a resident archivist.' Rumbelow speculates that because Miller's Court is only five minutes' walk from Bishopsgate police station (City) it is possible that City officers were present at the murder scene. It is not clear who took the Kelly photographs. Such written information as there is implies that photographs of corpses were for identification purposes only, not as part of a forensic investigation.

Kelly's body was moved to Shoreditch mortuary at 4 p.m. The windows of her room were boarded up and the door padlocked. Two uniformed constables stood guard at the entrance to Miller's Court in lieu of the blue and white tape which had yet to be invented.

The post-mortem took place the next day, carried out by Phillips with Dr Brown in attendance and a new name in Ripper pathology, Dr Thomas Bond. And there, almost, the medical testimony on the Kelly murder comes to a sudden stop. When the coroner implied that the public would hear more from Dr Phillips, he was either lying or was forced to change his mind later because the inquest did not contain any more medical observations. The excuse was that the cause of death – the severance of the carotid artery – was all that was required for inquest purposes. This ignores the fact that at all earlier inquests a great deal more information had been given and was daily reported in the press. Conspiracy theorists have had a field day with this. What made the coroner and Phillips clam up? What were they trying to hide?

Luckily, more evidence came to light in 1987 when an envelope with a Croydon postmark was sent anonymously to Scotland Yard. The following year of course, was the centenary of the Whitechapel murders and at least four books were being penned at the time. The envelope contained important Ripper artefacts which had been feared destroyed or at least had not been seen for decades. The Crippen case of 1910 was covered, as was the 'Dear Boss' letter, the most famous of the hoaxes sent to the media. What was far more important and relevant, however, were the notes of Dr Bond.

The man, as we have seen, was police surgeon to A Division, based in Whitehall and he lived in the Sanctuary that ran past Westminster Abbey into Parliament Square. He became involved because the Assistant Commissioner asked him to and clearly Anderson was impressed by Bond. His report was written up in *The Lancet* and makes it clear that he had attended the crime scene at 2 p.m. on the afternoon of the Kelly murder, the body still in place. The next day, he described what he saw and it is unfortunate that he makes a mistake in the very first line. 'The body was lying naked on the bed ...' Actually, as we have seen, Kelly was still wearing a chemise. The shoulders were flat but the body's axis was turned to the left side of the bed (from which the famous photograph was taken). The arms were as described above and the fingers clenched. The legs were wide apart, the left thigh at right angles to the trunk. The surface of abdomen and the thighs had been removed and the abdomen 'emptied of its viscera'. In other words, Kelly had been disembowelled. The breasts had been cut off and there were jagged cuts on the arms. The face had been mutilated beyond recognition (which has led some theorists to speculate that this was not Mary Kelly at all). The neck tissues were cut through to the bone. The uterus and kidneys, along with one breast were under the victim's head, the other breast by the left fist. The liver was between the feet, the intestines to the right and the spleen to the left. Flaps of skin from abdomen and thighs lay on the bedside table. The right side of the bed and the walls were covered in blood and the wounds to the face included the partial removal of nose, cheeks, eyebrow and ears. The lips were nicked several times. The throat wounds were deep through the larynx and the carotid cartilage. Both thighs had so much flesh removed that the femurs were visible, especially on the right and the calves were slashed too. There were minor cuts to the hands (which today we would assume were defensive wounds as Kelly tried to fight off her attacker). Her stomach contents (and this could only have been discovered during the post-mortem), included fish and potatoes. Perhaps most shockingly of all, Mary Kelly's heart was missing – another trophy for a serial killer.

Bond believed the murderer to be strong and very cool, but he did not believe that he had specialized anatomical knowledge. This was a bizarre conclusion, perhaps designed to take off the pressure of accusation against the medical profession, because the systematic *separation* of body parts screams just such knowledge. Someone who had no clue what they were doing would simply hack in all directions.

I find it very hard to believe that no photographs or drawings were made at the mortuary. Perhaps it was considered too gruesome to record. Alternatively, we have seen already in this chapter how criminal evidence is routinely stolen and discarded, so perhaps such photographs may yet turn up.

If Thomas Bond had left it there, he could be bundled into a clutch of other 'pathologists' whose work is not particularly helpful or insightful but in fact, unlike any of the others, he went *much* further. On 14 November, five days after the Kelly murder, he wrote to Robert Anderson with a summary of all the murders to date, beginning with Polly Nichols and providing what is perhaps the first attempt at psychological profiling ever undertaken in Britain and possibly the world. Nowadays, of course, profiling is not the purlieu of a forensic pathologist, however much he/she might itch to comment, and the whole industry of forensics has become minutely compartmentalized (see Chapter 1).

The report that Bond wrote took the whole subject into the realm of what today would be the domain of the forensic psychologist. Bond had no specific training in this (nobody had in 1888) but he may have read Richard von Krafft-Ebing's seminal *Psychopathia Sexualis* published the previous year, which not only discussed a murderer's motivation but used actual cases as examples. How far the other doctors who joined Bond at Miller's Court – Charles Hebbert, Gordon Bernard and John Gale – agreed with him is not known, but Phillips certainly did not and, as the 'lead' pathologist of the Ripper murders, must have had his nose put well and truly out of joint by Bond's intrusion.

The weakness of Bond's report was that he had only attended the murder scene of Kelly and was relying on second-hand information on Nichols, Chapman, Stride and Eddowes. He did not consider Tabram because she was not part of his brief – in other words we can only fall back on Macnaghten's 'canonical five'. All five Bond believed were killed by the same individual and were lying down when they were murdered. This has to be debatable in the case of Stride. He could not decide on the time of death in the pre-Kelly cases, making a judgement call that Stride was found immediately after her murder, and Nichols, Chapman and Eddowes 'three or four hours could have elapsed'.

Police evidence and witness statements make it clear that this is nonsense. In all cases, the time frame is much smaller than that. Bond concluded there were no signs of a struggle, despite what may have been defensive wounds on Kelly's forearms. The murderer would have *some* blood on him, but not the gouts both the police and public assumed. The killings were all about mutilation carried out by someone with no scientific or anatomical knowledge (which again flies in the face of the evidence). This extended to butchers and horse slaughterers. The murder weapon was a straight-bladed sharp instrument, at least 6 inches long and an inch wide. Contrary to his findings above, it could have belonged to a butcher or a surgeon.

It was now that Bond landed himself into a world nobody fully understood: what makes a serial killer tick? We have seen elsewhere in this book that no two were alike and the Thames torso killer could not have been more different from Jack. Bond surmised that the Whitechapel murderer would possibly be 'a quite inoffensive looking man' (think H.H. Crippen or John Christie rather than 'Dr' Tumblety) and a host of deranged individuals on the streets of the Abyss). He was probably middle-aged and respectably dressed. Again, most of the suspects picked up by the police wore scruffy, ragged down-and-outs. He must have worn a cloak or overcoat to disguise the blood on his cuffs and hands, at once giving birth to the ludicrous memes of the cloaked, top-hatted toff, assumed by all and sundry today, to be the guilty party. A man dressed like that – 'a swell' in contemporary slang – would stick out like a sore thumb in the East End.

Bond's killer would be a loner and eccentric in his habits, probably not having a regular occupation but possessed of a small income or pension. The loner makes sense because whoever Jack was, he came and went at all hours of the night and would probably be missed from a connected family home. He may live with respectable people who suspect that he might not be 'quite right in his mind at times'. A survey through those arrested by the police (over 200 of them) and others reported by the public show an extraordinarily high number of disturbed and mentally ill men in the area at the time. Violent crimes which today still fill the media and shock us all, are still carried out by such people, to which is added the complication of drug abuse. Bond surmised that the respectable people around Jack would not report him because of the fear of 'trouble or notoriety'. Mental illness was not understood at the time and regarded as a shameful thing. Far better to have a family member locked up in the west wing (à la Mrs Rochester in *Jane Eyre*) if there was room, or quietly put away in an asylum like Colney Hatch.

As to motivation, Bond sticks his neck out further. The killer, he said, was 'subject to periodical attacks of homicidal and erotic mania, a condition known at the time as satyriasis [an uncontrollable lust]'. Krafft-Ebing called this *lustmordre*. Bond threw out the idea of religious mania as unlikely.

Fast forward to 1988, the centenary of the Ripper murders. Agent John E. Douglas of the FBI was tasked with compiling a profile of Jack from all the evidence available, not merely the medical. His conclusions, based on years of research working with American serial killers, were astonishingly similar to Bond's.

According to Douglas, the killer was 'an asocial loner'. 'Employment in positions where he could work alone and experience vicariously his destructive fantasies, perhaps as a butcher or hospital or mortuary attendant.' 'Dress neat and orderly.' 'Sexual relationships with prostitutes.' This is highly likely because of the ease with which Jack picked up his victims. 'May have contracted venereal disease.' This presumably provides a motive for targeting prostitutes. The disease must have been prevalent among the down-and-outs of the East End, but of the known victims Liz Stride had medical treatment for it and it may be that Mary Kelly's stay in a Cardiff infirmary was another example. Jack's final victim, Alice McKenzie, had syphilis. Douglas's expertise led him to pinpoint Jack's age as late twenties. The red-moustached man seen by Mary Cox going into Kelly's room falls within the age group, although others cited by other eyewitnesses are considerably older.

'Employed since the murders were mostly at weekends.' This is a little misleading because *all* the murders occurred late at night or in the early hours of the morning. Work patterns of the 1880s were not the same as today ('working from home' was an individual's pipe dream at the time). 'Free from family accountability and so unlikely to have been married.' 'Not surgically skilled.' In this context, Douglas has followed Bond's view, but as we have noted, this ran contrary to the opinion of most doctors involved, especially Phillips, the most experience of them all. 'Probably in some sort of trouble with the police before the first murder.' Serial killers do not spring fully formed. Today, when medical and educational histories are readily available on everyone, we can piece together delinquent – and escalating – bad behaviour. This is rarely possible in the Victorian period when so many records are missing. 'Lived or worked in the Whitechapel area and his first homicide would have been close to his home or place of work.' This is the key to Jack's success; he knew the place like the back of his hand and so was able to elude police and vigilante patrols. 'Undoubtedly, the police would have interviewed him.' This is possible, but it is equally likely that he ducked under their radar altogether.

By 2000, when John Douglas reviewed the Ripper murders for his book *The Cases That Haunt Us*, he had changed his mind on the killer's anatomical skills.

So, we have the bizarre situation that Thomas Bond's medical opinions are woefully wide of the mark, however much Robert Anderson hoped otherwise, but his psychological evaluation is uncannily accurate. 'No one,' wrote Robert Anderson years later, 'ever saw Jack the Ripper,' but in fact it is highly likely that a number of people did. One of them was Mary Ann Cox, a prostitute who lived at 5 Miller's Court across the narrow space between Number 3 and Number 13. On the night of 8 November, she saw a man in Kelly's company wandering down Dorset Street. He had an auburn moustache and was carrying a quart of beer. Kelly had clearly been drinking and, as the pair went into her room, Cox called out to her 'Good night Mary Jane,' and Kelly replied in kind, telling her she was going to have a sing. And sing she did, according to Cox, the schmaltzy *Only a Flower I plucked from my Mother's Grave*. There was also a female cry of 'Oh, murder!' but where it came from and how seriously it can be taken is anybody's guess.

Then Jack went to work, perhaps stripping to avoid being covered in blood, perhaps burning Kelly's clothes to provide more light for his ghastly work. Probably by dawn and certainly long before Tom Bowyer arrived, he had gone.

Alice McKenzie

The murder of Mary Jane Kelly was not the final spectacular full stop that many people, including eminent researchers, have held it to be. Jack killed once more, going out with more of a whimper than a bang, nine months after the killing in Miller's Court. It was to be George Bagster Phillips' last hurrah in the Ripper murders and he arrived in Castle Alley, off Old Castle Street, Whitechapel to a sight all too familiar.

It was 1.10 a.m. by the time Dr Phillips got to the narrow thoroughfare that led past the Whitechapel public baths. It was pouring down by now, the only murder night of truly bad weather. The victim lay between the costermongers' carts, her head turned to the right and her throat cut. Her skirts were pulled up and she was naked below the navel, with a stab wound to her abdomen. There were policemen there already which must have made the scene very crowded. Constable 272H Walter Andrews had found the body and blown his whistle to summon aid. He had been talking moments before to his superior, Sergeant Edward Badham, who had previously taken Annie Chapman to the mortuary and had interviewed witnesses in the Kelly case. He had come running and, as the senior man, sent Constable 423H Joseph Allen to fetch Phillips and to get the duty inspector from Commercial Street police station. Edmund Reid, who had been involved in the Whitechapel murders since Nichols ten months earlier, turned up too. He organized a house-to-house search. It was Reid who found a clay pipe and a polished farthing under the body once it was taken away to the Whitechapel Workhouse mortuary.

The inquest was held on the day the body had been found, again at the Working Lads' Institute, presided over by Wynne Baxter who by now must have been all too used to inquiries of this nature. The post-mortem was carried out by Drs Phillips, Bond and McKellar. The findings of another Ripper-related body after months of quiet, clearly rattled everybody, because at three o'clock that morning, James Monro, the Chief Commissioner, had turned up at Castle Alley to see the scene for himself.

Phillips' report for the inquest (22 July) is very long, a series of short sentences with sub-headings which was not his usual style. The neck wound was jagged, the genitals exposed. The body was still warm where covered by clothes, cold in exposed areas. Her eyelids were open and the blood from the neck wound had run into the gutter, washed slightly downhill by the rain. There was no sign of anaesthetics or drugs. At the mortuary ('the shed used as a mortuary' as Phillips pointedly says), the doctor talked things over with Superintendent Arnold and Chief Inspector West and insisted that the victim was not to be touched.

Once he had the go-ahead for an inquest, Phillips contacted the Chief Surgeon (McKellar) and Dr Brown who had both asked to be involved. McKellar turned up with a friend, a Mr Boswick who appears to be something of a ghoul. He was not there long and it is easy to read between Phillips' lines that the doctor sent him packing. Phillips was accompanied by his assistant, Mr Clark.

The dead woman was 5ft 5in tall. Rigor mortis had set in. The body was well nourished. Intriguingly, the clay pipe found under the body had been thrown to the ground by 'one of the assistants' and broken. It had subsequently disappeared even though Phillips himself had picked up the pieces for preservation. The abdominal wounds made were far shallower than in previous cases, almost scouring the skin here and there. There was no sign of recent sex.

The cause of death was syncope arising from the slashing of the throat vessels. The murder weapon was sharp and the killing was carried out on the ground by someone who knew his way around the human body. There were no signs of struggle but the murderer had held the woman down by the shoulder. The victim's clothes were tight, which perhaps explains why various cuts had not been successful. Dr Frederick Brown had concurred with Phillips' findings and Dr Bond viewed the corpse at 6 p.m. By this time the body had been washed.

Phillips' overall conclusion was that the Castle Alley victim was not murdered by the Whitechapel fiend because the mutilations were relatively slight and no body parts had been removed. But Bond disagreed, an example of the bickering among doctors that plays into the hands of defence counsel in trials and causes confusion in the minds of jurors. Before the 17th was out, the police knew the identity of the victim – she was Alice McKenzie, known as 'Clay Pipe' Alice, a prostitute with a penchant for drink. She had been living at a doss house in Green Street with John McCormick for six years and was 40 years old. On the night she died they had argued. He believed that she came originally from Peterborough but had no idea whether she had ever married or had children (Phillips thought not). Bond's report was for Robert Anderson and he clearly believed that the Whitechapel murderer had struck again.

So, who was right? We have seen that Phillips had far more experience than Bond in the Whitechapel case and that Bond's medical (as opposed to psychological) opinions are a little suspect. The problem is partly one of timing. Serial killers' murder patterns vary. Most of them experience a number of phases in their quest for a victim, the murder itself and the aftermath. In some cases, the murders take place in rapid succession; in others, gaps of days, weeks, months or even years can intervene. Of course, if such a killer is imprisoned for an unrelated case, he/she is effectively taken out of circulation for a particular period before the cycle can begin again.

The doctor pathologists in 1888/9 gave it their best shot. It was not good enough, but neither was the work of the police or the integrity of the media. They all conspired unwittingly to let the Whitechapel killer escape undetected and to give rise to what has become the Ripper industry. Despite all they could do, Jack the Ripper still walks the streets of the Abyss.

Chapter 9

Poison for Cats

'Florence Elizabeth Maybrick, aged twenty-six, was indicted for having, at Garston, on the 11th of May [1889] feloniously, wilfully and of her malice aforethought, killed and murdered one James Maybrick.' So ran the opening comments at the Liverpool Summer Assize court.

If only it were that simple!

The Maybrick case, like that of William Palmer thirty-three years earlier, is awash with doctors, both before and after the cotton merchant's death. The first was the family physician, Dr Hopper, who was called in by Florence Maybrick as a friend rather than a medical man. James Maybrick was many years older than his wife and what had once appeared a happy marriage was now falling apart. Maybrick had a wife already (unbeknownst to Florence) and frequented brothels on his various business trips to Virginia. He had at least one mistress in his native Liverpool. Florence in turn was having an affair with Alfred Brierley, the couple having spent two days at a London hotel in late March. Hopper was consulted by Florence and a friend, Mrs Matilda Briggs, on 30 March.

It was as a doctor that he was questioned at Florence's trial on Wednesday, 31 July. He testified that he had known the Maybricks since 1881. James was generally healthy but he complained of dyspepsia and nervousness and the doctor clearly thought him something of a hypochondriac. In June 1888 he began dispensing nerve tonic. He had never prescribed arsenic but he had had conversations with Maybrick about it. Arsenic, in minute doses, acted as an antiperiodic, largely used in the case of intermittent fevers.

Hopper told the court that about 30 March meeting with Florence. He noted her black eye and remembered that she had told him that she could not bear her husband to come near her. The next day, Hopper played the marriage guidance counsellor at their home, Battlecrease House in Aigberth, and was under the impression that the pair had patched things up.

The doctor explained that Maybrick was in the habit of self-dosing with various drugs, often doubling the dosage of those prescribed by Hopper himself. He was also aware that Maybrick was taking strychnine and nux vomica, prescribed for him by an American doctor, as an aphrodisiac. Both the judge and counsel wanted to know more and Hopper explained that Maybrick's self-dosing included quinine, iron, hypophosphates, arsenic and strychnine.

Today, most of us would be horrified at the potential risk of taking this dosage, but in Victorian England, attitudes were different and scientific knowledge limited.

On the second day of the trial, Dr Charles Fuller gave evidence. He was the doctor of James's brother Michael, a famous songwriter of the day and something of a national celebrity. James was staying in London with Michael early in April and Fuller was called in because James was complaining of headaches, numbness and a fear of incipient paralysis. Fuller put the whole thing down to indigestion and prescribed an aperient and liver pills, both totally harmless. There was no mention of arsenic in the session and Maybrick showed no symptoms of having taken any. The doctor also explained that arsenic, unlike opium, was not addictive.

Later that day, another family doctor, Richard Humphreys, was in the witness box. He attended Florence and the two children but never James until Sunday, 28 April. Maybrick was in bed, complaining of pains in his chest and head and reiterating his fear of paralysis. He put this down to a cup of tea he had drunk, and that this had happened before. It did not say much for the doctor's reliability when the judge asked him if tea could cause these symptoms – 'Not usually,' Humphreys said, 'but I have known it to have done so.' Maybrick had complained of feeling ill at the Wirral races on the previous day, with stiff legs and feeling dazed. The doctor prescribed dilute prussic acid and advised soda and milk for the rest of the day.

Later that day, Humphreys saw his patient again and told him to discontinue Fuller's prescription. Maybrick agreed. 'He was a man,' Humphreys told the court, 'who prided himself on his knowledge of medicine.' The doctor prescribed bromide of potassium and tincture of henbane (itself a poison, of course, in certain proportions). Maybrick stayed in bed with a 'furred' tongue. Humphreys prescribed a diet of coffee, toast, bacon, Revalenta and, on alternate days for dinner, fish and bacon. He gave him iridium as a laxative and papain to help digestion. Two days later, Maybrick was worse, complaining that Humphreys' medicine had not agreed with him. Florence said that her husband always said that about any dosage given to him.

By that evening, the patient was in great pain in both legs and the doctor rubbed turpentine on them. Humphreys attributed the pain to a Turkish bath Maybrick had had earlier in the day. He had also been sick and the doctor gave him a morphine suppository. The symptoms worsened and Humphreys tried other remedies – Valentine's beef juice and Condy's fluid to wash out the mouth. The doctor asked Florence if she wanted a second opinion but she declined – James had seen so many doctors and none of them had done him any good. Humphreys provided Fowler's solution, which contained arsenic. He also administered a blister to the stomach and Maybrick appeared better.

It was now that Humphreys was joined by Dr William Carter whose presence had been requested by James's brother Edwin. Together, the doctors tried something else – jacharandi and antispyrine to ease Maybrick's sore throat.

By Wednesday, 8 May, Florence was worn out, administering the doctors' prescriptions several times a day. She requested a nurse to help and Ellen Gove turned up from the local hospital. Later that day,

Maybrick's condition was worsening and Michael arrived. His brother was complaining of 'tenesmus' (bowel pain). Humphreys found nothing amiss in his examination of the stools, but the ever-pushy Michael insisted on a second analysis. Accordingly, the stools were boiled and tested for antimony, arsenic and mercury. The results were negative; as they were for the urine tested later.

By the Friday, Maybrick's pulse was more rapid and he was weaker. One of his hands was white. His tongue was 'filthy' and he was very restless. He was now prescribed cocaine for his throat, prussic acid for his mouth. At the trial, Humphreys spoke of 'a suggestion' made to him the day before which led Dr Carter to examine a bottle of meat juice. This suggestion probably came from Michael and there is little doubt that both brothers now believed that Florence was poisoning James. By that night, Humphreys was really concerned for him and suggested calling his solicitor to set his affairs in order.

By 8.30 a.m. on Saturday 11th, Maybrick was dying and twelve hours later, he was dead.

Humphreys gave evidence at the trial with regard to the post-mortem on Monday 13th. Two other doctors, Carter and Barron were there, as was Superintendent Isaac Brynyng of the West Derby police. Carter made the notes and the examination took place in Maybrick's bedroom at Battlecrease.

In Scottish trials, the custom had arisen of reading post-mortem notes in court; the judge allowed it now, with the rather daft proviso that 'they cannot be called the strictest evidence'. What, in the days before tape or video recordings, could have been stricter?

Various internal organs – stomach, liver and spleen – were placed in jars, sealed and given to Inspector Baxendale of the local police. Humphreys told the court that the cause of death was arsenical poisoning, but that was based on the findings of the jars' contents, not the body itself. The cross-examination by Charles Russell for the defence, exposed Humphreys. He had never carried out a post-mortem on an arsenic victim; in fact, he had never carried out a post-mortem on anyone who had been poisoned. He had to hope that his medical colleagues would be able to bail him out.

When Russell resumed his attack on the third day of the trial, he went through the ludicrously long list of Maybrick's supposed ailments and Humphreys had to agree that they were all natural and at least some of them the result of hypochondria. He also admitted that in testing Maybrick's stools, he was not an expert and may have got it wrong. 'That is candid, doctor,' Russell sniped, and in Victorian forensic medicine generally, it is a pity that more doctors were not as candid. But Humphreys had to backtrack further. He admitted that until Michael Maybrick had put the idea of arsenic poisoning into his head, he would have ascribed James's death to gastro-enteritis. He also admitted that there was nothing in the post-mortem which would have pointed to death by arsenic either.

Russell then rattled through a number of drugs that Humphreys had prescribed. Some of these were 'homeopathic', in other words, not listed in the official Pharmacopoeia issued to all medical practices, hospitals and pharmacists. In others, Humphreys admitted, he did not know the chemical makeup. All in all, Humphreys must have been acutely grateful when he stood down to make way for Dr Carter.

William Carter told the court that he was experienced in cases of arsenic overdose and that he did not know the Maybricks until four days before James died. Rather bizarrely, he did not know that Humphreys had sent for him until the inquest. Neither he nor Humphreys suspected poison. 'It is the last thing – the very last thing – we [doctors generally] would think of.' By Thursday 9th, bowel straining (tenesmus) had set in and this had not been present before. Another nurse, Calley, was there, as was the ever-present Michael Maybrick.

The next day, he tested (again almost certainly at Michael's request) Newe's food which had been given to James. There was nothing wrong with it. Neither was there a problem with some brandy that he had drunk. On the Friday, Michael gave Carter the bottle of Valentine's meat juice, again for poison testing. The medicines that Carter prescribed were to help Maybrick sleep and would have no ill effects on him. Carter's tests carried out that night (in contrast to Humphreys') showed a metallic substance in the stool sample. By Saturday, Carter knew that the man was dying. He took the meat juice bottle to be analysed by Edward Davies, consulting chemist. Carter added his views, at the trial, about the post-mortem, stating that the inflammation of the stomach was evidence of arsenical poisoning. The fatal dose, he believed, had been administered on Friday, 3 May, but subsequent doses had probably been given too. As with Humphreys, Carter had no direct experience of death due to arsenic poisoning, although, tellingly, he was aware of cases where an overdose was the cause. Altogether, Carter's answers to Russell were prevaricating – 'It is often there, and often not' – leaving a completely unhelpful diagnosis. But he had found arsenic in the meat juice.

Dr Alexander Barron came next. He was Professor of Pathology at University College and a practising doctor in Liverpool. He attended the post-mortem on Mrs Maybrick's behalf and believed the cause of death was due to an irritant poison. Pushed by Russell to explain the symptoms of withdrawal from a drug – what today we would call 'cold turkey' – Barron described almost exactly Maybrick's symptoms. When Russell tried to show a medical book to the jury to make the post-mortem clearer, John Addison, for the prosecution, objected and the judge backed him. Once again, the jury was denied clarity in what must have been (as with William Palmer nearly half a century earlier) a difficult medical/technical line to follow.

On the fourth day of the trial, the medical heavyweight Dr Thomas Stevenson was called in. He was lecturer in forensic medicine at Guy's Hospital, London, and was the last witness before Russell summed up for the defence. Stevenson was the nearest thing to a Home Office pathologist the prosecution had at the time, with considerable experience of arsenic. He had tested various body specimens received from Davies the pharmacist and Inspector Baxendale on 22 July. He found no arsenic in the stomach but there were traces of it (and bismuth, prescribed by Humphreys) in the intestines. The spleen was so decomposed by this time it could not be tested. All arsenic was the white variety, .015 of a grain. Stevenson also found traces in the kidney and the liver. It was the liver that particularly showed intake of the poison and Stevenson stressed that this was based on personal experience and not 'from stories you find in [medical] books'. He concluded, 'I have no doubt that this man died from the effects of arsenic'; the symptoms which Stevenson outlined were exactly those experienced by Maybrick. The defence objected and the judge agreed; Stevenson was quoting other medical testimony he had not witnessed himself. Russell did his best to rattle the expert, but Stevenson would not be browbeaten.

There were still four doctors to come, called by the defence, in the same kind of tedious rebuttal we saw in the Palmer trial (see Chapter 5). Dr J. Drysdale was a Liverpool physician consulted by Maybrick the previous November. He had complained of headaches he had been having for three months and of a nasty taste in the mouth. All this became worse when he smoked or drank too much. Maybrick admitted to self-medication and Drysdale had him down as a chronic hypochondriac.

Charles Tidy was the expert witness to counter Stevenson. Examiner of Forensic Medicine at the London Hospital, he was employed by the Home Office as an analyst. He had personal experience of over forty cases of arsenical poisoning. This time, the explanatory diagram of a body was allowed for the jury's benefit and Tidy's job was essentially to sow doubt into their minds as to the general symptoms, which could have causes other than arsenic.

On the fifth day, Dr Rawdon Macnamara of the Royal College of Surgeons of Ireland took the stand. He agreed with Tidy that the retching by Maybrick was attributable to a number of other things than arsenic. Humphreys' use of a blister would have no effect on arsenic poisoning, but it would help in cases of gastro-enteritis. Russell also got out of Macnamara the fact that in many cases, not even post-mortem could provide a satisfactory cause of death, providing the jury with doubt in the context of the prosecution doctors' testimony. Despite

Addison's attempt, the Irish expert stuck to his guns – Maybrick died of gastro-enteritis and this had no links whatsoever with arsenic.

The next level down among the medical fraternity was as important as the doctors. Christopher Hanson was a chemist and druggist at nearby Gressington and on 29 April Florence Maybrick had bought two dozen flypapers from him. These were strips of cellotape, coated with arsenic, which were suspended from a ceiling to catch and kill flies.

Two weeks after James and Florence's row after the Grand National (caused, as it turned out, by her going off with Brierley) the family nurse, Alice Yapp, saw those flypapers soaking in a washbasin of water in Florence's bedroom. As other witnesses at the trial testified, white arsenic could be removed from the papers by this process, leaving a quantity of potentially dangerous liquid. As another witness testified, this was routinely used by ladies as a cosmetic, although surely other products could be obtained more simply over the counter.

If the evidence of Hanson and Yapp was circumstantially damning, that of the analytical chemist Edward Davies was even more so. On 11 May, Dr Carter had brought him a bottle of Valentine's meat juice and Davies found traces of poison in it – half a grain of white arsenic. He double checked with other samples and found no trace of the substance elsewhere. The samples, of intestines provided by Inspector Baxendale, also contained arsenic, but there was none in the spleen. Other deposits, taken from the plumbing of Battlecrease House as part of the police search, carried traces of arsenic too, as did the cloth of a handkerchief. A bottle containing liquid and a black powder had been found in Florence's bedroom, hidden in a hatbox. The black powder was charcoal, but there was also a quantity of solid arsenic. Edwards' tests were detailed and thorough but Charles Russell threw him by asking the judge to examine the glass with arsenic in court. Even with two magnifying glasses, Stephens could not see anything. Neither could Russell. What the jury made of it, only they knew.

Nurses Gove and Calley gave evidence of Florence Maybrick handing them various medicines to be given to her husband. As far as they knew, of course, these were innocent remedies provided by the various doctors and it was not possible for the prosecution to prove otherwise.

Until 1898, the accused in a court of law had no right to speak in their own defence, but in an unusual move, the judge let a statement be read which Florence had written. She argued that the flypapers were indeed for cosmetic purposes, that in her native United States she had been in the habit of using a facewash prescribed by a doctor which consisted of arsenic, benzoin and elderflower. She had lost the prescription and, to clear up skin blemishes in time for a ball on 30 March, had tried to make up a solution for herself. She had seen this done by friends in Germany, using a handkerchief to apply the liquid. In the context of the Valentine's meat extract, she told the court that James had asked her for some powder on Thursday 9th. She was tired and distraught, adding, rather tellingly that 'I had not one true or honest friend in that house' and that she had not been able to nurse the dying man or give him anything from her own hands. This time she managed to give the powder to him, not knowing what it was and left it by his bedside because he had fallen asleep. She complained, rightly, that no one had told her that a death certificate had been refused and that charges would be brought until Superintendent Brynyng turned up on the 14th with the relevant warrant for her arrest.

This was as far as the law could let Florence Maybrick go. The rest was to be fought out by counsel for the prosecution and defence and a summing up by the judge. James Fitzjames Stephen was not the man he used to be. He was only 60 at the time of the Maybrick trial but his rambling, sometimes incoherent summation proved that he was suffering from the early onset of Alzheimer's disease. That was not a diagnosis available in 1889 and it was a brave barrister indeed who would accuse a high court judge of being gaga! He had had a stroke in 1885 and should have retired then. Intriguingly, his son was Kenneth Stephen who was tutor to 'Prince Eddy', the Duke of Clarence and he died insane in 1892.

Stephen's summation lasted for the best part of two days and runs to seventy-five pages of solid text. A few examples will suffice as to the judge's incompetence. He referred to Florence's lover as Brierley throughout, without the courtesy of a Christian name or even a 'Mr' (and Brierley was in court!) He did not know what the Grand National was, calling it the 'Grand National something'. Defence counsel had to correct some of the judge's dates. 'There is no use,' Stephen said, 'in disputing about whether I used one word or another.' He claimed that Dr Hopper had last seen Maybrick in 1885, four years before he actually did so and read the word 'arsenic' in his notes even though he admitted it was not in Hopper's testimony. 'There are so many different circumstances,' moaned the judge, 'and it is so very difficult to tell what is done to each person, that it introduced a great deal of difficulty into the case.' But that was precisely the judge's job. A cynic would say that counsel might deliberately confuse or mislead the jury but the judge's summation should cut right through all that.

In the context of medical evidence, Stephen rightly pointed out the excessive amount of it, with various doctors trying various treatments, all to no avail. The judge believed that Dr Fuller's hour-long consultation with Maybrick was far too long. He reiterated the list of chemicals in the medicines prescribed – 'I do not know, gentlemen,' he said to the jury, 'whether these names convey much to your minds' – and once again, we are the heart of forensic medicine. The facts are vital in deciding guilt or innocence, but the rubric and the jargon were often way over the heads of jurymen. Unusually, we have a list of them – there are plumbers, farmers, barbers, grocers and woodturners; not one of them had any medical knowledge. The rambling judge confused doctors Tidy and Stevenson, which cannot have helped them much. He also dismissed the value of the doctors not directly involved in the case, because theirs were merely opinions (which, of course, was the whole point of expert witnesses).

Having said that motive for murder was not necessary in a murder trial, Stephen spent pages discussing Florence's relationship with

Brierley, the letters between them and the time they spent together in a London hotel. He also had the gall to mention the inequality of attitudes in terms of the morality of men and of women before proceeding to trash Florence for taking part in this 'disgraceful' affair.

There must have been huge sighs of relief when the windbag finished and the jury were back after only thirty-five minutes with a verdict of guilty. Florence's sole statement as prisoner at the bar was, 'Although I have been found guilty, with the exception of my intimacy with Mr Brierley, I am not guilty of this crime.'

In all probability, she was. The evidence was certainly tortuous, from doctors, forensic experts, servants, friends and family, but the balance of it suggests that the jury got it right. The weakness in the defence case was that James Maybrick was a junkie, self-medicating with arsenic, strychnine and other drugs, which not only accounted for quantities of poison in his system but the samples of it lying around Battlecrease House, including the fatal bottle marked 'Poison for Cats'.

But Florence Maybrick did not keep her appointment with James Berry, the public hangman. Heavyweights in the media, politicians on both sides of the Atlantic, weighed in on her side. The Americans were powerless; the crime had been committed on British soil and, by marrying Maybrick, Florence had renounced American citizenship.

The judge himself was booed and jostled as he left the court and *The Times* wrote, 'It has been noticed by [everybody] that the doctors differed beyond all hope of agreement as to the cause of death.' Half a million people signed a petition for reprieve, among them several doctors. All the major newspapers were bombarded with letters from medical practitioners, lawyers and arsenic-takers, arguing very ably with the prosecution. Auberon Herbert, writing to *The Times* asked why it was necessary to make enquiries into anything Mrs Maybrick had given her husband when, at his own connivance, Maybrick's stomach was 'a druggists' waste-pipe' containing strychnine, arsenic, jacharandi, cascara, henbane, morphia, prussic acid, papain, iridin' and God knew what else his doctors had prescribed.

Predictably, *The Lancet*, a medical journal written exclusively by the medical profession, struck back in defence of its own.

Such was the pressure on the Home Secretary, Henry Matthews, that Florence's death sentence was commuted to one of life imprisonment. The gallows was already being built in Walton gaol by that time and she must have been able to hear the carpenters at work from the condemned cell.

With a change of government in 1892, there were various attempts to get Florence Maybrick released. Over 3,000 people signed a petition for a public enquiry which Herbert Asquith, the new Home Secretary, ignored. Florence served fifteen years, during which she wrote a book on her prison experience and was released from Aylesbury in January 1904. As soon as possible, she went home to America, where she died, surrounded by cats, in 1941.

But there is a bizarre postscript to the Maybrick case. In 1992, Liverpudlian Michael Barrett contacted a literary agent, Rupert Crew, over a diary he had obtained which was purportedly written by Jack the Ripper. The last line of the diary read 'I give my name that all know of me, so history do tell, what love can do to a gentle man born, Yours truly Jack the Ripper, dated this third of May 1889.' James Maybrick died eight days later.

Crew put Barrett in touch with author Shirley Harrison and together they produced *The Diary of Jack the Ripper*, published by Smith Gryphon in 1993. High-profile hoaxes had been foisted on the public before, most spectacularly the Hitler diaries, bought by media mogul Robert Murdoch for $3.75 million in 1982. In 1968, Murdoch had offered $250,000 for the diaries of Benito Mussolini, the price difference presumably reflecting the levels of infamy rating of the dictators concerned. When both sets of documents were proved scientifically to be forgeries, heads rolled and companies collapsed. The British historian, Hugh Trevor-Roper, who had told everybody that the Hitler work was authentic, was utterly discredited.

Provenance is everything in the historic document world and the Ripper diary is about as shady as it can get. Barrett said he was given the diary by a friend, Tony Devereux, who subsequently died of heart failure. Devereux had not divulged the diary's source. Smith Gryphon and Shirley Harrison nevertheless became absorbed by the diary and set to work to prove its authenticity. This study in itself is a classic example of the two sides of forensic science – the technical world of objects and the far vaguer field of psychology. This book is about the former, but the latter cannot be ignored, so we will begin by looking at the mindset of the writer.

In facsimile form (I have not seen the original) the diary runs to sixty-two pages in a very clear handwriting. Having handled hundreds of Victorian documents in my own researches, this is one of the clearest I have seen. It purports to have been written by James Maybrick and, until the 'sign-off', has no dates at all. One expert who Harrison consulted was Dr David Forshaw, then an addiction consultant at the Maudsley Psychiatric Hospital in London. Forshaw believes that the writing becomes more disorganized, chaotic and unhinged as the Whitechapel crimes are catalogued in the diary – and as Maybrick descended into increasing drug-related paranoia. I cannot detect this. There are pages where the writing is larger and more scribbled than others, but essentially the last page is very much like the first.

The 'story' in the diary's pages is that Maybrick was furious that Florence was having an affair behind his back – and seemingly oblivious to his own mistresses, possible earlier wife and frequenting of brothels – and this drove him to take revenge on prostitutes generally.

This is not an uncommon motive among serial killers, but the link here is extraordinarily vague. If the Whitechapel victims were substitutes for Maybrick's unfaithful wife – he calls her 'whore' throughout – they were very poor examples. Florence was 23 in 1888. All the East End victims except one (Mary Kelly, who was 24) were middle-aged and looked older.

The diary says that Maybrick was influenced by the name Whitechapel in his native Liverpool and so decided to launch his murderous campaign in Whitechapel, London. But serial killers, especially before the age of the car, did not behave like this. Their first kill will be close to their home or workplace, radiating outwards as they gain confidence and experience. Deciding to strike 210 miles away (a train journey of five hours) makes no sense. Maybrick did have business contacts in London and his brother Michael, the songwriter, lived in Regent's Park. But Regent's Park is 5 miles away from the Whitechapel killing fields – the far side of the moon as far as serial killers are concerned. The diary says that Maybrick rented a room in Middlesex Street (Petticoat Lane) which of course puts him in the heart of Ripper territory, but there is absolutely no evidence that he did so. He also says that he walked the streets to familiarize himself with the area, but that does not compare with the experience of H Division of the Met who performed such perambulations daily. Are we to suppose that a relative stranger (even if Middlesex Street is valid) could outsmart them?

Everybody who knew Maybrick remembers how well dressed he always was. Such a 'toff' would stand out in the East End and would invite comment. Did he disguise himself by dressing down? The diary makes no mention of that.

The diary contends that Maybrick's first murder took place in Manchester – and this fits the serial-killer pattern. We have no dates but it must have been, from the context, before the summer of 1888 and there is no record of a prostitute murder by strangulation (the MO recorded in the diary) in that time period. Rather lamely, Harrison tells us that records are often lost and the media would not bother reporting the death of a single 'unfortunate'.

Early on, in the planning stages of the campaign, Maybrick conjectures what it would be like to eat parts of his victim. We know that this theme emerged after the murder of Kate Eddowes in Mitre Square (see Chapter 8) and the vexed issue of the kidney sent to George Lusk. Since that kidney is likely to be a hoax and its accompanying letter about eating the other half is equally a scam, we cannot seriously consider the Whitechapel murderer as a cannibal. It is not in his mindset. Maybrick plans to use his cane (many 'gentlemen' carried them) and insert it – 'ram a cane into the whoring bitch's mound and leave it there to see how much she could take'. While all this is deeply unpleasant, it never happened and Maybrick would be a different kind of lunatic altogether to leave his own cane at a crime scene.

There is no reference to the murders of Emma Smith or Martha Tabram even though, at the time, the media assumed they were both Ripper victims. That, says Harrison, is evidence that the diary is genuine. No, it is not. After a possible reference to the murder of Polly Nichols, Maybrick uses the phrase 'funny little games'. This is straight out of Jack's playbook, appearing in the infamous 'Dear Boss' letter sent to the Central News Agency on 25 September 1888. This was widely circulated in the press of the time and in most books on the Whitechapel murders since then. The recurrent 'ha! ha!' which litter the diary and the constant assertion of Maybrick's cleverness is also lifted from these letters.

In what is clearly a reference to the murder of Annie Chapman, the diary says that Maybrick returned to the body 'and cut out some more'. But on the morning when it happened, it was already dawn and no one would seriously take the risk of going back to the crime scene, when Whitechapel was already awake and moving. The diary claims that Maybrick 'ate all of it' (the viscera removed from Chapman) and refers to pills, farthings and rings found at the murder scene. We know that there were references to some of these in the press at the time and all of them have been included in discussions of the murder in recent books.

The diary claims that the time gap between the murders of Stride and Eddowes in the 'double event' was fifteen minutes. In fact, such a walk from one crime scene to the next, takes at least forty-five minutes.

The diary is obsessed with rhymes, with many words repeated as the writer struggled to find one that would fit. As explanation, Maybrick contends that he is trying to outdo his brother Michael, the lyricist, in some sort of fraternal competition. He planned to stuff such a rhyme into a victim's mouth, but, like the cane referred to above, this never actually happened.

The only two policemen that the diary refers to are Warren (Chief Commissioner) and Abberline (in charge of the investigation on the ground) even though many more officers were mentioned in the press at the time. I believe this is because Abberline stands out as *the* investigating officer today, with the 1988 *Jack the Ripper* movie starring Michael Caine as an obvious example. One 'rhyme' in the diary reads 'Abberline says he was never amazed/I did my work with such honour/ For his decree/he had to agree …' 'Decree' is an odd word to use in this context, unless you remember the 1979 movie *Murder by Decree*, a piece of hokum featuring Sherlock Holmes and the 'highest in the land'.

'The funny little Jewish joke' undoubtedly refers to the Goulston Street graffito found after the Eddowes murder and although this was deleted at the time to avoid an anti-Semitic backlash, it has featured in innumerable books on the Ripper case in recent times.

In reference to the Kelly murder, Maybrick says he left the victim's breasts on the bedside table, whereas in fact one was under her body on the mattress. In an odd paradox, he writes that he took nothing away (i.e. body parts) from the murder scene but later, 'May God forgive me for the deeds I committed on Kelly, no heart, no heart.' Most commentators believe that this refers to the removal of the woman's heart and point out that this was generally unknown until 1987 when Dr Thomas Bond's reference to it was sent anonymously in documents to Scotland Yard. For me, this is the crux of the hoax. It helps us to pinpoint precisely when the diary was forged.

The other forensics of the diary, scientific analysis of paper, ink and handwriting, is irrelevant. I have in my possession a Letts diary from 1885 which I bought in a junk shop years ago. The first few pages have been ripped out (exactly as Michael Barrett's was) and the remaining pages are blank. A scientific analysis of that diary would prove that it was consistent with the paper quality available in Britain in the 1880s. Later, I was given a gift of an earthenware bottle of red ink with a tight cork seal, labelled 'F. Morden's Alkaline Red Ink. For Metallic Pens, Albion Works, 326 City Road, London' which dates it to before 1914. Harrison asked Dr Nicholas Eastaugh, then a specialist in inks and paper working for the Museum of London and high-end art galleries whether it was possible for someone to forge a document had they 'located a bottle of ink of sufficient age that was still usable (though these seem to be quite rare)'. They may be, but I own one! I have not opened it, but the ink inside can be clearly heard sloshing about. I also have (and I have no idea where or when I got it) a cheap Victorian pen of the 'dip' type with a plain tapered wooden handle. Put these three together (as I have) and you have the makings of a perfect hoax.

As Dr Eastaugh says, 'Even if we could effectively determine the age of the ink and the paper, this would be insufficient to "authenticate" the document since we would still not know when ink and paper combined and the diary was actually written.'

Robert Smith of Smith Gryphon wrote in his introduction to Harrison's *Ripper Diary* book that a hoaxer would have to have specialist knowledge of ink and paper chemistry. Not so – all you need is ink and paper from the period; I have both. And a contemporary pen – I have that too. He would need to be a crime historian (me, again!) and be familiar with Maybrick and Ripper cases 'beyond the accessible published sources' (which takes us into the realms of unprovable fiction; if such sources are not accessible, do they still exist? Have they ever existed?). Dr Forshaw believes that only someone with an awareness of the effects of arsenic dependency could have written the diary. Such information is widely available online today. And only someone with a disturbing sociopathic mind, Forshaw says, could write such unpleasant and terrifying things. Crime fiction writers (also me, again!) write this stuff every day of our lives. It does not make us serial killers, but (hopefully) good at what we do.

1988 marked the centenary of the Whitechapel murders. It sparked a renewed interest in an 'industry' that had been growing steadily since the 1930s. *Everything* a hoaxer needed to know – details of the Maybrick and Ripper cases (including Kelly's missing heart information); drug dependency and its effects; the psychoses and mindsets of serial killers – all of this and more is easily accessible. And it gave somebody the idea to get hold of the mechanics of paper, ink and pen, do some solid research and let their imagination run wild. Why is there no official reference to Maybrick's 'first' murder in Liverpool? Why is there no remote mention of any anatomical knowledge in the diary that experts today agree was a feature of Jack's MO? The appearance of the letter 'M' at three of the murder sites is in the eye of the beholder. The cuts on Kate Eddowes' face are actually 'V's; they are not joined to form an 'M'. The 'M' on the envelope found near Annie Chapman's body was part of an address written innocently by somebody else. The blood-spatter on Mary Kelly's wall is just a random shape. The pocket watch which turned up so conveniently at the time that the *Diary* was published, with the words 'I am Jack' scratched inside, echo too closely the hoax tape sent to the West Yorkshire police in the Yorkshire Ripper case in 1980 – 'I am Jack' said a voice with a Wearside accent, leading George Oldfield and his murder team in completely the wrong direction.

I do not know if Florence Maybrick murdered her hypocritical and rather unpleasant husband. But I do know that he was not Jack the Ripper. Neither did he write the diary.

Chapter 10

'I am Jack the ...'

'Certain appalling events took place before the end of April, 1892,' said the Attorney General, Sir Charles Russell at the Old Bailey on 17 October of that year. He was referring to the murders of Ellen Donworth, Matilda Clover, Alice Marsh and Emma Shrivell, all of them killed by poison administered by the same hand.

'The setting,' wrote Richard D. Altick in *Victorian Studies in Scarlet* (1970) 'is the promenades and bars of certain London theatres and music halls, for decades the notorious haunts of prostitutes on the prowl and the pavements outside and ... the lodging houses and overnight "hotels" ... where the women took their pickups.' In the social hierarchy of prostitution, the victims of 1892 were above Jack's targets in the East End. They were smartly dressed, still attractive and would never consent to sex in the street. But, like their 'scarlet sisters' in the Abyss, they were vulnerable and easy prey.

Ellen Donworth

On 13 October 1891, John Johnson, an assistant at a clinic in Waterloo Road, was called to 8 Duke Street. The landlady, a lodger named Annie Clements and a local labourer, James Styles, were trying to cope with 19-year-old prostitute Ellen Donworth who was writhing in convulsions on her bed. Johnson recognized the symptoms at once – strychnine poisoning – and insisted, despite Donworth's protestations, that she be taken by cab to the nearest hospital, St Thomas's. By the time they got there, on what was a wet, wild night, the girl was dead.

An autopsy carried out at the hospital showed no obvious cause of death but by the time the inquest had been set up two days later, it was clear enough; Ellen Donworth's stomach, according to Dr Thomas Kelloch of St Thomas's, contained *strychos nux vomica* (strychnine) and morphia. The original inquest, held at St Thomas's under George Perceval Wyatt, coroner for London and Surrey, began on 15 October, but was delayed until the 22nd to allow Kelloch to make his examinations.

In her ramblings before she died, Donworth had told Annie Clements that she had been given a drink 'with white stuff in it' by a tall, dark man with a top hat and crossed eyes. They had met at the nearby York Hotel. All such cases of suspicious death were investigated by the local police – in the case of Lambeth, L Division of the Met. Their enquiries traced three labourers who had been seen with Donworth on the night she died; none of them was tall with crossed eyes.

The victims of Jack the Ripper are now nearly as famous as he is, because of recent research done on them, but the same is not true of other 'children of the streets' who remain in the shadows. We know that Ellen Donworth was the daughter of a labourer, had become pregnant at 16 and had left home to live with the baby's father, casual labourer Ernest Linnell, whose surname she occasionally used. She had been employed in a local factory sticking labels on bottles but they were both unemployed by the time she died. She had lost the baby and, according to Linnell, 'used to walk the streets and bring money home'. It is not clear whether she used the Duke Street address for soliciting purposes or whether she had some arrangement with a boarding house where rooms were let by the hour.

Donworth had collapsed in the street, trembling and twitching outside the Duke of Wellington pub and had been helped home by Styles. Although the medical findings were correct, the traditional view at the time (and for many years after) was that strychnine was very common among suicides. This is the first assumption relating to nux vomica in Aitchison Robertson's *Medical Jurisprudence and Toxicology* (1908) with 'homicide' as a secondary likelihood. This is all the more surprising because the symptoms are horrific. Donworth would have experienced a tightness in the chest some two hours after swallowing the drink. She would have painful cramps and her muscles would have begun to twitch, each spasm more painful than the last. The body arches backwards, with head and feet on the ground and each convulsion can last for up to five minutes. The eyeballs swell and the pupils dilate, the mouth forming the hideous *rictus sardonicus*, a ghastly grin. How anyone could *choose* this as a suicide method is beyond me.

The jury, as in the dark as most juries are, returned a verdict of death by poisoning 'but how administered there was no evidence to show'.

The police, from field officers to the top brass, showed an appalling indifference to what was clearly murder. Chief Inspector Colin Chisholm put it down to suicide and told the press: 'Police have ascertained that she could not be in the company of a tall dark man from the time she left home until she was found in Waterloo Road.' This ignored the fact that strychnine can take up to six hours to show symptoms after ingestion. Closing ranks, as the Victorian (and much later) police forces were inclined to do, Chisholm's boss, Superintendent James Brannan, told the media that, 'I do not think that there is the slightest evidence of foul play.' And in case the word of a superintendent was not enough, Robert Anderson, Assistant Commissioner and still, at the time, in overall charge of the Ripper case (where we have already noted his imbecilic involvement) wrote in a memo 'clearly a case of suicide'. The point about strychnine is that, although hideously painful, it leaves the mind clear; Donworth's claims about the tall man should have been taken seriously and were not.

And that same tall man had written a letter to his victim days before he killed her. Donworth's fellow lodger (and prostitute?) Annie Clements had seen it, complete with the odd instruction that Ellen should bring the letter and envelope with her to the assignation. And at the time, unbeknown to anybody, Coroner Wyatt had also received a letter, in the same handwriting:

To G.P. Wyatt Esq, Coroner,
I am writing to say that if you and your satellites fail to bring the murderer of Ellen Donworth, alias Ellen Linnell, late of 8 Duke Street, to justice, I am willing to give you such assistance as will bring the murderer to justice, provided your Government is willing to pay me £300,000 for my services; no pay unless successful.

It was signed 'A. O'Brien, Detective' and, unsurprisingly, Wyatt dismissed it as a prank.

The murderer of Ellen Donworth had got away scot-free. But other letters followed. On 6 November, F.W.D. Smith, heir and managing director of the W.H. Smith bookstall franchise, received a note at his Strand address signed H. Bayne. It said that Bayne had proof that Smith had killed Donworth and had received a letter to that effect from the girl on the day she died. Bayne claimed to be a barrister and that he could save Smith's bacon. An enclosure with the letter was addressed to Donworth:

Miss Ellen Linnell,
I wrote and warned you before that Frederick Smith of W.H. Smith and Sons was going to poison you and I am writing now to say that if you take any medicine he gave you for the purpose of bringing on your courses [period] you will die. I saw Frederick Smith prepare the medicine he gave you and I saw him put enough strychnine in the medicine he gave you to kill a horse. If you take any of it you will die.

H.M.B

Bayne suggested to Smith that a written request to meet him should be displayed in a window of the Strand bookshop. Smith contacted the police and followed up accordingly, leaving the note there until 12 November. There was no sign of Mr Bayne.

A copy of the letter was also sent to Alfred Dyke Acland, on the board of W.H. Smith, that same day – 'Mr Fred Smith wishes to see Mr Bayne, the barrister, at once.'

And it did not end there. Six months later, Dr Joseph Harper of Barnstaple, Devon, received a letter on 26 April 1892. With it was a cutting from *Lloyd's Weekly News*. By this time 'Fred' had added two more kills to his repertoire and the sender 'W.H. Murray' was threatening to tell the world that the doctor's son, Walter J. Harper, a medical student at St Thomas's, was guilty of those (and by implication, the Donworth murder) 'strong enough to commit and hang your son'. It was the same arrangement that would be offered to at least two people in the Matilda Clover murder (see below). Young Harper had no knowledge of this.

Louisa Harris aka Lou Harvey, 20–24 October 1891

Strictly speaking, Lou Harvey is not a murder victim at all, entirely due to her suspicions of her would-be killer. She cohabited with omnibus driver Charles Harvey, hence the assumed name, in Townshend Road, St John's Wood, and met a man at the Alhambra, another Music Hall theatre with a dodgy reputation, on one of the dates above. She bumped into him again outside St James's Hall in Regent Street. It was (to quote W. Teignmouth Shore in 1923) 'a well-known haunt of men-about-town and ladies desirous of their company' (what the police often called a 'knocking shop'). 'He came up to me and touched my shoulder and asked me to go with him.' Although the traditional greeting from prostitute to client was 'Are you good-natured, dearie?' it was the physical touching that was the signal for an assignation. They spent the night in a hotel in nearby Bewick Street.

The talkative client, who never expected to see Harvey alive again, told her that he was a doctor at St Thomas's Hospital and had recently come over from America. He did not say that was specifically Joliet Prison, Illinois, and, naturally enough, Harvey did not think to ask.

He asked her address and she told him, but, whether by accident or design, gave the wrong house number. The next morning, the client noticed spots on Harvey's forehead and said he could supply pills for that. They arranged to meet that evening near Charing Cross station and planned to go to the Oxford Music Hall – 'I told him I was a servant; that was not correct.'

Sensibly, Harvey took her husband with her that night and he hung back in the shadows, keeping a careful lookout. The client duly arrived and went to the Northumberland Park near the Embankment and they drank wine. The doctor bought Harvey some roses, but he had to cry off the Music Hall date because he had an urgent appointment at St Thomas's. Harvey was to go alone and meet her client outside the Music Hall prior to going back to the same hotel. Before they split up, he gave the girl some figs and two pills wrapped in tissue paper which he urged her to swallow there and then. With sleight of hand that would have impressed any Music Hall audience, Harvey palmed the pills and showed him her two empty hands. He clearly had not heard the pills hit the pavement. The doctor gave Harvey her cab fare and walked away in the direction of St Thomas's. Perhaps surprisingly, having filled Charles Harvey in on what had happened, she went on to the Music Hall and waited for the doctor outside as arranged. He did not turn up, because he expected her to be dead, or at least dying.

She met him again a few weeks later, on the corner of Piccadilly and Regent Street. He did not recognise her at first, but took her for a glass of wine in a pub in Air Street. When she identified herself as the woman he had stood up in Oxford Street weeks earlier, he turned on his heel and walked away. Harvey saw him once more, three weeks later talking to a woman in the Strand.

In court, Harvey was grilled about what was clearly a loose lifestyle, but she feigned all innocence and defence counsel did not press the issue, because the Attorney General, Sir Charles Russell, the prosecuting counsel, had asked for leniency in her case.

Matilda Clover, 20 October

And history nearly repeated itself in the case of the next victim, Matilda Clover. Like Donworth, she offered her services to men she met in hotels, music halls and pubs. Like Donworth, she was first examined by an unqualified medical assistant, in this case Francis Coppin of 138 Westminster Bridge Road. He worked for Dr McCarthy and was called to 27 Lambeth Road, where the landlady, Mrs Emma Phillips (who also called herself Mrs Vowles) showed him into the room of her lodger, Matilda Clover.

The girl's pulse was quick and she was sweating and trembling. In the next ten minutes, she had a convulsion, with twitching and vomiting. Coppin diagnosed alcoholic poisoning, especially when Mrs Phillips told him that Clover liked a drink. Cross-examined in the trial that followed, Coppin admitted that although he had fourteen years' experience in this part of London, no one had mentioned poisoning as a possible cause of the symptoms. 'There was nothing to point out to me that she died from anything but delirium tremens.' In fact, the 'DTs', as they were known, are totally different from the convulsions caused by strychnine, while Coppin doggedly tried to cover his incompetence by claiming the similarity of such symptoms. The man had clearly been out of his depth and had recommended bicarbonate of soda!

Just as the police close ranks whenever their conduct is exposed, so too do doctors; in fact, usually more so. Dr Robert Graham was Matilda Clover's doctor and he was asked to attend, without Coppin, later that day. He had been Clover's doctor for a few days only and was treating her for alcoholism. The last time he had seen her was on the 19th and Mrs Phillips had come to report her lodger's sudden illness. Busy with other callouts, Graham had suggested she contact a colleague, Dr McCarthy of Westminster Bridge Road. By the time Graham got to Mrs Phillips', Clover was dead and he wrote and signed a death certificate – 'I certify that I attended Matilda Clover during her last illness [not quite true] … To the best of my knowledge and belief, the cause of her death was, primarily, delirium tremens; secondly, syncope [heart failure].'

Graham was rightly castigated by the court. 'In giving such a certificate in this way, I suppose you were aware you were guilty of a very grave dereliction of duty?' 'I am not aware of it,' Graham snapped back, although of course he should have been. The Victorian period is littered with careless and even murderous doctors using poison as their weapon of choice; you have read about one already. At the subsequent trial, Graham told the court that no one had told him about Clover's convulsions or the pain she was in. The mere mention of drink had sent him in the wrong direction. The doctor was lying; both Mrs Phillips and the maid, Lucy Rose, had told him specifically about the dead woman's symptoms.

It transpired that Clover regularly brought men to Number 27 and, on the evening she was taken ill, she was entertaining 'Fred', a tall, dark man with a heavy moustache, top hat and cape. He left shortly before ten. The ever-observant Lucy Rose had not only shown 'Fred' in, but knew that he had taken with him a letter to Clover which had arranged an assignation at the Canterbury Music Hall in Westminster Bridge Road, then the largest in London. She also knew that 'Fred' seemed genuinely fond of Clover, buying her an expensive pair of boots and offering to pay her to keep her off the streets over winter. The dead woman had told the maid, 'That wretch Fred has given me some pills.' Four of them, 'Fred' had told her, would 'prevent me catching the disease'. As we know, sexually transmitted diseases were an occupational hazard for prostitutes and their clients were running a serious risk. Lucy Rose had not seen 'Fred' leave, but when she returned from an errand, both the visitor and the letter had gone.

But the medical debacle effectively shut down any possible murder enquiry. Because Graham had been treating Clover for alcoholism and had signed the death certificate, no inquest was necessary. Matilda Clover was buried in a parish funeral at Tooting Cemetery, the brass plate on the coffin reading 'M. Clover, 27 years'. Few people noted her passing. As one local paper put it, Clover was a 'miserable street outcast, whose life was of no particular value to anybody'.

On 30 November, Dr William Broadbent of Seymour Street, Portman Square, received a letter. He was a prominent London doctor, working at St Mary's Hospital, Paddington. The letter accused him of murdering Matilda Clover and promised to hand over the incriminating evidence for £2,500 or it would be sent to the police. It was signed 'M. Malone'. Since Broadbent had never heard of Malone or Clover and had no links with 27 Lambeth Road (nor did he recognise the handwriting) he went straight to the police who followed the letter's instructions by agreeing to a meeting, in the columns of the *Daily Chronicle*. The doctor's house was watched and no one turned up.

At the trial which eventually followed, it transpired that 'M. Malone' was a private detective and that, according to the blackmail letter, Broadbent had been hired to kill her. The choice was Broadbent's – '2500l sterling on the one hand, and ruin, shame and disgrace on the other.'

The handling of all this by the Met was shambolic. There seems to have been little co-operation between L Division and Scotland Yard. At the subsequent trial, Inspector George Harvey told the court that he did not hear of Matilda Clover's death until 28 April (1892). The Broadbent letter sent to the Yard was not forwarded to him. In the witness box, Inspector John Tunbridge from the Met headquarters, explained that since no one turned up at the doctor's house to claim blackmail money, nothing was done – 'the letter remained in the department'. There were no enquiries made at 27 Lambeth Rd, which, for all Mrs Phillips' attempts to whitewash it, was clearly a house of ill repute. There were no enquiries into the death of Matilda Clover. Tunbridge, of course, claimed ignorance of the whole thing – 'the letter was looked upon as a letter from an insane person.'

The judge at the trial expressed his amazement. There was an accusation of murder; Scotland Yard was only fifteen minutes' walk from the crime scene and nothing was done. 'My surprise,' said his Lordship, 'remains.'

Alice Marsh and Emma Shrivell 11 April 1892

He would become, in the media, the 'Lambeth Poisoner' and his name would be known throughout the world, but as things stood in early April 1892, nothing could point to him as a killer. In fact, there was no hard evidence that murder or attempted murder had happened at all.

That changed on the night of 11 April. Constable George Cumley of L Division was on his beat in Stanford Street off Waterloo Road at about 1.45 a.m. A man was being let out of Number 118 by a young woman. In view of what happened later, Cumley remembered details. The man was about 5ft 9in tall, with a silk top hat, a moustache and glasses. It was less than forty-five minutes later when the officer was called to 118. A four-wheeled cab was standing outside and Constable William Eversfield was carrying the girl Cumley had seen earlier, into it. She was not the only one in distress. Another girl, about the same age, was lying over a chair in the passageway. He carried her into the cab and hopped on board, bound for St Thomas's Hospital.

Rather as doctors and the police had ignored the victims' statements in the earlier poisoning cases, so now, in court, the Attorney General did not believe that the statements the girls made were admissible as evidence. Not for the first or last time, the law was proving itself an ass. Cumley wrote a report when he had time, both girls having died in the cab.

The constable saw the man he had seen with the dead girl again, hanging around music halls and watching women. The net was closing in.

The first medical man on the scene in the case of the girls from Stanford Street was house surgeon Dr Cuthbert Wyman of St Thomas's. It was three in the morning. One of them, Alice Marsh aged 21, was dead. The other, 18-year-old Emma Shrivell, was experiencing tetanic convulsions – 'she showed all the symptoms of strychnine poisoning.'

Despite their best efforts, an emetic and chloroform, Shrivell died at eight o'clock. Wyman carried out both post-mortems later in the day and passed the stomachs and viscera to his assistant, George Hackett, in sealed jars. These were then passed on to Dr Thomas Stevenson, lecturer on medical jurisprudence at Guy's Hospital, who would feature in the Maybrick case later in the year. There was, at this point, no such thing as a Home Office Pathologist, but Stevenson held an embryonic post – 'one of the analysts employed by the Government'.

On 16 April, he examined three jars, one labelled 'Alice Marsh', another 'Emma Shrivell' and the third 'Matilda Clover'. Testing by colour, alkaloids and taste (!) Stevenson was able to say that all three women had died by strychnine poisoning. Matilda Clover, of course, had already been buried and this made a difference in terms of testing her remains. The tortuous way in which Clover's death was attributed to murder, rather than the original natural causes, was in connection with the arrogant blackmail letters referred to above and had nothing whatever to do with forensic medicine.

In court, the defence counsel was condescending to say the least. As forensic medicine improved and science became ever more exact, defence teams had to resort to ever more desperate (and often underhand) measures to discredit an expert witness. 'I suppose,' sneered Gerald Geoghegan for the defence, 'I may say your life has been spent in these studies and pursuits?' implying that Stevenson was an obsessive oddball. With all the clout that his experience gave him, he assured the court that there was no doubt as to the cause of death and rattled off facts and figures, running to sixteen pages in the written account, which must have left judge, counsel and particularly the jury, bewildered.

An odd interlude followed in court during the trial relating to the use of strychnine for medical purposes. That can of worms had been opened up by an earlier witness, John McCulloch, a Canadian who worked as a travelling salesman for a Toronto-based company. McCulloch told the court that, at the end of February, he had met a fellow lodger at

Blanchard's Hotel in Quebec. The guest told him that he was a doctor and showed him an impressive case of medicines, some phials of which he used to procure abortions. He even showed McCulloch a false set of whiskers which he wore while operating. Throughout the nineteenth century and well beyond, abortion was illegal. The only people who carried it out 'in the back streets' were struck-off doctors and midwives. The salesman with the drugs and the disguise admitted to having had fun with various women in London, especially Waterloo Road, Westminster Bridge Road, London Road and Victoria Road, often with three of them a night, for the princely sum of 1 shilling each.

The abortionist took morphine for headaches during his time with McCulloch and showed him pornographic photographs in his possession. His name was Dr Neill Cream.

Clearly, in the trial, the judge, Mr Justice 'Hanging' Hawkins, was uncomfortable with letting the jury hear this evidence, probably because of the bad light it shone on the medical profession. They could not possibly believe that Cream was the only doctor carrying out this illegal sideline. The judge's decision not to show the note to the jury is bizarre. He had already allowed McCulloch's verbal testimony which fingered Cream in no uncertain terms as a degenerate who accosted women in the very area of London where the Lambeth poisonings had taken place. How much worse could it get for him?

Geoghegan was not going to let Stevenson get off that lightly – 'Science, like the law, sometimes does make mistakes?' 'That,' said the doctor in all humility, 'is perfectly true.'

As if to underline such mistakes, other medical men were quizzed on Ellen Donworth's death. Dr Thomas Kelloch, another houseman at St Thomas's, saw Donworth in 13 October 1891 when she was brought in with convulsions. Although he could find nothing to explain her death, his subsequent tests on her stomach contents found 'an appreciable quantity of strychnine'.

As we have said, it was not forensic medicine that hanged Dr Cream but his own arrogance. He was careful to remove his letters from the women he targeted but more than happy to blackmail perfectly innocent people using an array of aliases, most of them claiming to be private detectives. In court, a new kind of forensic expert emerged, one who was not called in any capacity to comment on the welter of 'Ripper' letters still in circulation in 1892. This was Walter de Grey Birch, who had spent twenty-seven years in the Manuscripts department of the British Museum. The various letters were handed to the jury and Birch had no hesitation in claiming that all of them were written by Cream. All of the letters were clear and showed no attempt at disguise. The contents, of course, proved that the writer had inside detailed knowledge of the murders.

Thomas Neill Cream effectively hanged himself and in so doing has left us a bewildering picture of a serial killer, far removed from the dribbling lunatic the police were still searching for in Whitechapel. In his summing up for the defence, Geoghegan cited the case of William Palmer, the Rugeley poisoner (see Chapter 5) which was probably a mistake, as Palmer was, quite rightly, hanged. Geoghegan could not understand why Dr Stevenson rejected the diagnoses of Dr Graham and Mr Coppin, ignoring the fact that Coppin was not qualified and that Graham had signed a dodgy death certificate after a cursory ten-minute examination of Clover's corpse. He banged on about the woman – 'one of the legion of the host' – who drowned her misery in drink. She was 'sodden with drink'. The fact that Clover took several hours to die was, in Geoghegan's opinion, proof that 'medical science, great as it is, might have been mistaken'. Bizarrely, he criticized the fact that Birch, the handwriting expert, had not been cross-examined on the authenticity of the insinuating blackmail letters, but it was *he* who should have done so, if he thought it important.

Time and again, Geoghegan came back to Stevenson's evidence, condemning what the expert had said and done, belittling the tests carried out on a frog. Many other things, he told the jury, had a bitter taste as well as strychnine. Science, he claimed, could not help the prosecution. He tried to claim that no witness had seen Cream up close and personal and hinted that a man-about-town should not be blamed for living a spicy life in pubs and music halls. Hats on, hats off, backs turned, dim lighting – all of it played into Cream's hands. The tall, dark man with the top hat and heavy moustache could have been one of 30–40,000 on the streets of the largest city in the world.

Defence counsel argued, rather weakly, that Cream could have gleaned information on Matilda Clover's death from newspaper accounts and, as a medical man, drawn his own conclusions about strychnine poisoning. This gave him all the ammunition he needed to write the blackmail letters. He also pointed out that Cream had made no attempt to follow through on the blackmail or to make any money out of it.

Geoghegan was happy to brand his client 'peculiar' and all too familiar with prostitutes, but neither of these traits was a hanging offence. He went further, pointing out that four independent witnesses believed that Cream had a drug habit (specifically opium, morphia and sometimes strychnine) which may have made him come out with absurd statements, including the blackmail letters. The defence tried to rattle the jury by getting them to consider just how terrible the death penalty was and he left it, in the end, to the Genius of the Law of England to protect his client.

Charles Russell, for the prosecution, reminded the jury of the facts. In outlining the events surrounding Matilda Clover's death, he was contemptuous of Dr Graham's performance as a medical man – 'a state of things that called for reform'. He also wondered why, if Geoghegan was right about Cream learning of the woman's death and drawing the strychnine conclusion in all innocence, he did not go to the police with his theory rather than blackmailing Dr Broadbent. And why did he use an assumed name?

Russell defended Dr Stevenson over his professional view of the cause of death. What reason had he to lie? And surely, he would have used all the cutting-edge of forensic medicine to get to the truth.

On the fifth day of the trial, Mr Justice Hawkins delivered his summing up. He reminded the jury that there were eyewitness accounts of the murder of Matilda Clover, that verdicts could hardly ever be given with 'mathematical certainty'. Oddly, the judge copped out of Dr Stevenson's detailed toxicology evidence on the grounds that he 'could not pretend to have acquired one-twentieth part of the scientific knowledge possessed by that learned gentleman'. Graham and Coppin had got Clover's cause of death wrong. The only reason for Cream to accuse Broadbent of poison is that he *knew* the cause of death, at a time when the doctors were squabbling about it.

Hawkins went on to sing Stevenson's praises. He had many years' experience, employed regularly by the government in prosecution cases and his post-mortem work on Clover's exhumed body was exemplary.

Although not facing trial on the other cases, the judge alluded to the deaths of Ellen Donworth, the 'wretched girls' Alice Marsh and Emma Shrivell, and the attempted murder of Lou Harvey. This was tricky legal ground because British law excluded other 'bad acts' from court as being irrelevant to the case in point. Hawkins and counsel had argued this one behind closed doors and had decided that it was right and proper to introduce them. The judge also mentioned Cream's attempt to 'frame' Dr Harper, a fellow lodger in his house.

Hawkins raised the issue of the mysterious John Haynes. Most modern books on the Cream case state baldly that he was a New York policeman, in London either on holiday or in some semi-official capacity. Neither of these rings true. According to Haynes' own trial testimony, he was an unemployed engineer who had met Cream by chance and struck up an acquaintance with him. He became suspicious when the doctor talked constantly about the Lambeth poisonings and even took him on a grand tour of the scenes of crime. This in itself was weird, if only because Haynes' and Cream's landlord, the photographer Armistead, of Westminster Bridge Road, told both men that they were being followed. Cream explained to Haynes, according to his trial testimony, that Cream was being mistaken for another lodger, Walter J. Harper, a medical student at St Thomas's. Over dinner at the Café de Paris on Ludgate Hill, the American wrote down what Cream told him.

Harper was the son of a doctor from Barnstaple (true) but he was 'well known among a low class of people', had got a girl pregnant, sorted out an abortion for her and that he, Harper, was being blackmailed by Marsh and Shrivell.

Although the framing of Harper was utter rubbish, Haynes' role in the case remains obscure. He was with Cream on 3 June until shortly before he was arrested, having passed titbits of incriminating evidence on to the police.

Defence counsel was clearly suspicious of Haynes, asking him where he got his knowledge of British law, especially in relation to blackmail which Haynes and Cream had discussed. Rather limply, Haynes explained that he had picked up such trifles 'travelling about the world a good deal for forty years'. Geoghegan asked Haynes to write down the name of his former (engineering) employer, which he duly did. Acting on what information I do not know, defence counsel asked Haynes outright if he had ever been a detective. Haynes said he had not, but his next answer refuted that – 'or a private enquiry agent? Yes, in London and elsewhere, making enquiries for the British Government.'

Geoghegan implied that Haynes had effectively cajoled Cream into incriminating himself and that he, Haynes, was trying to get himself a job with the Met. Haynes denied both. When Sergeant Patrick McIntyre of the Met was called to give evidence against Cream, defence counsel asked him if he knew Haynes. The answer was that he did, as a shipboard engineer. He was a friend who had come over from America six months earlier – 'I knew he was in the Home Office Department as a secret agent to make enquiries about a certain class of suspected persons.' 'You yourself,' Geoghegan went on, 'were connected with the dynamite explosives …?' 'Yes,' Haynes admitted and, in this context, told the court that Haynes showed him a number of photographs of 'suspected people from America'.

In his summing up, Judge Hawkins pointed out, 'the jury must judge for themselves the credit they ought to attach to the evidence given by Haynes.' Geoghegan had let the man off lightly, almost certainly because of the sensitive situation regarding Anglo-Irish relations. As we have seen, the Fenian Brotherhood had brought a terrorist bombing campaign to London in 1881 and the Met's Special Irish Branch had been set up to cope with them. Some of the 'dynamitards' and a great deal of money came from the Irish immigrants of the United States (especially Chicago) and there can be little doubt that Haynes was over here acting as a liaison with the Branch. Whereas he was constantly 'making enquiries' into Cream (and mentioned that Cream was aware of this) he denied in court being a detective and clung to his rather unlikely 'cover' as an unemployed engineer. That alone should have had his evidence dismissed and he himself charged with contempt of court. The judge sailed on regardless.

It took the jury only ten minutes to find Cream guilty of the murder of Matilda Cover and he said nothing in response to the verdict.

What the jury did not hear, of course, was Cream's previous. If they had, even that ten minutes would seem inordinately long. Several times during the trial – and even more often since – people have posed the question: who was Thomas Neill Cream? And what made him tick?

Born in Glasgow in 1850, Cream moved with his family to Canada (many Scots did) in 1854 and later he enrolled in Montreal's McGill University to read medicine. His father's lumber business enabled him to lead the life of a 'swell', dressing elegantly, driving an expensive coach and pair, gambling, drinking and womanizing. He graduated MD from McGill in 1876 having written a thesis on 'The Evils of Malpractice in the Medical Profession'. He had also written an essay on chloroform. In an attempted insurance scam in April of his graduation year, he claimed $978.40, was given $350 and narrowly escaped prosecution for fraud and arson, which may have given him a sense of superiority in the context of future crimes.

In September, Cream became engaged to Flora Brooks, who was pregnant. Before the doctor could arrange an abortion, Flora's father found out about it and forced Cream to marry her at gunpoint. The day after the wedding, Cream left for Britain to continue his medical training and Flora died of consumption (tuberculosis) in August of the following year.

As a postgraduate student, Cream attended St Thomas's Hospital in London and lodged in Lambeth Palace Road. He failed his finals, but passed the double qualification of the Royal College of Physicians and Surgeons in Edinburgh. It must be said that, in the 1870s, medical qualifications were not particularly rigorous; examination was by viva (an oral examination that amounted to little more than a chat) which explains why forensic medicine was in such a grim state during virtually all the cases covered in this book.

During his time in practice in London, Ontario, Kate Gardener, a hotel chambermaid, was found dead in a privy behind premises that Cream rented. She had clearly been murdered by chloroform, with which Cream was more than familiar, but nothing could be pinned on him. The verdict was death 'from chloroform administered by some person unknown'. Alarmed by this near miss, Cream left for the United States, opening a surgery in West Madison Street, Chicago.

As a practising abortionist (as illegal in the States as it was in Britain) Cream was responsible for the deaths of at least two women in 1881 and he began his bizarre campaign of blackmail (without ever collecting a cent), this time from the pharmacist who had made up Cream's prescription. In June of that year, the doctor had an affair with Julia Stott, the young wife of the much older Daniel. The doctor's prescription as a remedy against epilepsy killed Daniel Stott in twenty minutes on 14 June. There the matter might have rested, with epileptic seizure being the cause of death, but Cream stirred things up (as he was to do again) by telling the coroner that the pharmacist was responsible by overdoing the ratio of strychnine in the compound.

Drawing a blank with the coroner, Cream made the same accusation to the District Attorney who had Stott's body exhumed. His stomach contained four grains of strychnine. Both Julia Stott and Cream stood trial for murder; he got life, she was set free. Thomas N. Cream was now prisoner No. 4374 in Joliet Prison, the Illinois State Penitentiary.

For his good behaviour here, the doctor's sentence was cut to seventeen years and he was actually released well ahead of even that, sailing to Liverpool aboard the *Teutonic* in September 1891.

By October, calling himself Dr Neill, he moved from hotel to boarding house to hotel on a large cash sum he had inherited from his father. That month, he began to pick up prostitutes in and around the Lambeth area, bought strychnine and morphia from various chemists, always flashing his credentials and his links with St Thomas's Hospital. On 9 October, two of the theatre girls he met, Elizabeth Masters and Elizabeth May, saw Cream going into a house in Lambeth Road with another woman. Her name was Ellen Donworth …

What are we to make of Neill Cream? He was peculiar in many ways, but we can be sure that he used his medical knowledge to murder by strychnine, which was perhaps the most excruciating of all poisons available. He knew that his victims, from Daniel Stott onwards, would die in agony. He was a narcissist, dressing like a toff, living the life of a man-about-town. He killed because he could and because of the need to indulge his sadism. But it was not forensic science that brought Cream to the gallows; it was his own arrogance in the various over-the-top blackmail scams he tried to carry out.

Dr Thomas Neill Cream met his maker at Newgate gaol (next to the Old Bailey) on 15 November 1892. The executioner was James Billington, who doubled as a barber in Farnworth, near Bolton. Using the alias 'Higgins' because he hated publicity, he arrived at the prison the day before, with top hat and black bag, just like a provincial doctor. It may be that on the morning of the execution, he wore his little black velvet smoking cap.

If anybody facing the drop can be said to be lucky, Cream was. Hanging in the past had been a slow, cumbersome, grisly affair, the victim often strangling slowly to death. Billington had reduced the process – pinion, procession, drop – from five minutes to a few seconds.

With the white hood over his head and the noose around his neck, Cream just had time to gasp 'I am Jack the ...' before Billington's lever cut him off in mid-sentence. Did he actually say it? And if so, was he claiming to be the Ripper? We do not know, but we know that he was not the Whitechapel murderer. While those crimes were being committed, Cream was safely behind bars in Joliet prison. Could there be a better alibi than that?

Chapter 11

'Lizzie Borden took an axe ...'

It was a sweltering Thursday, 4 August 1892 and Bridget Sullivan, known as Maggie, was hammering on the door of Dr Seabury Bowen along Second Street in Fall River, Massachusetts. It made sense to call Bowen because he had been the doctor to the Borden family for years. But Maggie had had her instructions; she was not to go to the Irish doctor (Kelly) even though he lived next door to the Bordens, nor to the French-Canadian (Chagnon) diagonally opposite the family home at Number 92. Only a Yankee doctor would do.

Bowen grabbed his leather bag with all the basics inside to deal with anything from indigestion to childbirth. He could not have been prepared for what he found across the street, however. 'Physician that I am and accustomed to all sorts of horrible sights, it sickened me.' Maggie showed him into the hallway where Lizzie Borden stood transfixed with a faraway look on her face. In the sitting room, fully dressed, 69-year-old Andrew Borden, her father, lay slumped on the sofa, his feet on the floor, his head, what was left of it, turned to the right, it and the furniture saturated with blood that was still warm, still seeping. Bowen felt for a pulse although he knew that was pointless; Andrew Borden was dead.

Where was the dead man's wife? Bowen and Maggie briefly searched the house. Halfway up the stairs they could see the body of Abby Borden, lying grotesquely beside the bed in the guest room. The doctor crouched over the body. Mrs Borden's head had been battered and gashed exactly as her husband's, her forehead on the carpet as if some maniac had shattered her skull as she was sweeping.

What was particularly shocking about the Borden murders was that the setting for slaughter was so genteel. Fall River, at least the Bordens' end of it, was a wealthy, upper middle-class neighbourhood where such violence rarely happened. The Bordens were financially very secure, with a large, comfortable house and a live-in maid. This was America in the 'gilded age' where greed was good and the well-to-do mixed with no one else, revelling in a gentility that was positively cloying.

The Bordens were not *quite* as rich as the folks who lived on The Hill, the *really* expensive end of town, but they were more than comfortable. Andrew had made his money in property and owned several textile mills in the area. He was a director of a local bank and several financial trusts and his net worth at the time of his death was estimated at $300,000 ($10 million in 2024). He was also known to be a miser ('frugal' was the polite word) only spending money on a few select favourites. His first wife, Sarah, had died a few years previously and he had married again, this time to Abby Gray, four years his junior, who, it was widely believed, married the old man for his money.

Their daughters, Emma and Lizzie, were brought up in the gentility of Massachusetts. But, as police discovered in the days following the murders, the Bordens were anything but a happy, Christian family and tensions lay beneath the surface of respectability. Both daughters clearly resented Abby, referring to her pointedly as 'Mrs Borden' and this antipathy worsened as Andrew began giving away properties to her family members. The girls rarely ate with the parents and in July there had been a huge row, perhaps over Andrew's killing of pigeons for which Lizzie had made a loft, and the daughters had stormed out. They moved to New Bedford nearby and even though they returned in the week before the murder, Lizzie took rooms at a lodging house in Fall River before returning home.

On the day before the killings, Sarah Borden's brother John Vinnicum Morse came to stay, coupling a family holiday with business talks with Andrew. He was put in the guest room where Abby would be found dead within hours. On that day, Wednesday, 3 August, people in the house became ill. Some accounts say only Andrew and Abby were affected, others imply it hit everybody. A combination of unusually fierce heat and the re-using of cooked mutton over several days contributed to this. At the inquest, however, it transpired that Lizzie had been attempting to buy Prussic acid from a local druggist, Eli Bence of S.R. Smith's Drug Store in town, and rumours abounded.

On the night of the murders, Thursday, 4 August, the police having rampaged through the house, missing clues left, right and centre and according perhaps too much courtesy and respect to the daughters, Lizzie's friend Alice Russell stayed in the house while, for obvious reasons, Uncle Morse slept in an attic room rather than his own, which was a crime scene.

In 1892 New England, 'crime scene' was not even a phrase, still less a reality. There was no fingerprint technology (that was being developed at the time, but 3,000 miles away in London), no sealing off of rooms with the famous yellow tape, no measurements of rooms and furniture. Crime scene photographs *were* taken of both victims and they were useful in establishing facts. For instance, at the trial that followed, Maggie Sullivan claimed to have removed Andrew Borden's boots so that he could doze on the sofa, yet the photograph shows them still clearly in place on his feet.

That said, the photographs leave a lot to be desired. It is not clear how many were taken. That of Andrew's body was taken from the front only and it is by no means clear how much room, if any, there was for a killer to strike from behind the sofa (which might account for a lack of blood on the murderer). In the case of Abby, from one angle, it looks as though she was kneeling when she died, but from a side view, this was merely the voluminousness of her skirts and she is actually lying on her front.

The next day, John Morse left, having to have a police escort through a ghoulish crowd, to get him out of town. Although he was not seriously regarded as a suspect, the fact of his arrival and departure – so neatly on either side of the murders – aroused suspicion in some quarters. By the middle of August, the Borden case was front-page news across the States.

A prominent campaigner for women's suffrage, Mary Livermore, complained of the 'discharged convicts, paupers, lunatics, imbeciles, illiterates, defectives ... who crowd out our native [New England, white] working men and women'. These people were 'aliens' and it was assumed that one of them was responsible for the Borden murders.

Led by Marshal Rufus Hilliard, local law officers put together a timeline for the Bordens' last day on earth. Emma, the elder daughter, was 15 miles away visiting friends in Fairhaven. Andrew had gone out after breakfast about 9.30 and was back an hour later, having visited a couple of his properties. Tired because of his age and the stultifying heat, he had gone into the sitting room for a nap, dozing on the sofa. He had asked his younger daughter, 32-year-old Lizzie, where Abby was. She told him that she had received a note from a messenger boy to visit a sick neighbour. In later police enquiries, Lizzie could not remember the name of the neighbour nor where she lived. Neither was there any sign of the note. In fact, of course, Abby Borden was already lying upstairs in a pool of blood, her head caved in. Lizzie later told police that she thought she had heard her mother come back from the alleged visit, but she had not seen her.

The only other person in the house was Maggie the maid who was busy, on instructions from Abby earlier, cleaning windows. At some point, Lizzie had gone out to the barn to the left of the premises to get iron (for an unspecified purpose) or lead (to make sinkers for fishing during some future picnic) from the loft. Lizzie was not a fisherwoman and there was no fishing rod in the house.

Just before 11.10 a.m., Lizzie shouted up to the maid on the top floor, 'Maggie, come quick! Father's dead. Somebody came in and killed him.' The maid was sent to fetch Dr Bowen.

What struck any number of policemen who arrived (as in all States, there was a confusing overlapping of police forces) was the calm that Lizzie showed. While Maggie was in various states of excitement, if not hysteria, the dead man's daughter was calmness itself. There was no sign of tears.

There was talk of an intruder – Lizzie's 'somebody came in' – with sightings of a number of strange, unidentified men in the area, although many of these had been seen days or weeks earlier and clearly had no relevance to the murders. Almost everybody 'in the know', be it police officers or the media, relied on the 'science' of Cesare Lombroso, professor of forensic medicine at Turin University – criminals could be identified by their appearance.

And Lizzie Borden, already morphing into a staid old New England maid, hardly fitted Lombroso's Neanderthal-jawed protype. She was 5ft 4in and was constantly referred to in the press as a 'lady'. Ladies do not kill their fathers and stepmothers. And if they do, they do not do it with an axe.

In their searches of the Borden house, police found two long-handled axes, used for chopping firewood. These were in the basement as was a peculiarly damaged hatchet, its wooden handle sawn off just below the head and showing signs of having been in a fire.

The Bordens were buried on Saturday, 6 August, but were exhumed for a secret post-mortem, performed in the ladies' lounge of Oak Grove Cemetery on 11 August and the officiators were Dr William Dolan, Bristol County's medical examiner, and Dr Frank W. Draper, his opposite number in Suffolk County. Some modern accounts have this carried out by Dr Bowen but that was impossible on two counts: he was not a qualified pathologist; and, as the family doctor, was a material witness in the trial that was bound to follow. The results of the autopsies were never revealed fully, but details of the wounds and cause of death were. While Lizzie and Emma offered a $5,000 reward for information leading to arrest and conviction and hired O.M. Hanscom of the Pinkerton Detective Agency, the police themselves closed in on Lizzie.

The inquest was held on 9 August at the Fall River police station with Second District Court judge Josiah C. Blaisdell in the chair. In accordance with the rather arcane legislative history of Massachusetts, this was heard in private, with no press or public present.

The man who would lead the prosecution at the later trial, District Attorney Hosea Knowlton, grilled Lizzie, particularly over the morning's events of 4 August. Her answers were vague and contradictory and at various times she did not appear to know what he was asking her. She did herself no favours and the police became ever more convinced over her involvement. Marshal Hilliard officially arrested her and she was held in a (surprisingly comfortable) prison.

Almost immediately, the press took sides. Either Lizzie Borden was the most appalling monster who had ever drawn breath, or she was an innocent dupe bullied by the all-male preserves of police and legislature. The 'shrieking sisterhood' closed ranks, ably led in the media by journalist Elizabeth Jordan who attended every day of the preliminary hearing, the grand jury observations and the trial itself. Each day during the trial, the number of women in the audience outnumbered the men by four to one. Denied, by state law, the right to sit on either the bench or the jury, they nevertheless made their presence felt in the courtroom and outside it, literally jostling each other for seats. For those who did not believe that a short, plump woman could wield a fatal axe, their cause was wholly undone by the loutish, not to say ferocious, behaviour of the 'monstrous regiment of women'.

When the preliminary hearing resumed on 25 August, the world heard medical testimony for the first time. This was Dr Dolan's first year as a medical examiner and it would be difficult to find a more high-profile case, according to the press. His evidence was clear and confident. He was, however, stopped from reading his autopsy notes by Lizzie's defence counsel, Andrew Jennings, and had to carry on from memory alone. What possible objection Jennings could have had is a mystery but with Americans' proclivity for such interruptions in proceedings (as opposed to British courts) it would be a regular feature by both prosecution and defence in the months ahead. Both defence counsel (Jennings and Melvin O. Adams) had a go at Dolan, trying to undermine his expertise in a tactic that was to become de rigueur for doctors in murder trials on both sides of the Atlantic.

There was a gasp in the courtroom when Dolan explained that he had removed the Bordens' heads for forensic purposes and had them in his possession. The doctor would not be shaken in his central testimony – Abby Borden had died first, perhaps up to two hours before Andrew. This was an important point because it made less likely the defence's notion that a stranger could have been hiding in the house. To have killed Abby and then Andrew two hours later would have meant that such a killer would either have had to sneak in and out twice or he had been hiding inside for a considerable time. Neither of these scenarios was viable.

The next medical expert proved to be anything but. He was Professor Edward Wood, a Harvard chemist who told the court that there was no poison in the Bordens' stomachs. This was important because police knew that someone resembling Lizzie had tried to buy Prussic acid from a local pharmacy – this had emerged at the inquest. The woman had said that she needed it for cleaning a sealskin cape. The prosecution's contention was that Lizzie had intent ('with malice aforethought' – the legal definition of murder) to kill Andrew and Abby by whatever means came to hand. Since Eli Bence had declined to sell the poison on the grounds that a doctor's prescription was required, presumably she had resorted to the axe instead. That said, Wood could find no blood or hair on any axe in the Borden home.

As in Britain, the law's machinery ground with glacial slowness. Unlike Britain, a Grand Jury was summoned to decide whether there was a 'true bill', i.e., whether the case should proceed to trial at all and there were three different indictments: one for killing Andrew Borden; another for the murder of Abby; and yet a third for killing them both!

While Lizzie's lawyers were happy to charge a total of $55,000 for their work (nearly $15 million today) the media speculated on whether or not she ought to be sectioned; everybody found her stoic coolness disturbing. Central to the whole argument, which would be covered by forensic psychiatry today, was the effect on Lizzie – on any woman – of menstruation. Because of the time (1892) and the class from which Lizzie came, the word itself could not be used; the police, the lawyers, even the doctors, tied themselves in knots to avoid direct mention of it. It was (and is) artificial nonsense and did little to further the cause of justice. Dr Hans Gross, an Austrian criminologist of the time, wrote, 'Menstruation may bring women to the most terrible crimes. Various authors cite numerous examples of sensible women driven to do the most inconceivable things – in many cases to murder.' In England, Dr Henry MacNaughton-Jones agreed that women's responsibility for crimes should be weighed against this.

The trial of Lizzie Borden began on Monday, 5 June 1893. Like the month in which the murders were committed, June was appallingly hot and the atmosphere in the overcrowded courtroom was unbearable. Nevertheless, a would-be audience queued around the block of the New Bedford courthouse and most of the crowd were, once again, women. With Cesare Lombroso firmly in mind, various reporters wrote, 'there is nothing wicked [or] criminal or hard in [Lizzie's] features.' She was, they all agreed, astonishingly self-possessed, prim and proper in black clothes. What they were looking at, of course, was a sociopath, one who did not or could not register emotions like most people. But no one in 1893 was qualified to think that, let alone say it.

In terms of forensics, there was a great deal of discussion over the murder weapon. Inevitably, focus fell on the damaged hatchet with the sawn-off handle. As is true of virtually every case in this book, the work of the police was less than exemplary, with officers contradicting each other all over the place. Several of them had been promoted since the murders, in the case of Philip Harrington from patrolman to captain, which seems particularly meteoric. One account was that the sawn-off handle was clean and freshly cut; another was that it was old and covered in the ordinary debris of a cellar, not the ashes of a recent fire. And why, the defence was entitled to ask (but did not), remove the handle in the first place? Without fingerprint evidence, there was nothing about the hatchet that could confirm it as the murder weapon.

While the judge (again, Blaisdell, along with two others) ruled that Lizzie's inquest testimony be excluded (a decision later judged to be wrong by *the* expert on evidential testimony, Joshua Henry Wigmore) the medical evidence from a clutch of doctors came on Monday, 12 June. Local doctor Albert Dednick testified that Abby was killed first, at least an hour and a half before Andrew. Journalist Julian Ralph of the *New York Sun* speculated that the medical evidence would be long-winded and boring and it would not lead to a solution to the murders. The second witness was Dr William Dolan who had given evidence at the inquest. Bizarrely (and this was a gift to novelists who later wrote their own version of the case), Dolan had passed the murder scene at about 11.45 a.m. on 4 August, so that his examination of the Bordens took place while Andrew's hands were still warm and blood was still trickling from his head wounds. He counted eight to ten individual blows, corrected after the autopsy to ten or eleven. Abby was found lying on the left side of her face. Her body was cooler than Andrew's and the blood was dark and congealed. There was a bloody handkerchief nearby. It was Dolan who had ordered crime scene photographs to be taken.

To establish the approximate time of death, he stripped Andrew's body and laid it on an undertaker's board in the room where he had been killed. He removed the dead man's stomach as well as Abby's and sent them, along with samples of milk from that day and the previous one to Professor Wood at Harvard.

Dolan studied the potential murder weapons. The claw-hammered hatchet appeared to have been scraped clean but still had two spots of rust or blood. There were also two hairs attached which he observed under a microscope. These he took to Professor Wood on 9 August. He also delivered a dress waist, a dress skirt and an under white skirt (Lizzie's clothes on the day) on which 'there is a minute pin spot of blood.'

At the autopsy two days later, he had cut off the Bordens' heads and cleaned the skulls. He may have done this at his home using lobster pots and he made plaster casts of the skulls. Andrew's wounds were 2 to 4½in in length, marked in blue paint for clarity at any forthcoming trial. Abby's skull carried eighteen wounds, ranging in size from ½in to 5½in. One wound – probably either the first or the last – was a horizontal one at the base of the neck. At some point, photographs were taken of both skulls. They show considerable damage (large missing areas) to the left parietal and occipital areas. In other words, the most savage attack came from a right-handed person – although nothing was made of this at the trial.

As Dolan explained to the court, the stomach and intestine contents of the couple differed, giving the different times of death. But it was the wounds which were, of course, of more interest. When asked by the prosecution if the blows could have been delivered by a woman, the answer was 'yes'. Oddly, the defence did not challenge Dolan's view, even if it was potentially damaging to Lizzie's case.

What the defence did was to try to undermine the medical evidence by implying police tampering with the crime scene. Patrolman Patrick Doherty had slid Abby's body away from the bed to check her pulse and Dr Bowen had touched her hand for the same reason. All in all, it did not make much difference, but the potential murder weapon did. Dolan had said at first that the claw-hammer hatchet had been used, then changed his mind having examined the skulls minutely. He also now doubted whether the hairs on it were human as he had first thought. It would not be the last time that an expert witness destroyed a case by doubt and incompetence.

As journalist Ralph summed the day up, 'Gone are the hatchets, axes, plaster casts that might have been borrowed from a Bowery chamber of horrors [the equivalent of Madame Tussauds], bloody garments, bits of bloody carpet and blood-spattered furniture ... these were the stage properties in this legal drama.' They were also, of course, the things that the public had come to see.

The next day, the defence went for Dolan over the times of death. Even today, with all the scientific paraphernalia of modern forensics, *exact* timing is impossible and there are so many variables, of temperature, weather, clothing, setting, that the best we can hope for is intelligent guesswork based on evidence. In 1893 all this was wide open. Melvin Adams pulled Dolan apart on this issue, introducing the intense heat of the day and the fact that the Bordens had been struck by food poisoning the day before they died. What about the supposed murder weapon with its missing handle, the so-called 'hoodoo' hatchet? Was it the right size for the wounds? Was it sharp enough to have split Andrew's eyeball? Dolan agreed that the killer must have been blood-spattered, especially on the hands and upper body, perhaps even the face. In Abby's case, the first blow was probably struck while she was standing; the others rained down from above while she was lying on the ground.

Where Adams could not shake Dolan was on the strength of the assailant. The weight of the hatchet would do the damage – masculine muscle was not required. At that stage, the finger could have been pointed at either woman in the Borden house that morning – Lizzie or Maggie Sullivan.

Relatively little was made of the maid. The fact that she was known by an invented name – Maggie as opposed to Bridget – gave her something of an air of mystery. But although various modern crime writers have pointed a finger at her, this was barely considered at the time. There was no known bad blood between her and her employers and however much hard, physical work she carried out, she was no more likely, as the forensics made clear, to have swung a hatchet with any more power or dexterity than Lizzie. And Lizzie, for all the defence's endeavours to cover it up, *did* have a motive.

At the trial, the Harvard expert Professor Wood, variously described in the press as 'stalwart', 'handsome', 'a heavyweight pugilist' and like 'an army officer burned brown by a long life on the plains', explained that he had examined the Bordens' stomach contents, dresses, a hatchet, carpet and hair samples. He agreed with Dolan on the time of death, found no trace of poison in stomachs or the milk samples he had been sent. The bloodstains on the carpet told him nothing. The chemical and microscopic tests he carried out on a supposed murder weapon likewise revealed nothing. As for the hairs on the weapon (by now reduced from two to one) it was animal, probably from a cow. This conclusion was, of course, guesswork in 1893. The 'hoodoo' hatchet with its sawn-off handle was covered in a white, ash-like dirt, indicating fire. To a barrage of objections from defence counsel, Wood stuck to his guns. As to the clothing, the single blood spot on the skirt was minute; it may have been menstrual. It was certainly not contiguous with a dress worn by somebody hacking two people to death, but of course, as the prosecution pointed out, Lizzie had changed her dress on the day of the murders and later burnt it 'because it was covered in paint'.

Once again, the gentility of New England in the 'gilded age' was allowed to obscure the truth. 'The defense claim,' wrote Joe Howard of the *Boston Globe*, 'for reasons *not necessary to publish* [my italics] ... that this blood is natural.' He missed the point that *all* blood is natural – the issue was, had it come from the smashed head of a Borden? There *was* discussion over bloody towels found in a bucket in the cellar, but this too was believed to be 'ordinary monthly sickness' and glossed over.

Dr Frank Draper was another Harvard alumnus. He was Medical Examiner for Suffolk County and had been present at the autopsy. He had, by this time, investigated 3,500 suspicious deaths and would go on to write a *Textbook of Legal Medicine* in 1905. Discussions about which blow was struck first and the exact position of the killer were likely to confuse the jury and would provide endless disagreement between the doctors.

Draper produced the plaster casts of the skulls and told the court that four of Andrew Borden's ten or eleven cuts had gone through the bone into the brain. Later that day, he produced the actual skulls (Lizzie was allowed to be in an ante-room for this). It was the first time that such grisly exhibits were seen in an American court and it shocked everybody. Andrew's lower jaw moved, as if he himself was trying to testify.

The doctor tried the various axe-heads in the wounds to show that virtually all of them fitted and he pointed out that Andrew's skull was particularly thin – anyone could have done the damage. In Abby's case, Draper believed, the first blow was delivered while she was still standing, facing her attacker; the rest (overkill) while she was on the floor. There were arguments over the amount of blood in both cases. If Andrew's carotid artery had been cut, there would be blood everywhere. It was a measure of the infancy of forensic science in 1893 that led Draper to say that there was no rule for blood spatter. Today, we know that there is and a scene of crimes officer will spend considerable time photographing and cataloguing such evidence.

Last among the doctors came David W. Cheever, professor of surgery at Harvard Medical School. He had thirty-five years' experience and was the heavyweight of the medico-legal team. He agreed with the findings of the others in terms of timing of death and use of weapon. With a panache worthy of the great pathologists of the twentieth century, he raised the 'hoodoo' hatchet and brought it slicing down from the full stretch of his arm to stop alarmingly close to the head of Melvin Adams for the defence. Everybody gasped.

On 20 June 1893, the twelve 'good and true' men of the jury acquitted Lizzie Borden of murder. The press, all over the States and indeed around the world, went into overdrive. But the hysteria did not last long and the friends of Lizzie Borden, who had clung to the femininity of the accused, disappeared with startling rapidity.

Long before that, the doggerel had broken out. There are various versions but the best known is:

Lizzie Borden took an axe,
Gave her mother forty whacks.
When she saw what she had done,
She gave her father forty-one.

The number of blows is exaggerated and technically, it was a hatchet, not an axe, that did the job.

There can be no doubt that the jury in the Borden case did not acquit on the evidence; they acquitted on Lizzie's social standing and her sex. Supporters scream that the evidence was circumstantial, but that is the case in 99 per cent of murders.

Cesare Lombroso got many things wrong in his studies of criminals. It is very telling that his most famous work is *L'Uomo Deliquente* (Criminal *Man*) but he has a special word for females. 'As a double exception,' he wrote, 'the criminal woman is a monster … the peculiarity of the female criminal lunatic … is that her madness becomes more acute at particular periods.' He was referring to menstruation, the 'time of the month' when, traditionally, females become more tetchy and emotional than at other times.

So, what is the case against Lizzie Borden? She hated her stepmother and possibly her father for marrying her. We have seen something similar in the case of Constance Kent thirty years earlier.

I believe that Lizzie intended to kill her stepmother – the attempt to buy prussic acid the day before was the first evidence of this. Her excuse to the pharmacist was that she wanted to clean as sealskin cape, and Lizzie owned two of them. It was her (understandable) lack of scientific knowledge that prussic acid is not a cleaning agent.

She took the 'hoodoo' hatchet from the cellar, seething with hatred at the woman who had invaded the family space and confronted her in the guest bedroom. Even though Abby was standing up facing Lizzie, she probably had no time to cry out or defend herself before the first blow felled her. In the blind rage that only a deranged killer can explain – or perhaps cannot – she rained a further seventeen cuts down on Abby's head.

She now had to contend with Andrew – and he was as guilty as Abby in allowing the woman into his household and his bed. He was probably back from his walk by now and she had made sure that he was dozing peacefully in the sitting room. Had Andrew been fully awake, he would have seen blood on Lizzie's dress, her hands, perhaps even her face. But he had no time to react before she killed him too.

Now, she had to think quickly. Maggie was on the third floor, cleaning windows. The murders had happened quickly and almost silently on the floors below. Lizzie changed her dress and washed her hands, looking clean and innocent before giving the alarm. She went back to the ground floor and came out with the first piece of misinformation of many – 'Maggie, Maggie, come quick! Father's dead. Somebody came in and killed him.'

Lizzie's icy calm in the face of so much hysteria alerted the police from the start. Her nonsensical 'alibi' of being in the barn at the time of the murders made no sense. The police search of the premises was woeful and not arresting Lizzie on suspicion immediately gave her ample opportunity to destroy the condemning bloodstained dress.

Then, the prejudices of the time kicked in. The jurors forgot that the forensic evidence made it clear which hatchet was used and that an averagely built woman could have wielded it. They believed – to a man, since the verdict was unanimous – that genteel 'ladies' do not commit crime at all, certainly not butcher their fathers and stepmothers. If there was evidence of disruption in the household – and there was – it could not, surely, lead to butchery on the scale of the Borden murders.

As for forensic science, it could prove the how and the where of murder, but it could not prove the who or the why.

And in that fatal absence, Lizzie Borden walked free.

Chapter 12

'Jack the Ripper ... at last'

'Now, gentlemen, antimony is a well-known poison, but although in the pharmacopeia it is rarely used now, its effects are well known. It is spoken of as a poison that has certain fine and well-known characteristics and it is generally used in the form of tartar emetic ...'

Mr Justice Grantham's comment on the MO of the prisoner at the bar at the Old Bailey in March 1903 did not refer to the fact that it was used in high-profile cases by the Rugeley poisoner, Dr William Palmer in 1846; Dr Edward Pritchard in 1865; and by the murderer of Charles Bravo eleven years later. Antimony is colourless, odourless and virtually tasteless, which is what makes it so dangerous. As tartar emetic (a compound of potassium antimony and tartrate) it dissolves easily in water. In general use, it was used to make patients sweat, empty bowels and reduce coughing. A fatal dose of antimony is difficult to quantify because it affects people in different ways. Four hundred grains have been swallowed with no fatalities whereas some victims have died having ingested only 1½ grains. The actual cause of death is heart failure, which is why a number of medical men missed the poison in 1903. Constriction of the throat and cramps add to a victim's discomfort in their final hours.

The lethal powder looks like Epsom salts, one of the generic 'cures' for just about anything in the Victorian period, but it causes painful and almost incessant vomiting, bloody urine, depression, delirium and coma. Deaths usually occur within twenty-four hours. Small amounts of the substance given over time give rise to natural-looking symptoms, nausea and vomiting, which of course can have a number of causes.

Interestingly, in the 1903 murder case, antimony was used in pubs to clean lead pipes and vessels.

Mary Isabella Spink

Four years after Neill Cream faced Billington's drop at Newgate, Dr J.F. Rodgers was called to the Prince of Wales pub in Bartholomew Square off the City Road in London's East End, on Christmas Day 1897. The landlord, George Chapman, was worried about his wife, Mary, who was vomiting and in pain. Christmas was not the extended national holiday it has become today so both the pub staff and the doctor were routinely working. Mrs Chapman had blonde hair, close-cropped like a man's, and her husband had been giving her doses of medicine prescribed by a local doctor for a few days. Rodgers may have been keen to get away to family festivities because his examination of the by now dead woman was brief to say the least. The death certificate put the cause down to phthisis (tuberculosis) which has *none* of the symptoms of antimony poisoning or any other stomach irritant. As author Richard D. Altick says in *Victorian Studies in Scarlet* (1970) the 'medical profession was not consistently one of the nation's first lines of defence against crime'.

Mary Spink, it transpired later, had been married to a railwayman, Shadrach Spink, but he had left her largely because of her drinking. She had a certain amount of money and gave £500 of it to Chapman when they became an item. The couple met in March 1896 when they had both boarded at the Forest Road house of John Ward, whom Chapman had met as a customer in William Wenzel's barbershop. Ward's wife had seen them canoodling on the stairs, but Chapman explained that all was well – they would soon be married. Whether they actually went through with the legal process is open to conjecture but they soon moved to Hastings, where they ran a barber shop, George shaving customers and giving haircuts while Mary sang and played the piano.

For a while, the business did well, allowing Chapman to buy a sailing boat, the *Mosquito,* but by September 1897 they called the barber shop quits and returned to London to begin the Prince of Wales tenancy.

And there, according to the death certificate, tragedy struck due to natural causes, as it did so often in one of the most unhealthy cities in the world. Nurse Elizabeth Weymark said later, 'I prepared the body for burial. It was a mere skeleton.' Mary Chapman was buried in Leyton cemetery and her husband moved on.

Elizabeth Taylor

Just as Mary Spink died on a 'special' day, so too did Elizabeth 'Bessie' Taylor, St Valentine's Day, 1901. Born to a loving family in Lynam, Cheshire, she had moved to London and by the time she met George Chapman was managing a restaurant, quite a high-profile job for a woman at that time. Like Spink, Taylor went through a lightning courtship with Chapman, claimed a marriage of sorts and began to receive verbal and physical abuse from him. At one point, according to her friend Elizabeth Painter, he threatened her with a revolver.

None of this was known to the doctor who examined Taylor and suggested she undergo surgery to cure the symptoms. The records are very vague on this. I have not found the name of the doctor, nor the hospital nor even the disease which led to the procedure. Whatever it was, it did no good and Taylor's symptoms continued. For a while, the Chapmans moved to Bishop's Stortford in Hertfordshire, where they ran The Grapes pub. They were soon back, managing the Monument Tavern in Union Street in the Borough. It was probably here that the now notorious photograph was taken, of the 'happy couple' smiling at their bar, Bessie plump and every inch the barmaid, George scowling beneath his peaked cap and sporting a huge moustache. As many writers have commented, he does look very like his far more famous contemporary, Frederich Nietzsche. But 'Superman' he was not.

Each day that Elizabeth Painter came to see her ailing friend, Chapman would tell her she was dead. This was a sick joke, because Bessie was still alive, albeit losing weight fast. On 15 February, Chapman's response to the usual question was 'Much about the same', except that this time, Bessie Taylor/Chapman really was dead. The family doctor had been no help; he could not account for Bessie's weight loss or her vomiting and diarrhoea. The cause of death was exhaustion as a result of both.

And for Chapman, a new love and a new death called.

Maud Marsh

In mid-October 1902, Dr Grapel was called. He was the Marsh family doctor from Croydon and what he found alarmed him. Maud Marsh was seriously ill in bed, a once healthy 19-year-old was now underweight and clearly suffering. The doctor spent some time with the woman's husband, George Chapman, and was told that both he and Maud had eaten rabbit earlier in the day and perhaps it had been 'off'. Standards of hygiene were nothing like they are today. There was no such thing as a sell-by date and meat of all sorts was hung up both inside and outside butchers' shops open to the elements and all manner of germs and bacteria. Grapel was an unusually careful – and suspicious – doctor. He could find nothing in the remains of the rabbit meal to explain what he was sure was a case of poisoning.

Days earlier, a Dr Stoker had been called to the rooms over the Crown pub to examine Mrs Chapman, the barmaid. Up to that point, any medicine the woman had taken had been administered by her husband. Now Stoker insisted that a nurse, Jessie Toon, be brought in to carry this out. Maud had been ill since July. In fact, Chapman told her sister Louisa that she was dying and Louisa was made of stern stuff. She insisted that Maud be taken for an examination to Guy's Hospital, the nearest to the Crown. She was there from 28 July to 20 August and seemed to recover. The doctors, however, could not agree on a diagnosis of the illness. Once back home, Maud's symptoms returned and she was effectively back to square one.

At some time in September, Maud's mother, Eliza, was visiting her daughter when Chapman gave his wife some brandy. As suspicious as Dr Grapel was weeks later, she waited until Chapman left the room, then sipped the brandy. It gave her a burning sensation in her throat and she was violently sick two hours later.

On 22 October, with Eliza at her bedside, Maud Chapman, née Marsh, died. Dr Stoker refused to sign a death certificate without a post-mortem taking place and the work was carried out by Dr Thomas Stevenson, the well-respected expert who had given court testimony against Neill Cream. In the dead woman's stomach, he found traces of tartar emetic – antimony. Three days later, George Chapman was arrested by Sergeant George Godley of J Division, accused of murder.

Maud had been hired by the man in August 1901 as he needed a replacement barmaid following the death of Bessie Taylor. Born in February 1883, Maud was listed in the 1901 census as a maid working for a local Croydon family. In October of that year, she turned up at her parents' home with Chapman, now her fiancé, both of them riding bikes. In the following June, they moved from the Monument to the Crown, shortly after the Monument caught fire and Chapman put in a hefty insurance claim (which was never paid out). Once again, there is a photograph of the couple, she looking adoringly under her 'Gibson girl' hairstyle, he looking stern and immobile.

In view of the extraordinary similarities between the deaths of Spink, Taylor and Marsh and the fact that Chapman was the common denominator, the police applied for – and got – exhumation orders on the first two. When they were dug up, on 22 November and 9 December respectively, both bodies were particularly fresh-looking, without the usual amount of decay that might be expected. This is typical of the post-mortem appearance of antimony. In searching the Chapmans' house, Godley and his team found a medicine bottle that also contained traces of tartar emetic.

The police in the meantime were busy doing their homework on George Chapman. Although he subsequently denied it, he was born Severino Antonovich Klosowski in the village of Nagornak, Poland, the son of a carpenter. He attended a school in Krasseminsk between 1873 and 1880 and was apprenticed under Senior Surgeon Moskko Rappaport for the five years after that. He may have learned Yiddish at this time, although he was not Jewish. He was a medical student in Praga Hospital, Warsaw, where no doubt he became thoroughly familiar with various poisons and their effects. By 1887, he was a *Feldsher* (assistant surgeon) in the Infant Jesus Hospital in Praga.

He moved to England in June 1887, perhaps because his Jewish associations made him a target for the Tsarist pogroms which were frequent in Russia and Poland at the time. Foreign doctors were not regarded with much favour in Britain at the time and Klosowski had to eat humble pie and work as a hairdresser for Abraham Radin in the West India Dock Road. Between 1888 and 1891, he lived in Cable Street in the East End and from 1890 he worked as a barber in a shop below the White Hart pub on the corner of Whitechapel High Street and George Yard, near the site of the murder of Martha Tabram in August 1888 (see Chapter 8). He quickly took over the business.

In view of later events, Klosowski's love life is interesting. In July 1889, he met Lucy Baderski and they went through the semi-legal marriage process that he used in the cases of his three victims. Most accounts contend that a Polish wife turned up at this point and that Klosowski paid her off to go away. In 1890, Klosowski and Baderski had a son, Wohystaw. The family moved around in this period, from Cable Street to Greenfield Street. Wohystaw died in March 1891 and within a month Klosowski had emigrated to Jersey City in the States where he again worked as a barber. The move to America is not as bizarre as it might be today. For many Eastern Europeans, Britain was merely a stepping off point en route to the land of the free which was seen as an impossible paradise to which the downtrodden could aspire.

By February 1892, Lucy was back in London and gave birth to a daughter, Cecilia. Klosowski joined her briefly, but left and disappeared from the record for several months. By 1893, he was living with Annie Chapman (no relation to the Ripper victim) in Tottenham, still working as a barber. She walked out the following year, disapproving of her 'husband's' attempts to arrange a threesome.

It was now that Klosowski took to calling himself George Chapman. He also claimed to be American, possibly as a result of his stay in New Jersey. Two years later he was working for William Wenzel in Leytonstone, then moved to Hastings with his new inamorata Mary Spink. The rest is criminal history, but the Hastings stay proved Chapman's undoing. A vital witness at his trial which began on 16 March 1903 was a Mr Davidson who ran a pharmacy in Hastings High Street. The reason that poison had been such a common murder method in Victorian England is that pharmacists were notoriously casual with their record keeping and the law was surprisingly vague on the issue of potentially lethal medicines. Unfortunately for Chapman, Davidson's records were meticulous and he produced his ledger in court. On 3 April 1897, Chapman, using his adopted name, had bought 1oz (28 grains) of tartar emetic, enough to kill ten people.

Under the watchful eye of the presiding judge, Mr Justice Grantham, Chapman's defence counsel, George Elliott, Arthur Hutton and V. Lyons, had a difficult job in the face of so much evidence. Chapman was charged only with the murder of Maud Marsh and the defence pointed out the total absence of motive in their client. He *had* obtained money (£500) from Bessie Taylor but nothing from the others. Neither was there hard evidence (despite Maud's mother's testimony re the brandy) that Chapman had administered the poison.

The jury disagreed, however, and took only twelve minutes to find Chapman guilty. The homicidal hairdresser collapsed in the dock of the Old Bailey and had to be half-carried down the stairs to his cell by the warders. It was the same story at his hanging. Lucy Baderski tried to visit the condemned man, awaiting justice in Wandsworth, but he refused to see her. He spent his last night pacing his cell and barely touched his last meal. William Billington gave him a brandy and water on the scaffold while Henry Pierrepoint pinioned his legs.

As with Neill Cream, defining a motive for Chapman is difficult. The sadism which marks Cream is not apparent in Chapman. He was probably misogynistic (a very common trait at any time in the past) and seems to have had scant regard for the women in his life. That said, he did form relationships with them and had children with two. He even sent a wreath to Maud Marsh's funeral in Croydon inscribed 'From a devoted friend, G.C.'. Many modern commentators have rather limply suggested that Chapman had no idea how to end relationships and that murder seemed his only solution. This is weak in the extreme and does not really merit analysis.

The most damning element in the whole case was the verbal lashing that Mr Justice Grantham gave to the medical profession – the fact that Chapman could have pulled the wool over the eyes of supposedly qualified doctors for so long.

There is a bizarre P.S. in the case of Chapman/Klosowski. When Hargrave Adam wrote the Introduction to *The Trial of George Chapman* (1930), he said:

> Chief Inspector Abberline, who had charge of the investigation into the East End murders [the Ripper case] thought that Chapman and Jack the Ripper were one and the same person. Abberline never wavered in his firm conviction … When Godley arrested Chapman, Abberline said to his confrere, 'You've got Jack the Ripper at last.'

Godley had assisted Adam on his book and the man was a confidant of senior policemen at the time of the Ripper murders like Robert

Anderson and Melville Macnaghten. By 1903, however, Abberline had long retired so the actual words quoted above were probably never spoken. Adam went further in claiming that Abberline had interviewed Lucy Baderski in 1888, which is nonsense in that she and Klosowski did not meet until the following year.

In *Forty Years of Man-Hunting* (1932) ex-Superintendent Arthur Neil adopted the same approach. He was working under Godley as a sergeant in the Klosowski case and wrote of the Ripper–Chapman link:

We were never able to secure definite proof that Chapman was the 'Ripper' but the strong theory remains just the same … As we discovered, Chapman had been a surgeon in Poland and would therefore, be the *only possible fiend* [my italics] capable of putting such knowledge to use against humanity instead of for it … Why [Chapman] took to poisoning his victims on his second visit to this country can only be ascribed to his diabolical cunning or some insane idea or urge to satisfy his inordinate vanity.

Neil is another in the far-too-long list of retired coppers who claimed insider knowledge just before the Ripper case developed into an industry. When he (and Adam) wrote, there was virtually no accurate, modern analysis of what makes a serial killer tick and phrases like 'fiend' and 'diabolical cunning' merely underscore that point. These men were basically making it up on the basis of Klosowski's medical background, the fact that he lived briefly in Ripper country and (subconsciously) that he took the surname of Jack's third victim.

Chapter 13

Blood on their Hands

Göhren is a little village in Rügen, a holiday island in the Baltic Sea off the coast of Germany. Soon after sunrise on Monday, 2 July 1901, a searching party made a gruesome find in local woods. Half-hidden under shrubbery lay the bodies of Hermann Stubbe, aged 8 and his brother Peter, 6, sons of a local carter. Their skulls had been smashed, probably with a rock and their arms and legs had been cut off. Both boys' hearts had been ripped out and Hermann's was never found.

The boys had disappeared the day before and when they did not come home for supper, their distraught parents organized a search. Locals lit flaming torches and combed the area. Police set about recreating the brothers' known sightings and this led them to a greengrocer who had seen them talking to a carpenter, Ludwig Tessnow. Tessnow was a reclusive misfit who had recently returned to the island after travelling around Germany and the previous evening, a neighbour had seen him going home with stains on his Sunday-best suit. He was duly arrested on suspicion and his house searched. Some of his clothes were still wet from washing, but that was hardly suspicious. Under a stone sink in the kitchen, police found a pair of boots, equally wet and stained red. Tessnow claimed that this was wood dye – as a carpenter, he used it all the time.

But the police would not let this one go. Their enquiries uncovered the fact that three weeks earlier, a farmer reported the killing and disembowelling of seven of his sheep on his farm near Göhren. Macabre examples of animal mutilation have occurred from time to time throughout the world – in our own time, they have sometimes been attributed to alien attacks; earlier generations believed they were linked with witchcraft. But the farmer had seen the all-too-human culprit running away from the crime scene and could identify him if he saw him again. At an identity parade held in the prison yard at Greifswald, he picked out Tessnow.

The magistrate, Johann-Klaus Schmidt, knew his business and had the memory of an elephant! Three years earlier, he remembered, there had been a similar case of child murder in Osnabruck and he contacted the police there.

At dusk on 9 September 1898, the dismembered body of 7-year-old Hannelore Heidemann had been found naked in the woods near the village of Lechtingen, body parts scattered in the bushes. An hour later, a second body had been found – 8-year-old Else Langmeier had been butchered like her friend. Hannelore's mother, Jadwiga, had gone to her daughter's school earlier to be told that she had not turned up; Irmgard Langmeier was told the same thing.

Schmidt's contact with the Osnabruck police threw up the name of journeyman-carpenter Ludwig Tessnow. He had been seen in the Lechtingen woods and his clothes were stained when he was arrested. He gave the same story he would give later to the Göhren police – the stains were wood dye. An enterprising detective visited the carpenter's premises and 'accidentally' knocked over a tin of dye which spilt on to Tessnow's trousers. The result was indistinguishable from the stains found earlier and the murder enquiry was closed. In fact, Tessnow stayed in the Lechtingen area for another four months before going on to Mecklenburg-Vorpommen in search of work.

To Schmidt, the coincidence of similar crimes involving the same man was too much and the area's chief prosecutor (the equivalent of America's District Attorney) had heard of the recent pioneering work of Dr Paul Uhlenhuth, then a professor at the Greifswald Institute of Hygiene. Uhlenhuth, building on earlier researches of Louis Pasteur, had found a means of distinguishing human from animal blood. He could also tell the scientific difference between blood and wood dye! We have to remember that there was always a huge time lag between investigative laboratory work by a scientist and its acceptance and application by police forces. The police of Osnabruck and Göhren had no idea of the revolutionary work being carried out, especially as scientists (as we have seen in courtroom dramas throughout this book) were often at odds over the results. There was also a high degree of professional – and even nationalistic – jealousy. Jules Bordet, for instance, working at the Pasteur Institute in Paris, established the basic principles of serology (the study of bodily fluids) and his work led to the execution of a murderer in France in 1902. But Uhlenhuth had beaten him by over a year.

At the end of January 1901, the doctor was sent parcels containing Tessnow's Sunday-best clothing and his work overalls, as well as a stained rock from the Göhren woods which was believed to be the murder weapon of the Stubbe boys. Over four days, Uhlenhuth tested the items by soaking them in distilled water or salt solution. The overalls were indeed stained with dye (the policeman's somewhat illegal ploy) but all garments had traces of blood – seventeen human and nine sheep.

Tessnow's trial took place over ten days in the spring of 1902 (if anything, German justice was even slower than in Britain) and Uhlenhuth was the prosecution's chief witness. Nobody could dispute his findings, but the prisoner's state of mind was another matter. Six psychiatrists were brought in to testify that the 'mad carpenter', the 'monster of Rügen' as the press called him, was insane at the time of the murders. His consistent calm and rational response to police questions and his behaviour in custody seemed to belie this and he was found guilty. He appealed his sentence (a Court of Appeal was still three years into the future in Britain) but the court at Leipzig rejected it.

In a curious postscript to the case, the actual fate of Ludwig Tessnow is unknown. Some accounts claim that he was executed by guillotine (the standard German method of execution as it was in France) in Greifswald prison in 1904, but there is no official mention of it. There is a theory that his death sentence was secretly commuted and that he died in prison in 1939. For our purposes, the Tessnow case marked a milestone, one that was stained with blood.

The history of blood analysis, so crucial to solving crime, began soon after William Harvey, physician to Charles I, expounded his views on *The Motion of the Heart and Blood in Animals* in 1628. Just over twenty years later, the architect Christopher Wren invented the first hypodermic syringe, a quill attached to a bladder. It cannot have worked too well, but it established a gadget and a principle that would be radically developed by later generations. Blood transfusion – the passing of blood from human to human and even animal to human – had been in progress for some time, but the chances of it working were strictly limited and often resulted in death. No one knew why until 1875 when the German physiologist Leonard Landois's experiments led to a realization that there must be a variety of blood groups, some incompatible with others.

The solution was found in 1900 by Dr Karl Landsteiner of the Institute of Pathology and Anatomy in Vienna. In a series of experiments using his own blood and that of six colleagues, he was able to identify these blood groups, which he labelled logically A, B and C (later O). Two years later, Landsteiner's assistant, Dr Adranio Studi, was able to identify an AB strain which clarified matters still further.

In terms of crime scene evaluation, the various tests had their limits. Uhlenhuth's colleague Max Richter proved that examination of old bloodstains was far less conclusive than fresh blood at recent crime scenes. There would be a double need now for the police to act quickly in terms of carrying out their investigations.

But it was not all about blood groupings. The extent and shape of blood spots, smears and spatters at a crime scene was clear evidence of what had happened. In this context, as in ballistics (the study of bullets) Alexandre Lacassagne pointed the way. His *Précis de Medicine* in 1878 was the culmination of years of service as a surgeon with the French navy and by 1880 he was professor of Forensic Medicine at Lyon. Blood patterns were only part of the work determined by Lacassagne in the series of murders near Lyon from 1894. Such was his grasp of every aspect of violent crime that the 'father of forensics' brought Joseph Vacher, the French 'Jack the Ripper' to the guillotine four years later.

Eugenie Delhomme, a mill worker from Beaurepaire, was found raped, strangled and disembowelled behind a hedge in May 1894. Three similar crimes followed – two teenaged girls followed by 58-year-old widow. The killer struck in open countryside and in the sanctity of the victim's home. In September 1895, he changed tack; his MO was the same, but now his victims were boys, like the shepherd Victor Portalier, whom he castrated. Another shepherd followed, aged 14, and another girl, 16-year-old Alice Alise.

The extraordinary body count was halted for six months, but then the wife of a shepherd, Marie Moussier, aged 19, was murdered, as was a shepherdess, Rosine Rodier. The occupation of many of the victims had most relevance because they worked alone in the country, far enough from the nearest settlement to give the killer time to carry out his mutilations. In May 1897, 14-year-old Claudius Beaupied was butchered in an abandoned property, but his body was not found until six months later, by which time all the evidence of blood type and blood patterns was useless. The last to die was yet another shepherd, 14-year-old Pierre Laurent, who had been sodomized and castrated like the others.

'L'eventreur du sud-est' as the press dubbed him was finally caught on 4 August of that year when the family of a woman under attack rescued her and dragged Joseph Vacher to a nearby inn to wait for police. There he casually played the piano accordion while awaiting arrest.

The oddest thing about Vacher was his peculiar behaviour and appearance. We saw in Chapter 8 that police and public hunting the Whitechapel murderer nine years earlier had been looking for a dribbling maniac who would have stood out in a crowd. Such stereotypes did not exist, yet there he was, playing the accordion in a French pub! Vacher was 26 (*exactly* in the age range of serial killers as identified in the FBI's psychological analysis of a century later), had been in and out of asylums for years (hence the six-month cessation of murders) and had a deformed face caused by trying to commit suicide with a revolver. In an age far less sensitive than ours to people with obvious mental and physical impairment, it is astonishing that no one had pointed a finger at him earlier.

Vacher claimed that he was insane having been bitten by a rabid dog as a child. Lacassagne did not buy it, testified accordingly and the man was found guilty of the murder of Portalier and guillotined on 31 December 1898.

Although later work on blood patterns in the twentieth century has given us the highly organized knowledge we have today, it was Lacassagne who first noted the relevance of such patterns to the position of a body at the crime scene. It was almost impossible to remove bloodstains from such a scene. In 1869, the French detective Gustave Macé of the Sûreté was sitting in a living room where he believed a murder had recently taken place. There was no sign of any blood and the suspect was sitting with him. Macé took a jug of water and poured it onto the floor tiles which lifted under the water pressure. The tiles' undersides were caked with blood.

It was William Jones who first realized that something was wrong. The 16-year-old turned up punctually for work at Chapman's Oil and Colour Store at 34 High Street, Deptford, as he did every day of the week. It was Monday, 27 March 1905 and it was 8.30 in the morning. There was a time when Deptford in South London had been a rough and ready, dangerous neighbourhood, the docks and shipyards of Henry VIII and the murder scene of Shakespeare's contemporary, Christopher Marlowe. By the early years of the twentieth century it had calmed down considerably, although the events of earlier that March morning told a different story. The boy's knock elicited no response, even though he knew that the Farrows, who owned the premises, lived over the shop. James looked through the window and saw that some chairs inside had been overturned. Still getting no reply to his increasingly frantic knocking, he ran next door to find shopkeeper Louis Kidman and the pair broke in to Number 34.

Thomas Farrow, 71, was lying in a pool of blood in the parlour, and there were blood spots and spatters over the floor and on the stairs. In the bedroom, they found Ann Farrow, 65, battered around the head and unconscious. In a case of murder, it was routine for the local division to call in headquarters at Scotland Yard. Accordingly, Detective Inspector Frederick Fox arrived to control the crime scene, but not before Sergeant Albert Atkinson had moved an empty cash box with his bare hands. Fox knew that his boss, Assistant Commissioner Melville Macnaghten, would be interested in this case, not because it appeared to be complicated (it was obviously a robbery that had gone wrong) but because it would be a means of testing a hypothesis which had already proved solid in a case three years earlier.

Derby Day 1902 was the usual brouhaha with the great and good of the racing world and high society mixing, all too unaware, with the low-life pickpockets who also had a field day on such occasions. Of the fifty-four thieves arrested that day, twenty-nine had previous convictions. The police knew this because of the Yard's new Fingerprint Bureau, set up under Sergeant Charles Collins. Later in the year (27 June) Harry Jackson made history as the first felon to be convicted solely on fingerprint evidence. A careless house-breaker, he had left his dabs on the newly painted windowsills of a house in Denmark Hill, London, and had stolen billiard balls. Collins testified in court where a brilliant brief, Richard Muir, explained to an astonished jury exactly how the 'miracle' of fingerprinting worked and introduced them to the previously unknown world of plain and tented arches, simple, double, central pocket and lateral pocket loops and plain whorls – all the technical jargon that went with fingerprint identification. The scientific reality was that no two sets of fingerprints were identical and crime would never be the same again.

It was one thing to prove a case against a pickpocket or burglar; an entirely different one in a capital case of murder where suspects' lives were at stake. But the killers had not only been careless in emptying the Farrows' cashbox of its £13 (about £1,800 today), they had been spotted leaving the premises an hour before William Jones arrived and two of those eyewitnesses gave police a name – Albert Stratton. He was arrested by Inspector Hailstone in Deptford High Street on 3 April, just a day after his brother Alfred had been collared by DS Frank Beavis in the King of Prussia pub in Albany Street.

The Strattons were low-lives, well known in the area for rowdy behaviour. In fact, during the subsequent inquest into Thomas Farrow's death, they laughed and joked and shuffled their feet as if they had been at a Music Hall, much to the annoyance of the coroner.

Their trial, under Mr Justice Channell, opened on 5 May. The prosecution was led by Muir, once again, who was determined to establish fingerprint evidence as the new norm in serious crime. Forty prosecution witnesses were called including the Stratton brothers' girlfriends, Ann Cromarty and Katie Wade, who effectively shopped their menfolk by not providing alibis and, in the case of Cromarty, telling the court that Alfred had asked for a pair of her stockings on the day of the robbery. These were made into rough and ready masks which were, along with the cashbox, produced in court.

The case made headlines solely on the issue of fingerprint evidence. A 'disgusted magistrate' (who sensibly did not give his name) wrote to *The Times*, 'Scotland Yard, once known as the world's finest police organization, will be the laughing stock of Europe if it insists on trying to trace criminals by odd ridges on their skins.' Ironically, Richard Muir may once have agreed with him, but he was not a believer in the efficiency of eyewitness testimony, and hard science made more sense.

Ann Farrow had died of her injuries on 31 March, so the Stratton brothers faced a double murder charge. The defence pulled in some heavyweights for its legal team, anxious to pour scorn on the 'new-fangled' technology that was about to revolutionize crime-solving. H.G. Rooth, Harold Morris and the famous Curtis-Bennett did their best, but they were undermined by the eyewitnesses and by their own expert witness.

Dr John Garson was not a fingerprint expert but was highly regarded in the world of anthropometry (effectively Bertillonage), but

Muir discovered that the man had offered his services to both defence and prosecution in the Stratton case. When the judge asked Garson why he was in court, he explained that he was an expert witness (a new phrase in 1905) and the judge hit back with, 'Yes, an absolutely untrustworthy one.' Despite Channell's direction to the jury not to commit on fingerprint evidence alone, the jury spent less than two hours deliberating before returning a guilty verdict.

On Tuesday, 23 May, the Strattons were hanged at Wandsworth by John Billington with assistance from John Ellis and Henry Pierrepoint. I doubt they were still laughing and joking that day.

The exposure of John Garson was a seminal moment in criminal history. Rather than scientists being relied upon and trusted, it was obvious that the expert witness business was merely a racket, not unlike the stance taken by counsel. In the rarefied atmosphere of crime fiction, lawyers of the old school never took on a case if they believed a potential client guilty. So, for example, Erle Stanley Gardiner's Perry Mason was always on the right side of criminal history. In reality, lawyers take on cases because they are paid (handsomely) to do it and a win in court brings in cash and kudos. But, just as laws are insufficiently tight to avoid various 'interpretations' of the same thing, so is medical science. We have seen examples in this book – especially the poisoning cases like those of William Palmer and Florence Maybrick – the endless bickering of professional men who did forensic science no favours at all. Nor did they have all the answers. In the 1886 poisoning case of Edwin Bartlett by his wife Adelaide, she was acquitted because the prosecution could not work out how the lethal chloroform was administered. Apocryphally, surgeon Sir James Paget posed the question after the trial, 'Now she's acquitted, she should tell us, in the interests of science, how she did it.' She never did. And this issue has never gone away.

Fingerprint technology, in terms of the written record, goes back to Dr Nathaniel Crew in 1684 and the first book on the subject to 1788 when J.C. Mayer published an anatomy work in which he wrote, 'the arrangement of skin ridges is never duplicated in two persons.' These works, like those of the Polish scientist John Purkyne in the 1820s, were scholarly and largely unknown to later researchers. Most prominent among these was William Herschel, an engineer in India, who used fingerprinting to stamp out fraud among his contractors. In 1877, when he was appointed senior magistrate near Calcutta, he used the same techniques on all legal documents and criminals in his remit.

As with the invention of the internal combustion engine taking place at roughly the same time, a number of men were all working on the new science simultaneously, unbeknown to each other. Dr Henry Faulds ran the Scottish Medical Mission in Japan and involved himself, like Virchow in Berlin, in local archaeology. He realized that ancient pottery finds had fingerprint marks that were probably a form of signature. He experimented with trying to remove skin ridges, using pumice and even sandpaper – nothing worked. He wrote a paper in 1880 explaining the importance of all this in the field of criminology. This he called Dactylography and an undignified war of words ensued between him and Herschel over whose discovery came first.

Third into the field, very much backing Herschel, was Dr Francis Galton, a highly respected anthropologist. He had his own research laboratory in South Kensington and, building on the work of Herschel and Purkyne, established categories of prints which he published in *Finger Prints* in 1892.

The torch was passed to Edward Henry, who became assistant magistrate in Herschel's India in 1873. As Inspector-General of Bengal by 1880, he made fingerprinting a routine part of police procedure. Henry's system differed from Herschel's and those of Juan Vucetich, deputy chief of police in La Plata, Argentina, with five distinguishable patterns – whorls and loops.

The Troup Committee of 1893 studied the various options and, rather conservatively, perhaps, stuck to Bertillonage, but with fingerprints thrown in. In 1901, the Belper committee adopted fingerprints alone, putting Edward Henry in the post of head of the CID.

On 1 July 1901, the Fingerprint Bureau was set up at the Yard, on the basis that because Galton's estimate was that chances of an identical print was 1 in 64,000 million, there was every chance that the Met could get their man! In fact, today's statisticians have moved that to an impossible figure.

Fingerprints could be 'lifted' from most surfaces and the collection of samples was quick and cheap. Any policeman with basic training could carry this out, long before specialist Scenes Of Crime Officers and the data was stored in cabinets in the increasingly crowded Yard offices, known as shoeboxes. In 1906, the technology went further when it was realized that it was possible to take fingerprints from bodies. The anonymous individual the Americans called 'John' or 'Jane Doe' could now be given an actual identity. Charles Collins was in charge of all this for several years, having worked originally with Inspector Charles Stedman and Constable Frederick Hunt.

Despite the nay-saying of the establishment and no doubt to the horror of the criminal community, fingerprints and bloodstain technology were about to make Britain, at least, a safer country.

But there was one more scientific breakthrough that would have a huge impact on crime and criminals. Edmond Locard studied medicine and law at the University of Lyon and became assistant to Professor Lacassagne, the ballistics expert. In 1910, he established his own laboratory and helped French police with their enquiries for years after that. To him belongs the Locard Exchange Principle – 'every contact leaves a trace'.

It is not *quite* as simple as that. Crime scenes can still be misinterpreted; clues can be missed, but by the time Locard was operating on his own, there was in Britain a professional whose expertise made judges take note, counsel defer and the accused quake in their boots. He was the Home Office Pathologist.

Chapter 14

The Home Office Pathologist

The early photographs are typical. At the age of 8, three years before the Ripper struck, he is a studious-looking little boy, wearing his Sunday-best and looking up from an outsized book in the photographer's studio. Six years later, as the young barrister Edward Marshall Hall defended the indefensible – the murderer Marie Hermann who had battered a cabman to death, he is still solemn, but sitting this time with a cute white dog at his feet.

It is the next photograph that is compelling. In this, he is at work, in his laboratory at St Mary's Hospital, Paddington, with rows of glass chemical bottles on the shelves behind him and a microscope on his desk. He is wearing an upright Edwardian collar and a white coat – the trademark of his profession. The shy slight smile is gone and he turns to the camera with a lantern jaw, cold penetrating eyes and a solemn mouth. He is the 'greatest detective of us all', according to various hard-bitten officers of Scotland Yard and his evidence, acute, accurate and devastating, sent dozens of people to the gallows. He is the Home Office Pathologist, Bernard Spilsbury.

The Spilsburys lived in the elegant spa town of Leamington in Warwickshire where genteel people lived in the Regency houses along the Parade and even more genteel people came to take the waters in the Pump Rooms. It was very near here that Bernard was born, in Bath Street, in January 1877. His father was a chemist who had wanted to go into medicine himself, but his mother disapproved of the 'trade'.

Until he was 10, he was taught at home by a tutor, not untypical for boys of the middle classes and then went to Leamington College, a grammar school with a good reputation. He boarded there, because the family were on the move to London and his parents did not want to upset the boy's education. When he left the school, his reports were average – 'could do better' was the stereotypical phrase. His new school was University College School, then in Bloomsbury, London, but it moved, complete with Spilsbury, to Frognal in Hampstead. Then the family moved again, this time to Manchester, and the boy enrolled in Manchester Grammar School, later to be one of the best in the country; three schools in four years did not faze him at all. As his biographers Brown and Tullett wrote in 1951, 'He was still exasperatingly normal.'

In 1893 as the con man Alfred Monson got away with murdering his wealthy protégé, Charles Hamborough, Spilsbury joined the alumni of Owens College. He was a loner, uninterested in competition and prizes. His favourite sport was ice-skating which he could do alone. An accident left him with a shortened index finger on his right hand so he taught himself to be ambidextrous and in later life he usually used his left.

He decided to become a doctor (against his grandmother's wishes) was carrying out animal dissections and reading the papers of Dr Almoth Wright, the bacteriologist. In 1895, he sat the necessary exams in science, chemistry and biology and went on to Magdalen College, Oxford.

In accordance with Oxford tradition, Spilsbury left the university after three years with a BA degree. This was a hangover from Medieval times and bore no relation to the physiology course he had followed. He went on to St Mary's Hospital Medical School with an Exhibition worth £26 5s a year. A contemporary said, 'I regarded him as a nice, very ordinary individual and certainly never expected him to do anything brilliant.'

St Mary's was the home of three well-established forensic scientists – A.P. Luff, William Willcox and A.J. Pepper. None of these made it into *Chambers Biographical Dictionary* (always a yardstick of success) – Spilsbury did. Morbid anatomy was looked down on by most of the medical profession, referred to as 'a beastly science'. And it did itself no favours. We have already seen the unseemly bickering in the trials of Palmer and Maybrick, the myriad theories about the anatomical skill of the Ripper. The case of Dr Thomas Smethurst, accused of murdering Isabella Bankes in 1859 was another case in point. Alfred Taylor (a *genuine* expert witness) admitted that his arsenic test was flawed. Two other pathologists argued with each other over the findings 'in matters,' said *The Lancet*, 'where there could be no possibility of doubt.' Smethurst was found guilty, but not because of the medical evidence, and because of this he was released by the judge. 'Taylor,' wrote the *Dublin Medical Journal*, 'brought an amount of disrespect upon his branch of the profession that years will not remove.'

Under advice from his mentors, Spilsbury got a state-of-the-art microscope and specialized in scar tissue, joining an elite group of scientists under Almoth Wright, which included Alexander Fleming. He was already a loner, working long hours into the night in his laboratory, refusing to share work and disliking to be touched. He was promoted within the pathology department, still uninterested in prizes and accolades. He was quite long in the tooth (28) when he got his degree – M.B, B.Ch.

Dr Pepper was the Home Office Pathologist, the senior man chosen by the government department to offer expert testimony in serious criminal cases. It was a prestigious position and when Spilsbury got the job, it was elevated to almost legendary heights.

The DPP (Directory of Public Prosecutions) had been set up in 1879 but the Director was then merely an adviser to the Treasury and it was not until 1908 that the DPP was a department in its own right. Edward Henry was already the driving force in the Met by then and his CID worked hand in hand with the DPP. Commissioners came and went, but there was only one Honorary Pathologist to the Home Office.

For Spilsbury, discussion over lunch or coffee with Luff and Pepper revolved around the Moat Farm murders of 1903, in which Samuel McDougal, prone to bicycling in the nude with maidservants, murdered a rich widow and was hanged for it. Other topics included the murder of his wife and two children by Arthur Devereux. Having poisoned them with chloroform and morphine, he sealed their bodies in a trunk using glue and boracic acid, leaving the luggage in a warehouse in Harrow. Henry Pierrepoint hanged him at Pentonville in August 1905.

An innovation kept Spilsbury busy. London County Council set up a new system in which two pathologists had to investigate sudden deaths in the area by post-mortem. The fee was 2 guineas per autopsy.

By 1905, Spilsbury was Resident Assistant Pathologist to Pepper with a comfortable salary of £200 a year. His carefully kept records of all his autopsies were hand written into black bound notebooks with additional notes on separate cards. All this was intended for a book which, in the event, he never got around to writing. By the time of his death in 1947, he had carried out over 25,000 post-mortems.

He joined the Medico-Legal Society in 1908 and was a regular attendee at meetings. His lectures were always packed. He also attended meetings of the Crimes Club – 'our Society' as members called it – made up of doctors, actors, writers, anybody with a penchant for the macabre. He was not a great orator, leaving the theatrics to the Marshall Halls of the world; but his flat, matter-of-fact explanation struck a chord with juries, court audiences and newspaper readers and was streets ahead of the jargon-filled gobbledegook we have heard, for example, in the Palmer and Maybrick trials. He was fast, he was accurate, he was certain – and he could use *both* hands!

He and his new wife, Edith, lived in Hindes Road, Harrow-on-the-Hill, then a small town distinct from London and he travelled to work each day at Paddington on the newly electrified Metropolitan Railway. The law was changing rapidly in Spilsbury's early years as a pathologist. From 1898, an accused could speak on their own account in a court of law and from 1907, the Court of Appeal gave felons the right to challenge a death sentence. From now on, more than ever, a Home Office Pathologist had to get it right. By 1910, he succeeded Pepper at St Mary's, later that year to discover that Dr Hawley Harvey Crippen was buying quantities of hyoscine …

Bernard Spilsbury single-handedly made pathologists into household names. Before him, they may well have been known in medical circles but from 1911 and the Crippen case, Spilsbury's name was never off the front pages of newspapers and other forensic scientists bathed in the same spotlight. The first three decades of the twentieth century are often referred to in Britain as the golden age of crime. And there was no one with more of the Midas touch than Bernard Spilsbury; he had made the 'beastly science' respectable and glamorous for the first time.

There would be no going back.

Bibliography

Adam, H.L., *CID: Behind the Scenes at Scotland Yard*, Samson Low

Adams, Blessin, *Thou Savage Woman*, William Collins, 2025

Altick, Richard D., *Victorian Studies in Scarlet*, J.M. Dent, 1970

Begg, Paul and Bennett, John, *Jack the Ripper: CSI Whitechapel*, Andre Deutsch, 2012

Begg, Paul, Fido, Martin and Skinner, Keith, *The Complete Jack the Ripper*, John Blake, 2010

Browne, Douglas G. and Brock, Alan, *Fingerprints*, George Harrap, 1953

Browne, Douglas G. and Tullett, E.V., *Bernard Spilsbury*, George Harrap, 1951

Budworth, Geoffrey, *The River Beat*, Historical Publications, 1997

Camp, John, *A 100 Years of Medical Murder*, Granada, 1983

Castle, H.G., *Case for the Prosecution*, Naldrett Press, 1956

Cole, Herbert, *Things for the Surgeon*, Heinemann, 1964

De Vries, Leonard, *'Orrible Murder*, BCA, 1974

Eddleston, John J., *Jack the Ripper: An Encyclopaedia*, Metro Publishing, 2002

Evans, Stewart and Skinner, Keith, *Jack the Ripper Source Book*, Robinson, 2001

Fido, Martin, *Murder Guide to London*, Grafton Books, 1987

Fido, Martin, *True Crime*, Sevenoaks, 2004

Friedland, Martin L., *The Trials of Israel Lipski*, Macmillan, 1984

Gaute, J.H.H. and Odell, Robin, *Murder 'Whatdunit'*, Pan Books, 1982

Goodman, Jonathan, *Bloody Versicles*, David & Charles, 1971

Graves, Robert, *They Hanged my Saintly Billy*, Cassell and Co, 1957

Guy, William, Ferrier, David and Smith, William, *Victorian CSI*, History Press 2009

Harrison, Shirley, *Diary of Jack the Ripper*, BCA, 1993

Havelock Ellis, Richard, *The Criminal*, Walter Scott, 1890

Holding, David, *Forensic Science Basics*, Scott Martin, 2020

Horton, Sarah Bax, *Arm of Eve*, History Press, 2024

Innes, Brian, *Bodies of Evidence*, Silverdale Books, 2001

Innes, Brian, *Body in Question*, Amber Books, 2005

Irving, H.B. (ed), *Trial of Mrs Maybrick*, William Hodge, 1912

Jackson, R.L., *Gross's Criminal Investigation*, Sweet and Maxwell, 1962

James, P.D. and Critchley, T.A., *The Maul and the Pear Tree*, Sphere Books, 1971

Jobb, Dean, *The Case of the Murderous Dr Cream*, Algonquin Books, 2021

Joyce, Christopher and Stover, Eric, *Witness from the Grave*, Grafton, 1993

Knott, George H. (ed), *Trial of William Palmer*, William Hodge & Co, 1922

Lambton, A., *Thou Shalt Do No Murder*, Hurst and Blackett

Lane, Brian, *Encyclopaedia of Forensic Science*, BCA, 1992

Lane, Brian, *The Murder Guide*, Robinson Publishing, 1991

Lazarus, Richard, *Unnatural Causes*, Futura, 1991

Lock, Joan, *Dreadful Deeds and Awful Murders*, Barn Owl Books, 1990

Logan, Guy, *Masters of Crime*, Stanley Paul, 1028

Naphy, William, *Sex Crimes*, Tempus, 2002

Robertson, Cara, *The Trial of Lizzie Borden*, Simon and Schuster, 2019

Robertson, W.B. Aitchison, *Medical Jurisprudence and Toxicology*, 1921

Ruddick, James, *Death at the Priory*, Atlantic Books, 2001

Science Against Crime, Marshall Cavendish, 1962

Summerscale, Kate, *The Suspicions of Mr Whicher*, Bloomsbury, 2008

Teignmouth Shore, W. (ed), *Trial of Thomas Neill Cream*, William Hodge, 1923

Thorwold, Jurgen, *Dead Men Tell Tales*, Pan Books, 1966

Trow, M.J., *Abberline: Ripper Hunter*, Pen and Sword, 2012

Trow, M.J., *The Thames Torso Murders*, Pen and Sword, 2011

Wilkinson, George Theodore, *The Newgate Calendar*, Sphere Books, 1991

Wilson, Colin and Pitman, Pat, *Encyclopaedia of Murder*, Pan Books, 1961

Wilson, Colin, *Written in Blood*, Equation, 1989

Index